# Genoa's Response
## to Byzantium
### 1155–1204

# Genoa's Response to Byzantium

## 1155–1204

*Commercial Expansion
and Factionalism
in a
Medieval City*

GERALD W. DAY

*University of Illinois Press*

URBANA AND CHICAGO

*Publication of this work was supported in part
by a grant from the University of Miami.*

Library of Congress Cataloging-in-Publication Data

Day, Gerald W. (Gerald Wayne), 1945–
  Genoa's response to Byzantium, 1155–1204 : commercial expansion
and factionalism in a medieval city / Gerald W. Day.
    p.    cm.
  Revision of dissertation (Ph.D.)–University of Illinois, 1978.
  Bibliography: p.
  Includes index.
  ISBN 0-252-01496-0 (alk. paper)
    1. Genoa (Italy)–Commerce–Byzantine Empire–History.
2. Byzantine Empire–Commerce–Italy–Genoa–History. 3. Genoa
(Italy)–Politics and government. 4. Genoa (Italy)–History–To
1339. 5. Byzantine Empire–History–1081–1453. I. Title.
HF3590.G4D39 1988                              87-29517
380.1′0945′182–dc19                                CIP

CORAE
uxori meae
quae sola me sustinuit
D. D. D.

# Contents

# *Preface*

WHILE I WAS STILL an undergraduate student at Illinois State University, Richard P. Kressel introduced me to the study of medieval Genoa. My interest in that old city grew into fascination as I discovered that the number of historical materials relating to Genoa's medieval past exceeds those from any other city and often forces historians to use the Genoese experience as the basis for generalizations about the development of European urban and economic institutions. The Genoese system of the twelfth century offers a classic example of an unfettered economy at work, and the relative abundance of sources allows historians to observe its day-to-day operations. This study, then, aims to look closely into the methods by which the Genoese translated their economic and political predispositions into actual practice. By analyzing Genoa's responses to the opportunities and problems presented in a sharply defined and well-documented area, the Byzantine Empire, this study provides a more accurate and complete description of the Genoese approach to cultivating the city's considerable commercial and political growth in the twelfth century.

Since this study is an extensive revision of my doctoral dissertation done at the University of Illinois at Urbana-Champaign, one can well imagine the degree to which I am indebted to others for what I now claim as my own. Donald E. Queller, the director of my dissertation and an indefatigable dispenser of encouragement, suggestions, and corrections, has had the greatest influence on the character of this work. The advice of Bennett D. Hill and Richard E. Mitchell, who were the other members of my doctoral committee, was the source of several insights that have, I am sure, improved on my overall views. I am especially grateful to Professor Michel

Balard of the University of Rheims for his words of guidance in the early stages of my research. Similarly, Professor Hilmar C. Krueger cordially shared with me a part of his vast knowledge of Genoese archival material. I also must express my appreciation for the efficient and gracious cooperation accorded me by Dr. Aldo Agosto, Director of the State Archives in Genoa, and by his staff both in making their holdings available for my study in Genoa and for microfilming large numbers of notarial documents for me. Closer to home, Martha Freedman, History Librarian at the University of Illinois Library, and Martha Landis of the Reference Department, were of substantial assistance in acquiring from scattered locations several hard-to-find items that were necessary to my research. All in all, the book in many ways is a very cooperative effort on the part of several people who are dedicated to reconstructing the past.

I must also thank the Research Board of the University of Illinois for its generosity in giving me a grant to help defray my expenses in Genoa. The University of Miami has been most supportive of my efforts by awarding me a Research Initiation Grant to acquire some necessary sources and a Summer Award in Business and the Social Sciences to give me the time to complete most of the revisions of the manuscript. I am especially grateful for the generous demonstration of continued support shown by Sidney Besvinick, the Dean of the Graduate School and Associate Provost for Research, and the Research Council of the University of Miami, who provided a Research Support Award as the work neared completion, to allow the final publication of my research.

Coral Gables                                                          G. W. D.

Genoa's Response
to Byzantium
1155–1204

## Chapter One

❧·❧·❧

# Genoa, Privileged Trade, and Byzantium

THE CITY OF GENOA, today the bustling port for the industry and commerce of northern Italy, has a singular importance for our understanding of the medieval world. Not only did the city build a commercial power with the accompanying political influence that lasted into the final years of the fifteenth century, but also its abundance of source material, especially for the twelfth century, when the histories of other European cities were still very obscure, furnishes scholars of the Middle Ages considerable economic, social, and political information. For most people, Genoa's important story has been overshadowed by the awesomeness of Venice and Florence, and a major gap in medieval scholarship is the absence of a good modern history of Genoa in English.[1] This is not to say that Genoa has been overlooked or underrated by scholars, for the list of historians who have concentrated on medieval Genoa is a very long one. The Genoese, however, were consummate businessmen, as is reflected in the medieval saying, "civis Ianuensis, ergo mercator," and their contribution to the cultural heritage of Western society pales in comparison with those of their Venetian and Florentine counterparts. But looking back into the twelfth century, Genoese galleys and roundships were ubiquitous throughout the Mediterranean, and wherever they went, they carried men who brought perhaps a unique viewpoint into the broader historical picture. This study is not economic, nor is it preponderantly diplomatic, for those histories have been written,[2] but it is an investigation into the interaction of twelfth-century Genoa's internal affairs and its deepening involve-

3

ment with a far-distant political climate. It concentrates on Genoa's Byzantine involvement not only because it establishes a clear focus, but also because that connection exerted a heavy influence on internal affairs; and of all Genoa's external relations of the twelfth century it alone generated sufficient surviving documentation to study it in some depth. The study begins around 1155, when Genoa first became seriously involved with the eastern empire, and ends in 1204, when the Fourth Crusade ended Genoa's twelfth-century involvement with Byzantium. Within that time frame, Byzantine concerns would profoundly affect the development of Genoa's notorious political factionalism, and often factional maneuvering would direct Genoa's policy toward the Byzantines.

Genoa emerges from the obscurity of the early Middle Ages during the eleventh century, when its inhabitants were busiest in protecting themselves from Saracen pirates who infested the Tyrrhenian Sea. In the ninth and tenth centuries, the Saracens raided southern Europe just as fiercely as the Vikings harrassed the northern part of the continent. After these Moslems had captured Sicily in 828, they, with their coreligionists in Spain, made the Tyrrhenian Sea a Saracen lake. Quickly the Saracens dominated not only the waters of the Tyrrhenian, but also the southern French and Italian coasts. Around 880 the Saracens established their infamous pirates' lair at Le Frenet on the French Riviera, and for a hundred years corsairs from this base raided coastal Europeans. Genoa itself was pillaged in 935, and Pisa several times felt the Moslem fury, even as late as 1004. By the first years of the tenth century, however, the Genoese and the Pisans had turned the tables on the Saracens, and steadily men from the two Italian cities gained mastery over the Tyrrhenian. By 1087 the Genoese and Pisans carried the struggle into the heart of Moslem power when, under papal aegis, they raided the city of Mahdia, the port for North African Kairowan. Immense booty was taken, with which the Pisans began the construction of their glorious cathedral and the Genoese built the church of San Sisto, remodeled San Siro, and perhaps began the erection of the cathedral of San Lorenzo.[3] At the end of the century, Genoa's participation in the First Crusade and subsequent crusading conquests not only brought the city much booty, but also gave it solid and privileged commercial footholds in the great Syrian and Palestinian cities that had fallen to the crusaders.[4]

Genoa's commercial expansion into the Mediterranean had now begun in earnest, but to arrive at a true picture of the process, a distinction between ordinary or unprivileged trade and the privileged trade that the Genoese and their Venetian and Pisan rivals sought must be made. Medieval trade occurred on two different levels. At the lower level was regular trade. Medieval governments were notorious for extracting from merchants as much money as they could. All sorts of tolls and fees were imposed. Genoa itself had harbor fees, docking fees, storage fees, excise duties, gate tolls, and even imposed a one-penny head tax on foreigners doing business in Genoa.[5] The Byzantines charged the *kommerkion,* a ten percent excise on goods traded in the empire.[6] Moreover, merchants had to find proper facilities like offices, warehouses, and lodging. If these had to be rented, they could add considerably to merchants' expenses and would diminish the popularity of the place as a port of call. Merchants also had no guarantee of fair judicial treatment in disputes with natives and had no clear way of enforcing contractual obligations with them.

These disabilities did not prevent merchants from engaging in ordinary, unprivileged trade (as Genoa's brisk trade with Moslem Alexandria in the middle of the twelfth century testifies), but they did move the Italian commercial cities to obtain from the rulers of particular markets privileges that would reduce imposts (sometimes to the point of exemption), provide physical facilities, and give some assurance of fair treatment to the Italian traders. This higher level of privileged trade was sought not only by the Genoese, but also by all medieval merchants; and wherever a city's merchants enjoyed privileged commerce, to that place the bulk of their activity would go. For that reason, the diplomatic development of privileged trade has understandably been presented as the history of commercial development itself.

The physical facilities given to merchants followed the example established by the Byzantines in the early Middle Ages in the *mitata* of Constantinople.[7] The Byzantine government customarily grouped merchants from a particular region together so that their activities could more easily be monitored and controlled by imperial officials. From these merchant compounds developed the

framework of the *fondaco,* or merchants' compound, found throughout Moslem lands. By the twelfth century merchants preferred
having their own compounds in major emporia because of the
convenience they offered. In the *fondaco* would be various docks,
warehouses, offices, and living quarters. Baths, ovens, churches,
and open areas for assembly, recreation, or future building completed the physical elements of the *fondaco.* Sometimes, especially
in Moslem cities, the compound might have been surrounded by a
wall, but in Constantinople and the crusader-held cities, these
merchants' quarters usually blended into other physical features of
the city.

Within these *fondachi* merchants were given certain freedoms,
although they were subject to the administration of officers of the
native political authority at first. Usually traders could use their
own weights and measures and their city's coinage. Disputes between
the home city's merchants were adjudicated by the home city's
laws, but disputes involving native merchants were reserved for the
normal courts of the land where the fondaco was located. In the
crusading states after the Third Crusade, however, these privileges
were extended to give the home cities virtually independent control over their compounds in which everyone fell under the jurisdiction of governors sent by the home city. Indeed, after the
middle of the thirteenth century, these overly generous privileges
at various markets in the Mediterranean enabled Genoa, Venice,
and Pisa to develop far-flung commercial networks that often
overlapped and in the late thirteenth and fourteenth centuries led
to disastrous warfare among the three maritime republics.[8]

The Genoese were unusually slow to develop privileged trade. The
city enjoyed commercial liberties in the crusading states since the
First Crusade, but these were somewhat curtailed by the middle of
the century.[9] In 1154 Genoa enfeoffed three members of the
Embriaco family with the city's possessions in the Holy Land, and
for many years thereafter the Genoese government had to battle with
the Embriaco family to enforce compliance with the terms of the
enfeoffment.[10] Also, sometime in the 1160's King Amalric of
Jerusalem revoked some of Genoa's privileges in his kingdom,
although the extent of his action is not known.[11] Nevertheless, every
indication is of a strong trade for Genoa with the crusading states
throughout the twelfth century.[12] In the first half of the twelfth

century, Genoa also gained privileges in Barcelona, Valencia, Montpellier, and the French Riviera.[13] Outside of these areas, however, in Norman Sicily, in Alexandria, in Moslem North Africa, and in the Byzantine Empire, the Genoese had to pursue only ordinary, unprivileged trade. In the second half of the century, beginning with a drastic change in municipal policy in 1154, the Genoese began seeking privileges elsewhere. Ambassadors were sent to Moorish Spain and to Morocco, to Sicily and, of course, to Constantinople.[14] By the end of the century, Genoa had acquired from various potentates the concessions that enabled its merchants to enjoy a network of privileged commerce throughout the Mediterranean.

The Christian Byzantine Empire was a natural place for western commercial progress to be made. For hundreds of years the great capital city of Constantinople had served as an emporium for items coming west along the trade routes across Asia. Such commodities as furs, timber, and slaves came south from Russia to the great Byzantine city. Fine examples of the wealth of the Caliphate could be found in Constantinople's bazaars as well. The Byzantine Empire, moreover, was not without its own internal economic strength. Indeed, the Byzantine economy had never been stronger than it was under the great emperors of the Comneni dynasty in the twelfth century. On the political level, the emperors Alexius I (1081-1118), John II (1118-43), and Manuel I (1143-80) provided the leadership and stability that had brought the empire back from its catastrophic defeat by the Turks at Manzikert in 1071. There is evidence of urban growth, increased production, and widespread minting as indications of the prosperity the Byzantines enjoyed under the Comneni.[15]

The Comneni emperors, especially Manuel I, left long-distance shipping with areas outside of the empire to foreigners because of the Byzantine fear of foreign places and of seafaring in general.[16] Manuel I minimized foreign interference in the internal Byzantine economy by shrewdly limiting movements and activities to prevent the foreigners from doing much beyond hauling goods into and out of the empire.[17] The cities of Genoa, Pisa, and Venice would be the major beneficiaries of this twelfth-century Byzantine policy.

The great mercantile cities of Italy had varied histories of trade with the Byzantine Empire. Amalfi, Bari, and Gaeta enjoyed contacts with East Rome for centuries until these cities fell under the control of the hostile Normans in the eleventh century. Venice had never lost completely its economic and political relation to the Byzantine Empire, and in the late eleventh century, with the isolation of the southern Italian cities from Byzantium, it gained a decided advantage. Venice's naval assistance to Alexius I in 1081 in repelling attacks from the Norman leader, Robert Guiscard, gained for the Italian city extensive commercial privileges throughout the empire. As the twelfth century progressed, Genoa and Pisa understandably became interested in the potential profits that Constantinople offered. Pisa concluded its first commercial compact with the Byzantine emperor in 1111, but Genoa waited until 1155 before it made an agreement with the Byzantines.[18]

Throughout the second half of the twelfth century, Genoa's relations with East Rome were marked by disappointment and disaster. Only during the years from 1171 to 1182 did Genoese merchants enjoy a secure trading operation in Constantinople, although the city's attempt to regain or to improve its position there was a continual concern for its government during the later twelfth century. The Fourth Crusade brought an end to Genoa's twelfth-century Byzantine connection. Although the terms of a Veneto-Genoese treaty of 1218 formally allowed Genoese merchants to trade at Constantinople, the resultant commerce was trifling.[19] Nevertheless, the Genoese had tasted the riches that could be acquired in Byzantium, and wide-scale trade with the eastern world became a definite policy of the Genoese government. The culmination of Genoese activity in its concern with Byzantium came in 1261 when Genoa-supported Michael VIII Palaeologus's successful bid to return the throne of the Caesars to Constantinople, from which it had been excluded since the victory of the Fourth Crusade. In return for their aid, Michael granted the Genoese merchants an extremely advantageous commercial concession on which Genoa built an extensive Black Sea trade supervised from the Genoese base at Pera, across the Golden Horn from Constantinople.[20]

The Genoese who built their city's commercial strength in the twelfth century were in reality not bourgeoisie, as is often assumed, but feudal aristocrats whose feudal world view largely directed the methods they used to gain trading concessions throughout the Mediterranean. In the eleventh century, when the bishop of Genoa governed the city, the important men in Genoa were tied to the prelate by vassalage and made up his feudal court. After the foundation of the commune in 1099, many of these men became the leaders of the new government, supplying communal consuls, military commanders, and ambassadors to their city. In their service of military command and the exercise of their feudal prerogatives, they amassed considerable wealth both from booty and from manorial exactions. This wealth became the capital that they invested in commercial ventures. They themselves were rarely merchants, but they supplied the money that other Genoese of lesser social standing took on distant voyages around the Mediterranean. This group, indeed, was an urban patriciate that nearly monopolized positions of leadership in twelfth-century Genoa. Only toward the end of the century were the actual "merchant" classes of Genoa able to break into this socio-economic and political caste.[21]

The course of Genoese internal and external history in the twelfth century can best be explained in terms of the feudal attitude, with its emphasis on the personal bond, that these men brought into politics, diplomacy, and business. The feudally minded Genoese aristocracy of the twelfth century made the same type of personal relationship the basis for political maneuvering at home and for diplomatic action abroad; and Genoa's commercial success or failure was largely a function of the resiliency of the personal relationships on which the commune's far-flung mercantile interests depended.[22]

Very important in the context of Genoa's twelfth-century relations with Byzantium was the strong connection built up during the twelfth century between Genoa and the powerful northern Italian noble house of Montferrat. Both parties were vitally interested in foreign involvement, and on many occasions they cooperated to attain their respective goals. Genoa's position in Byzantium, the city's acquisition of an elaborate commercial operation in the crusading states during the Third Crusade, and Boniface of Montferrat's relationship to the Fourth Crusade can be more clearly understood by looking into the Montferrats' ties with Genoa. Within Genoa itself, the Guercio family demonstrated the overwhelming influence that private interests had in determining Genoese policy toward Byzantium and, as a corollary, the impact of private affairs on public policy in general in medieval Genoa, even to the point of blurring the distinction between public and private considerations. Private family and business considerations, and Genoa's relations with Byzantium also provide the context for political factionalism.

The development of the Genoese interest in the Byzantine Empire and the influence that this great empire brought to bear on the Genoese themselves are representative of the concerns and the methods by which the great Italian city expanded its commerce throughout the Mediterranean world during the twelfth century. The expansion of Europeans throughout this Mediterranean community did not just happen, but it was the result of energetic and capable people attempting to achieve particular private goals, as the case of Genoa makes clear.

## Notes

1. Probably the most respected modern history of Genoa is that of Vito Vitale, *Breviario della storia di Genova: lineamenti storici ed orientamenti bibliografici,* 2 vols. (Genoa, 1955). A more complete history of Genoa, but one that does not display the same scholarly meticulousness of Vitale's history, is that of Teofilo Ossian de Negri, *Storia di Genova* (Milan, 1974), which has as its strong point very useful discussions of the scholarship on many topics. Several works have been devoted to particular periods in Genoa's medieval history. Among these is Attilo R. Scarsella, *Il comune dei consoli,* which is the third volume of a larger history of Genoa, *Storia di Genova delle origini al tempo nostro,* 4 vols. (Milan, 1942). Also for the twelfth century is Erik Bach, *La cité de Gênes au XIIe siècle* (Copenhagen, 1955). For the thirteenth and fourteenth centuries, we also have Vito Vitale, *Il comune del podestà a Genova* (Milan, 1951), and for the fifteenth century, Jacques Heers, *Gênes au XVe siècle: activité économique et problèmes sociaux* (Paris, 1961). In English, the best capsulization of Genoa's growth in the twelfth century can be found in John K. Hyde, *Society and Politics in Medieval Italy* (London, 1973), 65–73. Hyde summarizes Genoa's economic importance in the twelfth century: "It must be stressed that in its dynamism, its concentration on commerce and its dependence on distant markets, the Genoese economy was altogether exceptional, comparable only with its deadly rival Venice . . . " (ibid., 73).

2. The history of Genoa's twelfth-century trade with Byzantium has until recently been handled in a cursory manner at best. In the nineteenth century Wilhelm Heyd spoke of the trade in *Histoire du commerce du Levant au moyen âge,* translated and revised by Furcy Reynaud, 2 vols. (Leipzig, 1885–86), and in *Le colonie commerciali degli italiani in Oriente nel*

*medio evo,* translated and edited by Giuseppe Müller, 2 vols. (Venice, 1866-68). Camillo Manfroni wrote a very long article that really should be considered a monograph on the relations of Genoa and Byzantium in the Middle Ages, but it includes some errors and suppositions no longer held by historians: "Le relazioni fra Genova, l'impero byzantino, e i Turchi," *Atti della Società Ligure di Storia Patria* 28 (1896-98): 575-858. At the beginning of this century, Adolf Schaube again briefly dealt with the twelfth-century Genoese trade with the Byzantines in *Handelsgeschichte der römanischen Volker des Mittelmeergebiets bis zum Ende der Kreuzzüge* (Munich, 1906). Scholars interested in Genoa's later commercial empire centering on the Black Sea have also mentioned the twelfth-century trade. The earliest of these works is Ludovico Sauli's *Della colonia di Genovesi in Galata,* 2 vols. (Turin, 1831). Georgi I. Bratianu devoted only a few pages to the topic in his work, *Recherches sur le commerce génois dans la Mer Noire au XIIIe siècle* (Paris, 1929). Although Michele Balard's treatment of the twelfth-century establishment is not extensive, it is very thoughtful (*La Romanie génoise,* 2 vols. [Genoa, 1978]). Charles M. Brand devotes a chapter in *Byzantium Confronts the West,* 1180-1204 (Cambridge, Mass., 1968) to the Genoese and Pisan colonies in twelfth-century Constantinople, but he touches only the high points of the diplomacy. Most recently Ralf-Johannes Lilie has written a lengthy book concerned with the twelfth-century relations of the Byzantine Empire with the three major Italian commercial cities (*Handel und Politik zwischen dem byzantinischen Reich und den italienischen Kommunen Venedig, Pisa und Genua in der Epoche der Komnenen und der Angeloi* (1081-1204) [Amsterdam, 1984]). Lilie's book deals so extensively with the diplomatic aspects of the topic that little else worthwhile can be said on the topic, even if one does not always agree with his conclusions.

3. Vitale, *Breviario* 1: 8-13; De Negri, *Storia di Genova,* 167-72, 185-89, and 209-12.

4. Genoa's involvement in the crusading states has been known to scholars for a long time and can be found in almost any work dealing with Genoa or with the crusades. Perhaps this information can most conveniently be found in two articles of earlier scholarship done by Eugene H. Byrne, "Genoese Trade with Syria in the Twelfth Century," *American Historical Review* 25 (1919-20): 191-219, and "Genoese Colonies in Syria," in *The Crusades and Other Historical Essays Presented to Dana C. Munro,* edited by Louis Paetow (New York, 1928), 139-82.

5. These were dues that went to Genoa's bishop, theoretically, and can be found in "Registrum curiae archiepiscopalis Ianue," edited by Luigi T. Belgrano, in *Atti della Società Ligure di Storia Patria,* 2, Part 2 (1862), and 18 (1887), Part 2: 2, 9-11. By the middle of the twelfth

century, however, the communal government had taken over many of the bishop's traditional revenues and was using them to pay communal officials. For the revenues diverted to the consuls, see *Codice diplomatico della repubblica di Genova dal MCLXIIII (sic) al MCLXXXX (sic)*, edited by Cesare Imperiale di Sant'Angelo, 3 vols. (Rome, 1936–42) 1: 164, doc. 128, and for those paid to the *cintrago*, ibid. 1: 141–42, doc. 119. In 1133 the consuls earmarked some harbor revenues to pay for street improvements (ibid. 1: 81–82, doc. 67), and in 1134 other revenues paid for oil for the lamps of San Lorenzo's altar (ibid. 83–85, doc. 68). It would be valuable for someone to work out a schedule of these revenues and to use them to investigate public finances in twelfth-century Genoa. By 1141 the practice of the *compera*, whereby certain communal revenues were leased to consortia of businessmen in order for the commune to obtain large sums of ready money, had been introduced (ibid. 1: 129–31, doc. 108).

6. On the Byzantine maritime and commercial regulations in general, see Hélène Ahrweiler, *Byzance et la mer: la marine de guerre, la politique et les institutions maritimes de Byzance aux VIIe–XVe siècles* (Paris, 1966).

7. Robert S. Lopez, "Foreigners in Byzantium," *Bulletin de l'institut historique belge de Rome*, Fascicule 44 (1974): 341–52. A good study of the Italian merchants' compounds was done by Vsevolod Slessarev, "*Ecclesiae mercatorum* and the Rise of Merchant Colonies," *Business History Review* 41 (1967): 177–97.

8. Gerald W. Day, "The Impact of the Third Crusade on Trade with the Levant," *International History Review* 3 (1981): 159–68.

9. For the documents in which these privileges were embodied, see *Codice diplomatico*, 1: 11–12, docs. 7–8 (Antioch, 1098); 16–18, doc. 12 (Antioch, 1101); 20–23, docs. 15–18 (Acre, 1104); 32–33, doc. 24 (Tripoli, 1109).

10. For the documents giving these possessions to the Embriaco family, see ibid., 296–98, docs. 246–48. As late as 1179 Pope Alexander III sent a letter to Ugo Embriaco, lord of Jubail, admonishing him to fulfill his obligations as a vassal of the Genoese commune (ibid. 2: 251–52, doc. 118). Several years later, in 1186, Pope Urban III wrote similar letters to Embriaco, the patriarch of Antioch, and Count Raymond II of Tripoli trying to get the lord of Jubail to acknowledge his feudal obligations to Genoa (ibid., 296–98, docs. 152–54). More general troubles in the crusading states started for the Genoese as early as 1155, when the commune sent an ambassador to the papal court to prompt Adrian IV to write to King Baldwin III of Jerusalem to demand that Genoese merchants be compensated for a ship and money seized by his men at Acre (ibid. 1: 331–32, doc. 273).

11. King Amalric had confiscated from the Genoese the golden tablet affixed to the wall of the Church of the Holy Sepulcher on which King Baldwin I had recorded his concessions to the Genoese. The dispute over this tablet raged between the kings of Jerusalem and the Genoese, who engaged popes on their behalf until Saladin's conquest forced the Syrian barons to negotiate more favorable terms with the Genoese. (ibid. 2: 252, doc. 119; 2: 298-299, doc. 155; 2: 302-4, docs. 159 and 160). King Guy of Jerusalem in 1191 agreed to restore the tablet (ibid. 3: 22-24, doc. 8). Perhaps Genoa's most serious loss came sometime in the early 1180's when Count Raymond of Tripoli for unknown reasons took away from them their third of Tripoli (ibid. 2: 304-5, doc. 161).

12. Joshua Prawer, *The Crusaders' Kingdom: European Colonialism in the Middle Ages* (New York, 1972), 398-400.

13. See below, chap. 2 and chap. 4.

14. See below, chap. 2.

15. Michael F. Hendy, "Byzantium 1081-1204: an Economic Reappraisal," *Transactions of the Royal Historical Society*, 5th ser., 20 (1970): 31-52.

16. Alexander Kazhdan and Giles Constable, *People and Power in Byzantium: an Introduction to Modern Byzantine Studies* (Washington, D.C., 1982), 37-43.

17. Gerald W. Day, "Manuel and the Genoese: A Reappraisal of Byzantine Commercial Policy in the Late Twelfth Century," *Journal of Economic History* 37 (1977): 289-301.

18. See below, chap. 2.

19. Michel Balard, "Les génois en Romanie entre 1204 et 1261: recherches dans les minutiers notariaux génois," *Mélanges d'archeologique et d'histoire*, 78 (1966): 476-502.

20. Michel Balard, in his perceptive study *La Romanie génoise*, has superseded previous scholarship on this later Genoese network, and G. I. Bratianu has also provided further important contributions in his *Recherches sur le commerce génois*.

21. The origins of the Genoese urban patriciate in the twelfth century are well known to scholars. The important pioneering studies were those of Robert S. Lopez, "Aux origins du capitalisme genois," *Annales d'histoire économique et sociale* 9 (1937): 429-54, and in the same volume, Andre-E. Sayous, "Aristocratie et noblesse à Gênes," 366-81. With regard to the direction that scholarly inquiry on the Genoese nobility should take, Jacques Heers has said, "Of fundamental importance is the fact that the description of institutions obviously does not allow us to grasp the realities of political life from the social point of view. Organs and functions are only abstract names behind which we must be able to place the

names of men located exactly in their familial, topographic, economic, and social environment." *Parties and Political Life in the Medieval West*, translated by David Nicholas (Amsterdam, 1977), 4.

22. The problems encountered by Genoa in developing its Byzantine commerce in the twelfth century have been a boon to modern scholars, because the ensuing diplomatic activity generated sufficient source material to offer more than a sketch of what was happening. Genoa's activities in other areas during the same period—Syria, Sicily, and North Africa—lack enough documentation to follow the story very far. David Abulafia has best described Genoa's early connections with Sicily in *The Two Italies: Economic Relations between the Norman Kingdom of Sicily and the Northern Communes* (Cambridge, 1977). Eugene Byrne wrote extensively on Genoese trade with the crusading states in two articles, "Genoese Colonies," and "Genoese Trade." The dissertation and article by Hilmar C. Krueger on Genoa's twelfth-century trade with North Africa is about all that can be gleaned from the scanty surviving material: "The Commercial Relations between Genoa and Northwest Africa in the Twelfth Century," (Ph.D. diss., University of Wisconsin, 1932), and idem, "Genoese Trade with Northwest Africa in the Twelfth Century," *Speculum* 8 (1933): 377–95. The most recent study is that of Geo Pistarino, "Genova e i'Islam nel Mediterraneo occidentale (secoli XII–XIII)," *Anuario de Estudios medievales* 10 (1980, issued in 1982): 189–205. The sources for twelfth-century Genoa, unique for their early date and volume, are well known to historians. Perhaps the best descriptions of these sources are available in the following three books: Bach, *Gênes*, 11–26; Abulafia, *Two Italies*, 8–24; and Steven Epstein, *Wills and Wealth in Medieval Genoa 1150–1250* (Cambridge, Mass., 1984). The many thousands of extant notarial entries give clues to personal associations through the identification of people making business contracts and through the accompanying witness lists, where indications of family relationships are often found and assumptions of personal association can be made when particular people recur in different documents with other certain people. Needless to say, relationships many times must be traced through several entries, and sometimes the small number of first names in use, the orthographic fluidity of surnames, and the propensity for some Genoese families to use matronymic surnames frustrate the historian's inquiry. These records have been well described in the works cited above and in the small volume by Mattia Moresco and Gian Piero Bognetti, *Per l'edizione dei notai liguri del secolo XII* (Genoa, 1938).

## Chapter Two

*ՏՐ·ՏՐ·ՏՐ*

# Genoa's Diplomacy with Byzantium,
## 1155–1204

BOTH GEOGRAPHY AND HISTORY had made Italy in the twelfth century a diplomatic and economic crossroads. Four political systems, the Holy Roman Empire, the Byzantine Empire, the papacy, and the newly formed Norman kingdom of Sicily, vied for dominance in the peninsula. Internally, many Italians themselves, especially the thousands in the north gathered in their fast developing towns, struggled to win their independence from all of these powers. On the economic level, three cities, Genoa, Pisa, and Venice, came to dominate the commerce of the Mediterranean as the century progressed. The leaders of these three cities learned how to take advantage of the diplomacy surrounding them to advance their own economic interests.

Italy was just a geographic expression since the disappearance of Roman power in the west had made Italy vulnerable to repeated depredations by various peoples. Theodoric and his Ostrogoths had won Italy from Odovacar, the barbarian Roman general who finally dispensed with the shadow of the Roman Empire in Italy; but the Byzantine heirs of Rome had in the mid-sixth century repossessed the peninsula only to lose much of the territory to the invading Lombards. By the late eighth century the papacy remained as the sole vestige of Roman power, and the pope's reliance on Frankish arms had brought the northern part of Italy under the control of a resurrected western emperor in Charlemagne. When this western empire, after a period of near extinction, was revived by the great German king, Otto I, in the late tenth century, the northern half of the peninsula would be under German administration. The growing rivalry for control over Christendom between the western emperors and the popes in the eleventh century would make political chaos out of northern Italy for centuries to come. Chaos also seems best to describe the situation in southern Italy during the eleventh century. Here residual Byzantine power, eclipsed by the Moslem conquest of Sicily in 828 and the survival of independent pockets of Lombard power, could not stave off the formidable drive of Norman adventurers to blanket the whole area with their feudal method of political domination. In 1130, the Norman leader, Count Roger of Sicily, was given a royal crown by the antipope, Anacletus II, and the Norman kingdom of Sicily quickly became one of the most advanced and powerful political units in the Mediterranean.

These Normans in Sicily and southern Italy were stout adversaries of the Byzantines. As early as 1081 the Norman leader, Robert Guiscard, had invaded the Balkans, only to be repelled by the Byzantine emperor, Alexius I Comnenus. For the next one hundred years the Normans would repeatedly attempt to extend their power across the Adriatic Sea into Byzantine territory. Guiscard's son, Bohemond, attacked in 1107; and in 1147 and 1148 King Roger II sent a navy into Byzantine waters. As late as 1185 William II of Sicily unleashed an attack that succeeded in the capture of Thessalonica before his forces were driven out. Not only did the Sicilian Normans pose a threat on land, but also the strong Sicilian navy had the potential of cutting off the sea lanes to Byzantium. The offensive was not wholly in the hands of the Normans, however, for the great Byzantine emperor, Manuel I Comnenus, was intent on reducing the Normans' power, not only to protect his own territory but also to regain the lost southern Italian possessions. In the 1150's Manuel had an army operating in southern Italy in the hope of achieving his goals.[1]

Frederick Barbarossa involved the Holy Roman Empire too in the struggle for Italy. His hope was to strengthen his control over northern Italy and perhaps to extend it to southern Italy as well. The reintroduction of Roman law into the West in the twelfth century had given Barbarossa rather grandiose ideas of his own imperial importance, ideas which Manuel I could not allow to go unchecked. Byzantine agents in Venice were able to confederate the cities of the Veronese Mark (Treviso, Vicenza,

Padua, and Verona) with Venice in an anti-German alliance that was the beginning of the Lombard League, and in 1167 Barbarossa unsuccessfully besieged Ancona, which had accepted a Byzantine garrison.[2] Barbarossa eventually won the diplomatic battle with the Byzantines when he engineered the marriage of his son and heir, Henry, to the heiress of the Norman kingdom. Henry VI finally made good his claim to the southern kingdom in 1194 and turned his efforts against the Byzantines. The young emperor's death in 1198, however, prevented him from achieving his goal of becoming the sole emperor over Christendom.[3] In the latter half of the twelfth century, then, the German and Byzantine emperors nursed at least a latent rivalry for domination that would finally find expression in the East-West confrontation of the Fourth Crusade.

Within the complicated diplomacy of this period, Genoa, Pisa, and Venice concentrated on expanding their commerce by using their naval power to make themselves indispensable allies to the ambitious participants in Mediterranean politics. The fleets from these cities greatly assisted the crusading forces in the early years of the century in capturing the coastal cities of the Holy Land, and the Italians' continued service of linking these crusader outposts with the western homeland made them vital for the welfare, if not the very survival, of the crusading states. These northern Italian cities could offer the Sicilian kings very little since these southern Italian monarchs had built up their own very strong navy, but Genoese, Venetian, and Pisan warships did make up a potentially hostile force with which the kings of Sicily had to reckon in plotting their Mediterranean strategies. Even Barbarossa would realize the usefulness of the northern Italian navies when, in the 1160's, he enlisted Genoese and Pisan aid in his unfulfilled plans to invade Sicily.

The Byzantines too would come to rely on Italian naval power. Much has been conjectured about the size of the Byzantine fleet in the twelfth century,[4] but the Byzantines, unlike their Greek ancestors, disliked seafaring and the adventures of leaving their own land.[5] Whenever a navy was necessary in the late eleventh and twelfth centuries, the Byzantines preferred to buy the services of the Italian maritime cities with commercial concessions.[6] Venice, long associated with the empire and at least a nominal part of it, was the usual supplier of warships, but when the Venetians became too arrogant for Manuel with their disrespectful behavior in his campaign against the Sicilian invasion of 1148, the emperor began looking around for more reliable naval mercenaries. The open break with Venice in 1171 over the latter's attack on the Genoese compound in Constantinople forced Manuel to deal even more extensively with the Genoese and the Pisans, who also capitalized on the situation. The Byzantines, like the crusaders, would pay for the Italians' services by opening the economy of their empire to merchants from the cities and by granting them ever more generous trading privileges. Byzantine reliance on Italian naval power was transformed into dependence on Italian shippers to manage the empire's long-distance trade. Manuel allowed the Italians to monopolize his empire's import-export business since his own people had little interest in it, but he was careful to restrict their involvement with the internal Byzantine economy.[7] The emperors of the Angeli dynasty, however, were in a weaker position than Manuel and, by the end of the century, Italian merchants were making devastating inroads into the Byzantine economy and consequently were becoming far more influential in Byzantine political affairs. In general, Byzantine xenophobia and fear of the sea led the eastern empire into shortsighted economic and diplomatic policies which, by encouraging deeper Italian penetration of the Empire's life, could only spell disaster. The notorious internal weakness of Byzantium under the Angeli rulers was the result rather than the cause of these policies.

The Italian maritime cities competed with one another for Mediterranean commerce, but there was a progression in their rivalry during the twelfth century. In the late eleventh century, Genoa and Pisa, concentrated on the western Mediterranean, while Venice focused its efforts on its privileged trade with the Byzantine Empire, a position it had received for giving naval assistance to Alexius I against Robert Guiscard in 1081. In this early commercial world, the Genoese, Pisan, and Venetian spheres of interest were quite separate. Even after the creation of the crusading states provided the first common focus for all three Italian cities, their spheres of interest were kept fairly distinct. The Pisans had an extensive concern in Jerusalem, the Genoese were strong in Antioch and Acre, and the Venetians enjoyed a virtual monopoly on the business of Tyre. Genoa and Pisa, as can be expected, first came to blows in the western Mediterranean, and from 1123 on these two cities were almost always at war with each other. Venice remained aloof until both Pisa and Genoa intruded into their Byzantine monopoly. In 1162 the Venetians helped the Pisans destroy the new Genoese compound in Constantinople, and in 1171 they took it on themselves to attack the reorganized Genoese facility there. In the late twelfth-century Byzantine Empire, then, the Italians' overlapping spheres first clashed. The rivalry took on a Mediterranean character after the redistribution of commercial privileges in the crusading states during the Third Crusade broke down the customary separateness of their interests there, and the opening of privileged trade with Moslem emporia put them elbow to elbow there as well, until the middle of the thirteenth century when the three Italian maritime cities struggled for Mediterranean commercial hegemony.[8]

Many of these developments happened after 1155, but the leaders of Genoa in that year decided to accept the promise of privileged trade from the commanders of the Byzantine army operating in southern Italy. Genoa for centuries had had some contact with East Rome. The city had been a *municipium* of the Roman Empire and the administrative center for the province of Liguria. When the political center of the empire permanently shifted to the east in the fifth century, Genoa retained at least a heritage of *Romanitas*. For the first half of the sixth century Genoa was part of the Ostrogothic kingdom, but in the Byzantine reconquest of the lost peninsula in the middle of the century, Genoa returned to Roman administration and became the seat of the Byzantine *vicarius Italiae*.[9] The continuation of Roman influence in its Byzantine form in Genoa is perhaps most clearly demonstrated by the title given to one of medieval Genoa's municipal officers, the *cintrago*, which has been traced back to the Greek word, *kentarchos*, or centurion.[10]

This antique Roman connection was permanently broken with the Lombard invasion of Italy. The Lombard king, Rothari, captured and nearly destroyed Genoa in 643 or 644. What was left of the city passed into the Frankish system with Charlemagne's conquest of the Lombard kingdom. Afterward, Genoa was securely within the orbit of the developing German empire, emerging from obscurity in the eleventh century under the imperially delegated government of the archbishop of Milan and his local deputies.[11]

Nevertheless, in this little-known epoch of Genoa's history, at least a faint association with the empire may have continued. One of the great Genoese families of the Middle Ages, that of Grillo, traced its lineage back to a certain Uberto, who in a siege of Constantinople in 806 supposedly was the first man to scale the city's walls. The impressed emperor, Nicephorus I, reportedly said, "See that cricket (*grillo*)! With what speed he climbs the wall!"[12] Of course, the story belongs to folk legend, and while there is no evidence of a siege of Constantinople in 806, perhaps the tale commemorates a time when men from Genoa and its environs, on an individual basis at least, saw service in the Byzantine world. Some evidence points to the existence of a "Lombard" contingent in the Byzantine army during the twelfth century, and although a gap of three hundred years makes it impossible to connect Uberto with the Lombard contingent, the story of Uberto Grillo does suggest a tradition of Genoese service to the Byzantines extending back into the nearly forgotten past.[13] In general, however, from the mid-seventh century onward, the Ligurian city's orientation was western. Genoese sailors in the eleventh century were clearing the Tyrrhenian Sea of Saracen pirates, at first cooperating with Pisa and then rivaling that city for control of Corsica and Sardinia, and by 1093 Genoa was assisting the forces of the *Reconquista* in the never-ending battle to expel the Moors from the Iberian peninsula.[14]

The Genoese participation in the great adventure of the crusades renewed the city's connection with East Rome. The Genoese annalist, Caffaro, and the Byzantine chronicler, Anna Comnena, have widely differing versions of what probably was a single naval encounter between the Genoese and the Byzantines. Caffaro reports that in 1101 the Genoese fleet returning from the capture of Acre and Caesarea met a Byzantine fleet off the coast of Ithaca. The Genoese destroyed seven of the ships and the Byzantine commander sued for a truce. Two Genoese, Rainaldo di Rodulfo and Lamberto Ghetto, accompanied the Byzantine admiral to the imperial court, but Caffaro says nothing about what transpired in any negotiations that may have taken place. In Anna Comnena's account of the confrontation, the emperor, Alexius I Comnenus, sent a flotilla in 1104 to maintain surveillance on a Genoese fleet heading for Syria, but the Byzantine ships were so badly damaged by a storm that the commander chose not to engage the Genoese force. Although the Genoese version is the less reliable since the city of Acre was captured in 1104, there is every reason to surmise that Genoese envoys around 1104 visited the Byzantine capital, because Caffaro is usually trustworthy in reporting the city's embassies, especially when he names the envoys. Various items of business could have been on the agenda. The Genoese had received in 1098 considerable commercial concessions from the Normans at Antioch, a city which Alexius Comnenus considered to be his own territory, and perhaps the Genoese saw a need to insure that their new position there would not be endangered should the emperor eventually regain control over the city. Perhaps the ambassadors also hoped that they could obtain some sort of commercial foothold in Byzantine territory as the Venetians had already done: if so, these talks were unsuccessful.[15]

By 1106 Alexius Comnenus attempted to enlist Genoese aid, along with that of other Italian maritime cities, against the impending invasion of Bohemond of Taranto, and Genoa realized from the beginning of the twelfth century that it could no longer disregard Byzantine considerations in its Levantine commercial enterprises.[16]

The evidence for early twelfth-century Genoese trade with Constantinople is found in an *ars dictandi* dated to the 1130's which contains two hypothetical letters involving a Genoese merchant, one G. Embriaco, in Constantinople. While the letters were admittedly concocted only to serve as examples for future merchants and notaries, they are, nevertheless, full of significance to the issue at hand. The particulars of these letters strongly indicate that the compiler of the *ars dictandi* considered Constantinople to be a normal, if little-used port of call for Genoese traders. His use of the name, Embriaco, is significant, since the Embriaco family controlled Genoese affairs in the crusading states and the name suited the informed author's eastern scenario. Thus, as early as the 1130's (providing the dating of the *ars dictandi* is correct) stopovers of Genoese traders in the Byzantine capital were sufficiently common to seem appropriate to the anonymous compiler.[17]

Further evidence of Genoese trade with the Byzantine Empire before 1155 comes from a list of 1142 of the perquisites of the *cintrago.* Among the collections from other ships, the *cintrago* was allowed to take one *mina* of grain from every ship coming into the harbor from Romania. The archbishop of Genoa in 1143 also could collect a duty of 22½ solidi from ships coming from the Byzantine Empire. The existence of these duties is strong evidence again for a normal expectation of commerce with the Byzantines.[18] This trade, however, was not extensive, and it was regular and not privileged trade.

While Genoa continued this unprivileged trade with the Byzantines until the middle of the twelfth century, the other major Italian mercantile cities had for years enjoyed special consideration and facilities in the Byzantine capital. The southern Italian cities of Bari, Gaeta, and Amalfi had long been within the Byzantine administrative system and had carried on a thriving intercourse with Constantinople until they fell to the Normans in the late eleventh century and the hostility between the Normans and the Byzantines blocked these cities' connection. Even in the twelfth century, however, Amalfi possessed a quarter in Constantinople. Venice was also an outpost of the Byzantine Empire, at least in theory, and had a long and close relationship with the east. Venice had traded in the empire in the tenth century, and its naval help to Alexius I Comnenus in 1081 earned the city a very strong privileged position in the empire's trade. Thirty years later, in 1111, the Pisans negotiated a treaty with the Byzantines that opened privileged trade for them as well.[19] The Genoese alone were outside the competition for Constantinople's markets.

Perhaps the best explanation for Genoa's slowness in acquiring commercial concessions in Constantinople is that the Genoese themselves were unconcerned in the first half of the century with developing a privileged position in the eastern empire. Genoa's favored markets in the crusading states attracted much of the attention, efforts, and capital of the city's merchants. Outside of the crusading states, the Genoese concentrated on the western Mediterranean. In 1108 Count Bertrand of Saint Gilles gave the Genoese both exclusive freedom of trade in his city and enough land to build thirty houses, but this concession itself was part of the bargain struck to obtain Genoese assistance in the count's planned conquest of Syrian Tripoli.[20] Count Roger of Sicily gave the Genoese a parcel of land in Messina and some concessions on export duties in 1116. Sixteen years later the archbishop and government of Narbonne accorded the Genoese privileged commerce.[21] The Genoese were, on the whole, far more interested in consolidating their control over the Ligurian hinterland and the coasts of the Tyrrhenian Sea than in establishing commercial links in the wider Mediterranean outside of Syria. Only in 1146 did the Genoese venture far afield, and then only to coastal Spain, where their help in the Christian capture of Almeria and Tortosa won them privileges there.[22] The Spanish adventure proved financially disastrous for the Genoese government, and for several years the city floundered in trying to find ways to pay off its debts.[23] Even in 1155 the Byzantines approached the Genoese to make a bargain, not the other way around.[24]

In 1154 Genoese policy changed dramatically.[25] The consuls elected for that year refused to take office unless they were allowed to make necessary changes. They said that the city had been asleep and was like a ship floating without a helmsman.[26] Among the new policies they and their supporters instituted to end Genoa's financial problems was a conscious effort to expand privileged trade. Two months after the consuls took office, a treaty made with the count of Marseilles gave the Genoese commercial concessions there.[27] Two ambassadors, the archdeacon Ugo della Volta and Caffaro himself, were sent to Frederick Barbarossa for secret negotiations. The tenor of these talks is not known, but perhaps the Genoese sought his approval for the city's new policies, including a rather independent foreign policy aimed at building up privileged trade.[28] In 1155, of course, the convention was made with the Byzantines. In the same year an embassy went to Pope Adrian IV to persuade him to force the prince of Antioch and the count of Tripoli to honor the privileges granted to the Genoese years before in those territories, demonstrating that the Genoese had neglected even their special position in the crusading states. In fact, in January 1154, the Genoese had invested members of the Embriaco family with virtually all of the city's properties in the Holy Land. Now a new municipal government wanted matters straightened out in the east.[29] In the next year a treaty providing for privileged trade was made with King William of Sicily.[30] In 1157 more ambassadors were sent out, Guido da Lodi to Rome again, Gionata Crispino to the crusading states, and Amico di Murta to Constantinople.[31]

Affairs closer to home involving Frederick Barbarossa's progress through northern Italy diverted Genoese attention for the next two years, but in 1160 Caffaro reported that many ambassadors were sent out, including Oberto Spinola to Moorish Valencia and Enrico Guercio to Constantinople.[32] Guglielmo Cassicio went to Valencia again the next year, Nuvelone d'Albericis went to Morocco, and Ansaldo Spinola to the crusading states.[33] From 1154 to 1161, as the Genoese moved to build a network of privileged trade throughout the Mediterranean their parochial attitudes changed to more cosmopolitan ones.

Only once before 1155 did the Genoese display any real interest in the Byzantines. In 1142 the city sent two ambassadors, Oberto della Torre and Guglielmo Barca, to treat with the emperor, John I Comnenus, who was near the city of Antioch.[34] From John's point of view, the Genoese delegation formed only one part of his broader policy of "protecting his rear," while attempting to recover Syria by insuring the good will of the Italian maritime cities and by arranging the marriage of his son, Manuel, to Bertha of Sulzbach, the sister-in-law of the western emperor, Conrad III.[35] Once again, the nature of any ensuing talks has not been recorded, but possibly the Genoese were concerned with safeguarding their commercial position at Antioch amid the hostility between the Byzantines and Raymond, the Latin prince of Antioch. The acquisition of commercial privileges in Constantinople may have come up, but whatever negotiations may have been under way were terminated by John's death in the following year. The Genoese did regard these negotiations as important, however, for at the end of the "Brief of the Company" of 1143 (a statement of Genoese law in the form of a long oath to which the consuls of the commune had to swear) a clause was inserted that held the consuls to abide by any agreements made with the Byzantine court.[36] Such a clause, the only mention of diplomatic affairs in the whole document, highlighted both the seriousness that the Genoese placed on relations with East Rome and their lack of interest in relations with other foreign powers.

The new spirit of expansionism initiated by the Genoese consuls of 1154 converged with Emperor Manuel I's policies toward the West to bring about the Byzantino-Genoese agreement of 1155. Emperor Manuel, who was known for his fascination for western ways and dreamed of reestablishing Byzantine hegemony over lost portions of his empire, was eager to win western allies for his expeditionary force then operating in southern Italy. With Genoa's geographic position beside the plain of Lombardy, with its neighboring nobility hostile to any real advance attempted by the German emperors, and most of all, with the city's growing maritime resources tailor-made to support and to protect a Mediterranean supply line against the Sicilian Normans, the Ligurian city was a welcome ally to the expansionist emperor at Constantinople.

In the early fall of 1155, Demetrius Macrembolites, an agent for the Byzantine commanders in Italy, came to Genoa and drew up a commercial agreement with the city.[37] As a guarantee of Genoese support, the Byzantine offered the municipal government an annuity of five hundred hyperpers and two *pallia* of silk for fourteen years. The money was paid on the spot in a lump sum of seven thousand hyperpers. In addition, the archbishop of Genoa was to receive every year sixty hyperpers and one *pallium* of silk. Still, the greatest incentive for Genoese cooperation was the gift of a commercial compound and a wharf in Constantinople and the same commercial privileges as the Pisans had in the empire at large, including a reduction of the usual *kommerkion* from ten percent to four percent.[38] The Genoese for their part swore not to enter into any alliance that would be detrimental to the empire, excepting the city's interests in Syria. The Genoese also agreed that their fellow citizens in the Byzantine Empire would help to defend it from attack.[39]

After the Byzantine commanders had made their promise to Genoa in the name of their emperor, the Genoese had considerable difficulty in persuading Manuel to carry through with the agreement. Making a complete diplomatic turn about, the Genoese in 1156 concluded a commercial treaty with King William I of Sicily, Manuel's archenemy.[40] The Byzantine emperor, who surely saw this Genoese maneuver as an ungrateful slap in the face and as a signal of Genoese refusal to assist him in his Sicilian campaigns, sent the Genoese ambassador in 1157, Amico di Murta, home with nothing. Only in 1160, after Manuel's Italian designs had been temporarily interrupted by the Sicilian victory at the Battle of Brindisi in 1158 did the emperor's attitude soften sufficiently for him finally to award the Genoese their promised quarter. Even then, he did not issue a formal chrysobull confirming the concession;

at least we have no record of one today, but the promise of 1155 served as the basis for the Genoese concession.[41]

The intrusion of the Genoese into what the Pisans and the Venetians considered their own sphere quickly aroused their ire. In 1162 the uneasy situation came to a head when the Pisans with Venetian help attacked the compound and drove the Genoese from the city.[42] In retaliation for this outrage in his capital, Manuel removed the Pisan compound to Scutari, across the Golden Horn from Constantinople itself.[43] The Genoese, almost simultaneously with the destruction of their facility, had concluded an important agreement with Frederick Barbarossa to aid him in his planned invasion of Sicily in return for granting virtual independence to Genoa. Manuel was now so suspicious of their intentions that he would not let the Genoese return to Constantinople.[44] A Genoese embassy in 1164, whose negotiating position was probably weakened by severe internal problems at home, failed to regain the lost quarter for its city.[45]

Manuel changed his mind in 1168 and invited the Genoese to send a new embassy to his court.[46] After considerable diplomatic confusion, the Genoese envoy, Amico di Murta again, was able to hammer out by April 1170 an advantageous agreement with Manuel. The Genoese received a compound in Constantinople, along with a wharf and a church (or at least the land for one), and they kept the customary tax reduction. The yearly stipends of cash and silk that were parts of the agreement of 1155 Manuel promised to continue. The Genoese were still forbidden to trade in the Black Sea area, but they were specifically granted immunity from the emperor's customary right of treasure trove. Finally, disputes between Genoese and the Byzantine government were to be handled at the governmental level at five-year intervals.[47]

The Genoese compound, called the Coparion, served as the permanent core of the Genoese establishment for the rest of the twelfth century. It was located on the northern side of the city and formed the eastern end of the whole sector of Italian concessions lying along the southern shore of the Golden Horn.[48] Directly to the west of the Coparion was the Pisans' compound, which had been restored to them by Manuel also in 1170.[49] Although a description of the quarter (called a "verbal process") is extant, a detailed physical reconstruction of the quarter is impossible on account of our ignorance of the sites named in the documents and on account of the imprecision of the description itself. The quarter covered an area containing both buildings and vacant lots. The condition of the area may have been somewhat dilapidated since the description speaks of many lots which used to have buildings on them. There was already some industry in the area, since woodworkers were mentioned in the description.[50] The name of the quarter itself may have come from the Greek word, *kope,* oar, since a later document speaks of buildings in which oars were made.[51] The Genoese were probably not given a specific church, since there is no mention of one in the description, but Manuel did provide them with a vacant lot on which they could build one.[52] Mention was also made in the description of the other usual appurtenances of medieval Italian compounds, such as ovens, mills, and wells. The Genoese may have extended their facility by renting neighboring buildings from local people as they undoubtedly did at the end of the century.[53]

The Genoese must have begun occupying their new quarter immediately in the summer of 1170. Within a half year, however, the Venetians sacked the compound.[54] The losses sustained by the Genoese were not as great as the ones suffered in 1162. The Byzantine chronicler, John Cinnamus, reported that the buildings and houses of the compound were destroyed,[55] but in Byzantino-Genoese negotiations of 1175 as part of the grievance procedure, the Genoese were concerned only with monetary losses suffered by individuals. The total Genoese claim amounted to only 5,674 hyperpers distributed among some eighty-five Genoese, some of the individual claims being less than ten hyperpers.[56] Nevertheless, the Venetians had resolved to destroy the regenerated Genoese colony before it had had a chance to develop into a serious rival for Constantinople's business. Manuel reacted strongly to the violence by expelling the Venetians in March 1171.[57] The Genoese honored their commitment to Manuel by giving him considerable naval support in his consequent war with Venice, but they received no additional concessions.[58]

The Genoese retained their compound this time, and they spent the last nine years of Manuel's reign trading peacefully. Manuel had especially favored the Genoese. So prominent was his regard for the city that in 1179 King Louis VII of France put his daughter,

Agnes, on board a Genoese galley captained by Baldovino Guercio, a trusted Genoese confidant of the emperor,[59] for a safe voyage to Constantinople and to her new husband, Manuel's son, Alexius.[60] At the time of Manuel's death in September 1180, the Genoese establishment was quite prosperous. Eustathius of Thessalonica's figure of sixty thousand Italians in Constantinople at Manuel's death may be excessive, but it certainly included many Genoese,[61] considering that the Venetians were still banned. The Genoese cultivated their new source of profit so intensely that they lost 228,000 hyperpers in the destruction of the Coparion in 1182.[62] This figure represents a forty-fivefold increase over the capital invested in 1171 at the inception of the current establishment, and it is eight times the amount lost in 1162.

After Manuel I died, the imperial honor was transferred to the great emperor's eleven-year-old son, Alexius II. The firm control that the forceful members of the Comneni dynasty had exerted over the government for a century disintegrated at once. The tragic reign of Alexius II was dominated by a three-sided court intrigue, with the regents—the emperor's mother, Marie of Antioch, and her lover, the *protosebastus,* Alexius—on one side; Alexius II's older sister, Maria Porphyrogenita, and her husband, Renier of Montferrat, on a second side; and an anti-Latin party led by Andronicus Comnenus on the third.[63] Needless to say, the Genoese became caught up in this factionalism, and in 1182 they, like the other western merchants in Constantinople, suffered severely in the great Latin massacre that accompanied Andronicus' violent and success-ful bid for the throne.[64]

The Genoese were now excluded from Constantinople, and it was only after the hated Andronicus lost his throne to Isaac II Angelus in 1185 that the Genoese could hope to return. Isaac II was far more amenable to the Latins than his predecessor had been. The new emperor almost immediately began negotiating with the Italians for their readmittance to his empire. A Genoese delegation that went east at the end of 1186 was unsuccessful.[65] In February 1187, the Venetians regained their long-lost privileges in the empire.[66] The Third Crusade, launched in response to Saladin's conquest of much crusader-held territory in 1187, caused Isaac to look for allies in the fast-changing diplomatic scene of the Levant and of the West. Unsure of his safety because of the instability brought about by the appearance in the East of the great kings of western Europe, including the German emperor, Frederick Barbarossa, Isaac also feared the imminent fusion of the Holy Roman Empire and the kingdom of Sicily through the marriage of Barbarossa's son, Henry VI, an enemy of the Byzantines and heir to the throne, to Constance, the heiress of Sicily. As a consequence of the touchy diplomatic situation, Isaac made overtures to the Italian maritime republics. The emperor came to terms with the Venetians over reparations in June 1189,[67] and by 1191 he had reopened his empire to the Pisans.[68]

Genoa, too, profited from Isaac's precarious position. In late 1189 the emperor sent a high Byzantine functionary and one of his court favorites, Constantine Mesopotamites, to Genoa. Unfortunately, when the Byzantine ambassador returned home with a Genoese envoy, Simon Bufferio, the emperor renounced his ambassador's action as going beyond his authority.[69] In late 1191 another Genoese ambassador named Tanto was refused an audience with the emperor because internal Genoese political confusion made Isaac doubtful of the man's credentials.[70] Isaac requested that the Genoese send a new legation, and soon Guglielmo Tornello and Guido Spinola duly arrived at the imperial court. After considerable diplomatic dickering with Isaac's logothete of the drome (an official similar to a modern foreign minister), Demetrius Tornices, Isaac himself stepped in and reached an agreement with the Genoese in a chrysobull issued in May 1192.[71] On August 2, Genoa's magistrates swore solemnly to abide by the terms of the agreement.[72]

Isaac was generous to the Genoese. The emperor agreed to the Genoese request for a larger compound and an additional wharf, and on his own accord, he extended the quarter farther west to the cistern of Antiphonitus, the water from which the Genoese were allowed to use. The emperor included in his grant the structures on either side of the Genoese facility that belonged to the monasteries of the Apologothete and of Patriarch Theodosius. Moreover, Isaac paid the Genoese the stipends for the past three years at the old rate and for the next year and one-half at a new rate of six hundred hyperpers to the commune and one hundred to the archbishop. He also reimbursed the Genoese for the exorbitant duties exacted on the ship that brought the ambassadors; of more importance, Isaac retained the old four-percent charge for the future both in Constantinople and in the rest of the empire. Any individual disputes that might arise over the payment of duties would be settled on a governmental level and at the same five-year intervals that had been set up by Manuel in 1170. In matters of military aid and Byzantine supervision of Genoese citizens in Constantinople, the twenty-two-year-old agreement between Manuel and Amico di Murta was to have force, and it was restated in the new chrysobull.[73]

Piracy in eastern waters would prevent the Genoese from enjoying the same untroubled commerce that they had had during the last years of Manuel's reign. The Latin massacre of 1182 had alienated many Italians from the Byzantines, and the subsequent pillaging of Byzantine territory by survivors of the masacre had given western merchants and sailors a taste for the illegal rewards of piracy.[74] Since even the policing power of the Byzantine navy had been severely crippled by its confrontation with the Sicilian navy in the mid-1180's, Italian and Greek pirates had been able to range the eastern Mediterranean.[75]

One such pirate was Guglielmo Grasso, a Genoese shipmaster who, with his crew, teamed up with a group of Pisan buccaneers to cause Isaac considerable trouble.[76] As the pirates' first combined venture, they raided Rhodes, hauling off property belonging to Isaac's brother, Alexius. Later the corsair band attacked a ship sailing near Cyprus and carrying the bishop of Paphos and a Pisan knight named Papino, who was a liege man of the Byzantine emperor. The crime that most infuriated Isaac, however, was the pirates' interception of a Venetian ship in imperial service that had on board Byzantine and Moslem ambassadors coming from Saladin's court. The enraged emperor dispatched letters to both Genoa and Pisa to complain of the pirates' deeds.[77] At the same time, Isaac rounded up the Genoese in Constantinople and demanded that they put up a bond of twenty thousand hyperpers. The Genoese government quickly sent to Isaac Guido Spinola and Baldovino Guercio, even though Guercio's nephew had been in Grasso's gang. The ambassadors persuaded the emperor to issue a chrysobull in October 1193, assuring Genoa that the matter would be forgotten and confirming the treaty of 1192.[78]

Once the Grasso affair had been resolved, Genoa's relations with Isaac remained peaceful. It must have been with much apprehension, however, that the Genoese received the news of the manageable emperor's deposition and blinding by his brother, who became Alexius III in April 1195. The new ruler could hardly have had a deep affection for the Ligurian city that had evaded paying him the fifty thousand hyperpers he claimed to have lost in Grasso's raid on Rhodes. Although Alexius should have harbored the same resentment toward the Pisans, he was nevertheless attracted to them, partly because their large numbers in the empire made them effective counterweights to the aggressive Venetians, who were quickly regaining their former dominance in the Byzantine economy. Since these two Italian cities were at war when Alexius usurped the throne, it was an easy matter for him to incite the Pisans to attack the neighboring Venetian sector, thus inaugurating a series of sporadic Veneto-Pisan clashes that lasted until the eve of the Latin conquest of Constantinople.[79]

Alexius may also have shown his favor to the Pisans to encourage the Tuscan city's government to take more active steps in policing the piracy of Pisan seafarers. With the Byzantine navy in a disreputable state of decay, Alexius III enlarged on the policy begun by his brother of using private Italian sea captains to police Byzantine waters. The emperor issued what would later be called letters of mark authorizing these seamen to search out and to destroy pirate fleets and rewarding them with a portion of the confiscated booty.[80] For the Byzantines, this practice was an inexpensive way to maintain some sort of order, but the dependence on privateers seriously weakened Italian respect for imperial authority, and the westerners, who by now virtually controlled the empire's business, came more and more to feel that the imperial policing power in their hands gave them a strong position in determining East Rome's destiny. This attitude would bode ill for the eastern empire in 1203, when the Venetians and crusaders sailed under Constantinople's walls.

The early years of Alexius' reign were uneventful for the Genoese merchants in Constantinople. The size of the Genoese operation, small when compared to the Venetian and Pisan establishments, must have freed them from Alexius' machinations to control the Italians. Sometime in 1197 or 1198, nevertheless, the Genoese became embroiled with the emperor in a manner strongly reminiscent of the crisis of 1192–93 and indicative of the policy Alexius intended to follow in dealing with problematic Genoese in his territory. A Genoese merchant at Constantinople named Gafforio fell victim to the widespread corruption of Alexius' officials when the admiral of the Byzantine fleet, Michael Stryphnus, levied an exorbitant fine on him.[81] Unable to gain satisfaction legally, the Genoese sailor, who had experience as a naval commander for his city in the Levant during the Third Crusade,[82] assembled a formidable pirate fleet and began pillaging Byzantine settlements in the Aegean Sea. After an especially destructive raid on Adramyttium, off the coast of Asia Minor, the emperor commissioned Giovanni Stirione, a Calabrian pirate who had given up his illegal career to become a privateer for Isaac II, to take a thirty-galley fleet against Gafforio. In the waters off Sestus, the pirates took the Byzantine force by surprise and defeated it, hauling off the ships' equipment and Stirione as loot. The emperor now offered the Genoese buccaneer six hundred pounds of gold and a sizable *pronoia* to leave off his depredations. Alexius' offer lulled Gafforio into a false sense of security that allowed the recently ransomed Stirione, now at the head of another Byzantine fleet strengthened by Pisan contingents, to seize the pirates and to execute Gafforio.[83] The Byzantine emperor, undoubtedly remembering his own losses in the Grasso affair a few years before, had no wish to let the Genoese evade their responsibility this time. Many Genoese in Constantinople were jailed as Gafforio's accomplices and their goods were seized. Genoa's commercial privileges were revoked, its compound confiscated, and its merchants banned. Alexius also confiscated the *pronoia* of Baldovino Guercio, the long-time faithful imperial servant who had held his reward since Manuel's reign.[84]

Although Genoa sent an ambassador to Alexius to resolve the diplomatic crisis, the emperor refused to change his position. Alexius may have wanted the Genoese to make some effort to help police Byzantine waters, and perhaps within this diplomatic context a surviving letter of mark, issued to Guglielmo Cavallaro during Alexius' reign, should be placed.[85] By May 1201 Genoa felt confident enough of the emperor's good will to send Ottobono della Croce to his court to regain for Genoa a place in the Constantinopolitan market.[86] Although the chrysobull recording the final settlement has been lost, a detailed description of the property conceded by Alexius has survived. Alexius returned to the

Genoese their old facility along with an additional wharf, but he was not willing to compensate the Genoese for their losses.[87]

Several months later, in summer 1202, a large crusading force assembled at Venice for transportation east. While the crusaders were wintering at Zara, they were enlisted by another Alexius, the son of the deposed Isaac II, to help him regain the Byzantine throne for his father and himself. With the coming of spring, the crusade began its journey that would end in the destruction of much of Constantinople and the replacement of the house of Angeli by a Latin emperor supported by Venetian naval power.[88] Nothing is known about the Genoese role in the capture of the Byzantine capital, but possibly they and the Pisans assisted Alexius III in resisting the initial Latin assaults on the city.[89] At any rate, the Genoese quarter, part of which had been destroyed in the Latin massacre of 1182, was totally devastated in a fire that broke out on August 19, 1203, soon after the enthronement of Isaac II and Alexius IV.[90] Consequently the Genoese must have been among the some fifteen thousand Latins who evacuated the capital and joined the crusading host to take an active part in the final siege and capture of the great city.[91] It is doubtful that the Genoese among the Latin evacuees gave much aid to the crusaders in the final conquest, for the Venetians felt no guilt in excluding Genoese merchants from Constantinople when open warfare nearly erupted between the two republics over the possession of Crete, which the Venetians had purchased from Boniface of Montferrat before the Genoese had the chance to close their own deal with the crusading leader.[92]

Genoa's twelfth-century experience with the Byzantine Empire was over; but in the period between 1155 and 1204 diplomacy with the Byzantines had been a growing and major concern for the Genoese. Although the city entered Constantinople's business much later than Venice or Pisa, Genoa's conscientious efforts to honor its commitments to Manuel I and to conduct business peacefully in his domains nourished the growth of a very cordial and profitable relationship between itself and the great emperor. Conversely, after the death of Manuel Comnenus, Genoese relations with the Byzantine Empire were quite troubled. From 1182 to 1192 the Genoese were officially excluded from the empire, although sporadic trade on an individual basis may have continued.

No sooner had the Genoese merchants been readmitted to Constantinople than Isaac's wrath fell on them for Grasso's piracy. The Ligurian city kept its facility in the capital, however, until 1198, when Gafforio's activities caused another period of banishment until the end of 1201. In the twenty-three years that elapsed from Manuel's death until the chaotic period of the Latin conquest, the Genoese enjoyed organized trade in Constantinople for less than half that time. Thus, while the Genoese relations with the Byzantine Empire in the twelfth century did not have as much economic significance for the Italian city as its merchants would have liked, its connection with the eastern empire held a place of importance in Byzantine and Mediterranean politics. In the late twelfth century, the insinuation of Genoese adventurers, or of men closely connected with Genoa, into the internal affairs of Byzantium helped determine the course of events at the same time as it seriously weakened the Byzantines' ability to manage their own lives and to protect themselves.[93] Isaac II considered Genoese sea power to be the deciding factor if a showdown between the eastern and western empires should occur and, in fact, Henry VI failed to conquer Sicily in 1191 because the Genoese fleet came too late, and he succeeded in 1194 with Genoese help.[94] Genoa's reluctance or inability to control the piracy of its citizens in Byzantine waters severely debilitated the already weakened empire.

The Angeli offered a sharp contrast to the strong Manuel Comnenus, who had been careful to maintain control over the Italians. Manuel may have been a Latinophile in his personal life, but as emperor he never forgot that the useful Italians were foreigners and had to be excluded from internal Byzantine political affairs. The Angeli, on the other hand, who succeeded to a complex political system stripped of military and naval power by the Sicilian and civil wars of the early 1180's, were compelled to use western might as their base of power. In 1198 Alexius attempted to revive Manuel's adamancy in dealing with Latin unruliness when he closed Constantinople to the Genoese, but while Manuel had kept the Venetians out of his empire for the last nine years of his reign, Alexius III found his economic and political world so intricately bound up with the Italians that he settled the crisis with the Genoese within three years. At the end of the twelfth century, the Genoese, having profited from other Mediterranean markets and distracted by political turmoil at home, could afford to wait before reaching an agreement, and they forced larger concessions from the vulnerable emperor.[95] The late twelfth-century Latinization of the Byzantine Empire did not make the Fourth Crusade inevitable, but it did make it necessary for anyone wishing to take the throne from Alexius III to use western military resources as the most favorable, although least controllable, source of power. Thus, Prince Alexius in his search for help in putting his father and himself on the Byzantine throne made his visit to the crusader camp at Zara.

The Genoese government, which had been willing to recognize its treaty obligations to defend the empire in 1171 when the Venetians threatened, made no attempt in 1203 or 1204 to use its naval power to break up the Venetian armada sailing under Constantinople's walls. However, the Ligurian city probably did not have the power to play the *deus ex machina* even if only sea power was needed. The Genoese must have realized that there was very little left to defend. In fact, the Byzantine government was in such disarray that it could not help in its own defense. Moreover, Genoa would have had to support a continued Byzantine empire by itself, and Alexius III's unpredictable nature made the probability of realizing a profit from such an immense effort very small indeed. In addition, the Genoese were suffering such internal political problems that the city's government could neither agree on a consistent policy nor present a united effort, whichever way the sentiments of its citizens may have led it. This last failure of the Genoese was only representative of the political fighting within Genoa itself that determined Genoa's overall foreign policy more than any general principles of diplomatic concerns. In the catastrophic events of 1203 and 1204, the Italian city consequently remained aloof and hoped to snatch a morsel of the carcass after the tragedy was finally over.

Perhaps the Genoese figured that they would win regardless of the outcome in Constantinople. If the crusade was repulsed, as all previous attempts to take Constantinople had been, Genoese merchants would surely gain from the Venetian mistake; but if the crusade was victorious, the leader of the expedition, Boniface of Montferrat, would probably reward his longstanding friends for their neutrality. Only when the Venetians engineered the election of Baldwin of Flanders as the Latin emperor over Boniface, the Genoese discovered that they were to be left out of the spoils. The Genoese became embroiled in diplomatic problems with Venice over the island of Crete, which the communally backed Count Henry Pescatore of Malta, Guglielmo Grasso's son-in-law, tried for years to wrest from the Venetians.[96] By 1218 the matter had been terminated when Genoa came to an agreement with Venice ceding Crete to the Venetians but allowing the return of Genoese merchants to Constantinople.[97] Only in 1261, when Genoa helped Michael VIII Palaeologus recapture the old Byzantine capital city from the Latin Empire and the Venetians, did Genoa acquire in the Byzantine world a real position of political influence and commercial prominence.[98]

## Notes

1. For Manuel's campaigns in southern Italy, see Ferdinand Chalandon, *Les Comnène,* 2 vols. (Paris, 1900-12), 2: 353-81. The diplomatic context of events in the twelfth-century Mediterranean world has been reconstructed by several scholars, but the most recent work, and the one with a special importance for this study, is Lilie, *Handel und Politik,* which must be consulted by anyone interested in the topic. Practically every note in this chapter should include a citation to the appropriate pages in Lilie's book, but for the sake of convenience, let me make just this one general reference to it. I do not agree with Lilie completely, and in the places where I think a comment is in order, I have tried to explain my position.

2. William F. Butler, *The Lombard Communes* (London, 1906; reprint 1969), p. 127. On Germano-Byzantine relations in general for this period, see Paolo Lamma, *Comneni e Staufer: richerche sui rapporti tra Bisanzio e l'Occidente nel secolo XII,* 2 vols. (Rome, 1955-57). The latest study of the topic has been done by Peter Classen, "La politica di Manuele Comneno tra Federico Barbarossa e le citta italiane," in *Popolo e stato in Italia nell'età di Federico Barbarossa: Alessandria e la lega lombarda* (Turin, 1970), 263-80. For the siege of Ancona, see Nicetas Choniates, *Historia,* edited by Jan Louis Van Dieten, 2 vols. (Berlin, 1975), 1: 199-203. A study of Ancona's role in Byzantine policy during this period has been done recently by David Abulafia, "Ancona, Byzantium, and the Adriatic 1155-1173," *Papers of the British School at Rome,* 52 (1984): 195-216.

3. Edgar N. Johnson, "The Crusades of Frederick Barbarossa and Henry VI," in *A History of the Crusades,* edited by Kenneth M. Setton, 5 vols. (Madison, Wisc., 1962-), 2: 116-22.

4. The latest discussion of the twelfth-century Byzantine navy is in Lilie, *Handel und Politik,* 613-43.

5. For Byzantine fear of water and of foreigners, see Kazhdan and Constable, *People and Power in Byzantium,* 42-43.

6. For example, Abulafia, *Two Italies,* 91, speaks of the Byzantines as buying Italian fleets. Many Genoese privately offered their services as mercenaries to the Byzantine emperor. Lilie, *Handel und Politik,* 635-36, gives a few examples.

7. Nicetas reports that the Venetian fleet mutinied against Manuel and mocked the emperor by regaling a black slave on one of their galleys, thus mimicking Manuel's own dark complexion (*Historia,* 1: 85-87). For Manuel's use of the Italians as long-distance shippers only, see Hendy, "Byzantium," 40.

8. See Day, "Impact of the Third Crusade," 159-68. See also Donald E. Queller and Gerald W. Day, "Some Arguments in Defense of the Venetians on the Fourth Crusade," *American Historical Review,* 81 (1976): 729-34. Lilie, *Handel und Politik,* criticizes the theory, which he attributes to me, that in the post-Saladinic economy of the Levant, trade had been transferred from Constantinople to Alexandria. That is not quite what I said in the two articles just cited. Rather, the Third Crusade opened alternative markets for Italian traders through the advantageous gains in concessions in Syria resulting from the crusade and from Saladin's diplomatic flirtation with the Italians. Constantinople was losing the nearly monopolistic position that it had enjoyed for generations in the eastern trade, and I still think that the Venetians did see the original Egyptian goal of the Fourth Crusade as an opportunity to build up trade in addition to Constantinople, but not in place of it. Although Lilie's contention—that goods from Alexandria differed from goods from Constantinople, and thus Alexandria could not replace Constantinople—may be true, there are very few data on which to base such a conclusion. As for Lilie's disagreements with me about trade routes, I can only refer him to the scholarly works listed in my notes on which I depended.

9. De Negri, *Storia di Genova,* 131-33; Vitale, *Breviario,* 1: 5; Lopez, "Aux origins du capitalisme," 431.

10. Girolamo Bertolotto, "Cintraco," *Giornale ligustico di archeologia, storia, e belle arti* 21 (1896): 36-40.

11. Vitale, *Breviario,* 1: 5-13; De Negri, *Storia di Genova,* 185-208.

12. Angelo M. G. Scorza, *Le famiglie nobili genovesi* (Genoa, 1924), 122.

13. John K. Fotheringham, "Genoa and the Fourth Crusade," *English Historical Review* 25 (1910): 36, n. 38, demonstrates that the Byzantines habitually called the Genoese "Lombards." On the existence of the

contingent, see Girolamo Serra, *La storia della antica Liguria e di Genova,* 4 vols. (Turin, 1834), 1: 357.

14. On the Genoese participation in the Christian campaigns in Spain from as early as 1093, see *Codice diplomatico,* 1: 10, doc. 5.

15. Caffaro, *De libertatione civitatum orientis,* edited by Luigi T. Belgrano, in *Annali genovesi di Caffaro e de'suoi continuatori dal MXCIX al MCCXCII,* edited by Luigi T. Belgrano and Cesaré Imperiale di Sant'Angelo, 5 vols. (Rome, 1890-1929), 1: 118; Anna Comnena, *Alexiade,* edited by Bernard Leib, 3 vols. (Paris, 1937-45), 3: 46-47; Balard, *Romanie génoise,* 1: 17-19. The Genoese had received from Bohemond of Taranto and Tancred valuable commercial privileges in Antioch in 1098 and 1101. See above, chap. 1.

16. Anna Comnena, *Alexiade,* 3: 53-54; Wilhelm Heyd, *Le colonie commerciali degli Italiani in Oriente nel medio evo,* translated and edited by Giuseppe Müller, 2 vols. (Venice, 1866-68), 1: 23; Manfroni, "Relazioni," 591-92.

17. Abulafia, *Two Italies,* 74-75.

18. *Codice diplomatico,* 1: 141-42, doc. 119; "Registrum curiae," 2, pt. 2:, 9. This latter passage is also mentioned by Abulafia, *Two Italies,* 71, and Balard, *Romanie génoise,* 1: 21.

19. G. L. Tafel and G. M. Thomas, eds., *Urkunden zur älteren Handels- und Staatsgeschichte der Republic Venedig,* 3 vols. (Vienna, 1856-57), 1: 43-54; Giuseppe Müller, ed., *Documenti sulle relazioni delle città toscane coll'Oriente cristiano e coi Turchi* (Florence, 1879), 52-54.

20. *Codice diplomatico,* 1: 28-31, doc. 22, and for Bertrand's concession after the capture of Tripoli, see ibid., 32-33, doc. 24.

21. Ibid., 34-36, doc. 27; 73-75, doc. 62.

22. Caffaro, *Cafari ystoria captionis Almarie et Turtuose ann. MCXXXXVII et MCXXXXVIII,* edited by Luigi T. Belgrano, in *Annali genovesi,* 1: 77-89; *Codice diplomatico,* 1: 204-17, docs. 166-69; 228-33, docs. 182-83; and 236-40, docs. 190-91.

23. Hilmar C. Krueger, "Post-War Collapse and Rehabilitation in Genoa (1149-1162)," in *Studi in onore di Gino Luzzatti,* 2 vols. (Milan, 1949), 1:117-28, passim.

24. Nineteenth-century scholars have left the strong impression that the Byzantines made the initial offer of a commercial facility in Constantinople. Wilhelm Heyd, *Histoire du commerce du Levant au moyen âge,* translated and revised by Furcy Reynaud, 2 vols. (Leipzig, 1885-86), 1: 203; Camillo Manfroni, "Le relazioni fra Genova, *l'impero* bizantino, e i Turchi, *Atti della Società Ligure di Storia Patria* 28 (1896-98): 598. A sentence in the agreement of 1155 reads, "Si vero Paleologus vel Sebastos promiserit vobis specialem embolum et speciales scalas, Dominus meus

Sanctissimus Imperator dabit vobis easdem" "Nuova serie di Documenti sulle relazioni di Genova coll'impero bizantino," edited by Angelo Sanguineti and Gerolamo Bertolotto, *Atti della Società Ligure di Storia Patria* 28 (1896-98):344. Clearly the promise was conditional and its mention denotes only the potentiality of a formal offer being made at some future time, that is, perhaps when the Byzantine commanders, Palaeologus and Ducas, would approve the results of Macrembolites' negotiations. The implication is that while the Byzantines may have initiated the negotiations, the Genoese were the ones who brought up the matter of a commercial quarter. There is no proof, therefore, that the Byzantines agreed to this stipulation in 1155.

25. Krueger, "Post-War Collapse," *passim.*

26. On this dramatic change in Genoese policy, see below, chap. 4.

27. *Codice diplomatico,* 1: 301-2, doc. 251.

28. *Annali genovesi,* 1: 38-39.

29. Ibid., 1: 43; *Codice diplomatico,* 1: 296-99, docs. 246-48.

30. *Codice diplomatico,* 1: 328-43, docs. 279-80.

31. *Annali genovesi,* 1: 48.

32. Ibid., 60.

33. Ibid., 62.

34. Ibid., 31.

35. Steven Runciman, *A History of the Crusades,* 3 vols. (Cambridge, 1951-55), 2: 222.

36. *Codice diplomatico,* 1: 166, doc. 128.

37. Sanguineti and Bertolotto, "Documenti," 343-45. Also in *Codice diplomatico,* 1: 327-30. All of the diplomatic materials are in *Codice diplomatico,* but I prefer to cite in the future "Documenti," which has fuller and better organized versions and gives the original Greek, which *Codice diplomatico* omits.

38. *Annali genovesi,* 1: 42. This customs reduction, not specifically mentioned in the agreement, must be what was implied in the reference to Pisan privileges in the promise. Other privileges accorded to the Pisans that are not mentioned in the promise of 1155 are minor, such as the reservation of spaces in Hagia Sophia and in the Hippodrome (Heyd, *Histoire du commerce,* 1: 193-94).

39. Sanguineti and Bertolotto, "Documenti," 343-45.

40. For the Sicilian treaty itself, see *Annali genovesi,* 1, 46, and *Codice diplomatico,* 1: 341-43, doc. 280, and 344-49, doc. 282 (the Genoese ratification). For the reasons lying behind this change of policy, see below, chap. 4.

41. *Annali genovesi,* 1: 48 and 60.

42. Ibid., 67-68. Much work was done in the nineteenth century on

the description of the Genoese compounds in Constantinople. Alexander Paspati, "To emporion ton Genouension en Konstantinoupolei kai Euxeino ponto," *Byzantinai meletai topographikai kai historikai,* 4 vols. (Constantinople, 1877), 2: 127–276. Cornelio Desimoni incorporated Paspati's research (even before it was published!) into his two articles on the Genoese quarter, "Memoria sui quartieri dei Genovesi a Constantinopoli nel secolo XII," *Giornale ligustico di archeologia, storia, e belle arti* 3 (1876): 217–35. Some scholars have believed that the original quarter was outside of Constantinople. Bratianu, *Recherches,* 64; and most recently, Balard, *Romanie génoise,* 1: 107–8. Balard places much emphasis on the use of the Latin preposition, *apud* (in the promise of 1155) to mean outside the walls of Constantinople. He attempts to prove this very narrow definition of the word by making reference to the description of a Genoese ship that was attacked years later in the harbor of Constantinople. The Latin of the description places the ship both *in portu* and *apud Constantinopolim.* Thus Balard surmises that *apud* was used to denote proximity to the city, but not actual presence inside. The word is used in general like the English "at." In the lists of losses sustained by the Genoese in Constantinople and in some contracts relating to voyages to Constantinople or to other places, *apud* is used indiscriminately to mean near or in the confines of the place mentioned. This lack of locative specificity made the word very appropriate for the text of the Byzantine promise of 1155, the validity itself of which would remain unspecific until the emperor confirmed it at some future time. The ease with which the Pisans attacked the Genoese compound in 1162 suggests that the two facilities were close together, that is, the original Genoese compound was inside Constantinople and not separated from the city by the Golden Horn. This latter situation would have required a seaborne assault by the Pisans on the entrenched Genoese, and would probably have taken longer to execute than one morning. Still, this whole matter is of little consequence since the compound existed for only two years.

43. Heyd, *Histoire du commerce,* 1: 213–14.

44. Contrary to Lilie, *Handel und Politik,* 460–64, I still believe that Manuel did not instigate the Pisan attack to punish the Genoese for concluding their treaty with Barbarossa; see Day, "Manuel and the Genoese," 293. Nor do I think that Genoese negotiating with Frederick prior to the signing of the treaty was sufficient cause for Manuel's alleged action. Scholars, including Lilie, forget that Genoa's "German friendliness" could only be expected since the city was an integral part of the German empire and only the treaty of 1162 gave it some degree of administrative independence from it. The treaty, far from binding Genoa closer to the western emperor, as is often assumed, in reality made Genoa a corporate vassal

with particular immunities and duties like other individual vassals. Scholars usually have said that the treaty gave Genoa its independence, an interpretation which overstates the case; but surely Manuel would not have been upset by this clear indication that Genoa was separating itself from his western rival, even if part of the treaty did require Genoese naval support for Frederick's planned invasion of the kingdom of Sicily. Genoa had always carried on a dialogue with the German emperors because of their overlordship, so Manuel could not have felt surprised by continuing negotiations in the very early 1160's (if they did take place) between Genoa and its suzerain. Manuel let the Genoese into his empire in 1160 when the city had an even closer relationship to the German ruler than it did after the signing of the treaty of 1162. Also, the Pisans were guilty of the same crime as the Genoese in signing a similar treaty with Barbarossa in April 1162 (Ludwig Weiland, ed., *Constitutiones et acta publica imperatorum et regum, Tomus I, Monumenta Germaniae historica, leges, sectio IV* [Hanover, 1893], 282–84). If Manuel was afraid of Genoese intentions, he should have been just as fearful of the Pisans; yet the emperor only removed the Pisans outside his capital, probably because they were more commercially valuable than the Genoese. Again, Manuel was powerful enough to evict the Pisans and Genoese from his capital if he had wished to punish them without resorting to childish tricks. If the Genoese treaty with Barbarossa did have any connection with the Pisan sack, it was that the Genoese treaty with Barbarossa aroused Pisan jealousy, since Pisa's own new independence of the emperor and the possibility of profit from a successful Sicilian campaign had in June been matched by the Genoese rivals. This whole issue is a good example of how historians sometimes build up intricate structures of diplomatic connections and considerations which exist only in logic and not in the realities of the past.

45. *Annali genovesi*, 1: 168. Manfroni suggests two reasons for the failure of the embassy: (1) a Genoese demand for indemnification; and (2) a Genoese refusal to enter into an offensive alliance against Barbarossa ("Relazioni," 608). On the matter of Genoese civil strife at the time and its possible effect on this round of negotiations, see below, chap. 4.

46. *Annali genovesi*, 1: 213.

47. Sanguineti and Bertolotto, "Documenti," 349–67, and *Codice diplomatico*, 2: 121–23, doc. 53, for a copy of Amico di Murta's convention that was presented to the Genoese parliament for ratification in the summer of 1170. This document was omitted from "Documenti." The actual chrysobull of the concession has been lost, but both di Murta's oath and the text of the chrysobull that was issued in 1170 were included in the later chrysobull of concession issued in 1192 by Isaac II. The complicated diplomacy surrounding this concession of 1170 will prob-

ably never be satisfactorily untangled. For my own view of it, see Day, "Byzantino-Genoese Diplomacy and the Collapse of Emperor Manuel's Western Policy, 1168-1171," *Byzantion* 48 (1978): 393-405. Lilie, *Handel und Politik*, 87-100, has better described what happened. In criticizing my statement that Manuel had tried to make Genoa a Byzantine "vassal" (which I did not say) and to bind Genoa to the role of a future staging area for possible Byzantine military operation in Italy, Lilie says that in the Middle Ages treaties bound signatories only so long as the treaty served the individual interests of the parties (ibid., 96-97, n. 32). Not only has Lilie denied the very basis of any treaty or diplomacy connected with it, but he has not accounted for the western medieval *mentalité*, which placed considerable importance on oaths. In the absence of strong enforcing authority, the whole western medieval society was held together by a complex system of oaths which underlay the feudal system. Indeed, Genoa's problems in Byzantium in the twelfth century stemmed from the city's careful adherence to what the Genoese perceived as a personal bond implied in treaties struck with individual emperors, even when the interests of the city could have been better served by abjuring such oaths. Also, Lilie's belief, taken from Bach, *Gênes,* that at the time there were at Genoa two factions, one pro-German and the other pro-Byzantine, is an oversimplification of internal Genoese politics, since a third faction, the della Volta group, was the most powerful and dealt with Barbarossa and Byzantine emperors alike.

48. For a quick survey of the topography of Byzantine Constantinople, see Raymond Janin, *Constantinople byzantine* (Paris, 1950), especially map 1, which outlines the Italian quarters. As mentioned earlier, much of the work in locating the Genoese quarters in Constantinople was done by Paspati and Desimoni. Since Desimoni was confused on the dates and the purposes of the documents relating to di Murta's negotiations and had a jumbled idea of events, his attempt to lump proposed and actual compounds into one and then to locate the amalgam was futile ("Memoria," 132-51). See also Heyd, *Histoire du commerce,* 1: 253-55. Balard provides the latest and perhaps the most comprehensive description of this quarter in *Romanie génoise,* 1: 109 and 180-81.

49. For the readmission of the Pisans to Constantinople in November 1170, see Heyd, *Histoire du commerce,* 1: 214.

50. ". . . cum egasteriis fabrorum lignariorum" (Sanguineti and Berto-lotto, "Documenti," 365).

51. Paspati, "Emporion," 150. The document referred to is the set of instructions sent to the Genoese ambassador in 1201 (Sanguineti and Bertolotto, "Documenti," 470).

52. See Gerald W. Day, "Italian Churches in the Byzantine Empire to 1204," *Catholic Historical Review,* 70 (1984): 385.

53. For evidence of rented property in the description of the Genoese quarter made in 1202, see Sanguineti and Bertolotto, "Documenti," 475–82.

54. Brand assigns the event to early 1171 (*Byzantium,* 207). The sack occurred sometime between August, 1170 (di Murta's final agreement with Manuel), and the expulsion of the Venetians, March 12, 1171. H. Simonsfeld, ed. *Historia ducum veneticorum,* (*Monumenta Germaniae historica, scriptores,* 14: 78.

55. August Meineke, ed., *Epitome rerum ab Ioanne et Alexio Comnenis gestarum, Corpus scriptorum historiae Byzantinae,* Bonn:1836, 26: 282.

56. Sanguineti and Bertolotto, "Documenti," 383–85.

57. *Historia ducum veneticorum,* 78.

58. Sanguineti and Bertolotto, "Documenti," 347–48. In the undated instructions themselves, the ambassador is not named, but Desimoni assigned them to di Murta because the margin of the manuscript has the note, "Dominus Amicus" ("Memoria," 156). We can surmise that di Murta was in Constantinople by the tenor of the document's introductory clause: "De maxima conventione de quo (sic) sepe mentio est si fueris appellatus . . . " (If you should be summoned (to the imperial court) concerning the very important agreement about which there is often mention . . . ") That the instructions belong to the period after the Venetian expulsion is demonstrated by the persistent use of the imperfect tense when references are made to Venetian concessions and privileges in the empire. At the beginning of the instructions, this expected new arrangement is called the "maxima conventio," reflecting the great hope that the Genoese placed in their possible reward for faithful service.

59. For a brief summary of Guercio's career in Byzantine service, culminated by Manuel's grant of a *pronoia* to him, see Sanguineti and Bertolotto, "Documenti," 471, and below, chap. 5. For Byzantinists interested in the relationship between the Byzantine *pronoia* and the feudal fief in the West, it is perhaps noteworthy that the Latin Genoese document describes Guercio's grant as "possessiones in feudi beneficium." Balard, on the other hand, goes to great length to point out that the Byzantines did not see the relationship between emperor and faithful man to be the same as the western lord-vassal relationship (*Romanie génoise,* 1: 463–65). The westerners, however, probably did understand the relationship to be the same. For an excellent discussion of this issue, see Jadran Ferluga, "La ligesse dans l'empire byzantin: contribution à l'étude de la féodalité à Byzance," *Zbornik radova Vizantoloskog Instituta* 7 (1961): 97–123.

60. *Annali genovesi*, 2: 13-14.

61. As reported in Heyd, *Histoire du commerce*, 1: 121.

62. Sanguineti and Bertolotto, "Documenti," 425. For the destruction of the quarter, see Heyd, *Histoire du commerce*, 1: 222-23, and below, chap. 3.

63. The most recent and available secondary account of the last Comneni, with extensive bibliographic notes, is Brand, *Byzantium*, 228-51.

64. William of Tyre, *Historia rerum in partibus transmarinis gestarum* (*Recueil des historiens des croisades, historiens occidentaux*, 1, Pts. 1-2), 2, 2: 1083. See also below, chap. 3.

65. *Annali genovesi*, 2: 21.

66. Tafel and Thomas, *Urkunden*, 1: 170-203, docs. 70-72.

67. Ibid., 206-11, doc. 74.

68. Müller, *Documenti sulle relazioni della città toscane*, 40-49.

69. *Annali genovesi*, 2: 30. The Byzantine's legation is known from a reference to it in the Byzantino-Genoese treaty of 1192 (Sanguineti and Bertolotto, "Documenti," 414). For more information on Mesopotamites, Nicetas' rival who enjoyed considerable influence under Isaac II and even under Alexius III, see Brand, *Byzantium*, 99, 144-46. For the reasons for the embassy's failure, see Manfroni, "Relazioni," 630-31 and n. 1.

70. Sanguineti and Bertolotto, "Documenti," 408-9.

71. Ibid., 410-33. The document actually states that the Genoese ambassadors had come before Isaac II to take their leave of his court when Isaac himself took over the talks to reach an agreement (ibid., 415).

72. Ibid., 445-48.

73. Ibid., 413-23.

74. William of Tyre says that the Latin pillaging of the Greek coast after the Latin massacre repaid the Italians many times over for their losses sustained in the riot (*Historia*, 2: 1085).

75. Lilie, *Handel und Politik*, 632-34, demonstrates the reliance of the Byzantines on Italian naval support. Helene Wieruszowski mentions the severe losses suffered by the Byzantines in William II's invasion of the empire in 1185 and in the Sicilian support of the renegade Isaac Comnenus' successful bid to establish his independence on Cyprus in 1186 ("The Norman Kingdom of Sicily and the Crusades," in *A History of the Crusades*, edited by Setton, 2: 36-39. See also Ahrweiler, *Byzance et la mer*, 282, and Brand, *Byzantium*, 172). As for military defense, Francesco Cognasso argued convincingly that the rebellion of Alexius Branas effectively destroyed the already weak Byzantine army ("Un imperatore bizantino della decadenza: Isaac II Angelo," *Bessarione* 31 (1915): 52). On Branas' revolt, see below, chap. 3.

76. Sanguineti and Bertolotto, "Documenti," 448-53.

77. The letter to Pisa has been lost, but reference to it is made in a later letter written by Isaac to Pisa in 1194 (Müller, *Documenti sulle relazioni della città toscane,* 66–67).

78. Sanguineti and Bertolotto, "Documenti," 454–64.

79. Brand, *Byzantium,* 211.

80. One such authorization, issued to the Genoese Guglielmo Cavallaro, is extant (Sanguineti and Bertolotto, "Documenti," 467–68). For a discussion of this document's possible significance, see chap. 2, note 85.

81. On Byzantine corruption in general, see especially Nicetas, although he is biased since he was out of office at the time (*Historia,* 1: 483). It is not known exactly what Stryphnus did. Nicetas says only that he extracted a large sum of money from the Genoese as a fine (ibid., 1: 482). One of the complaints made by Tornello and Spinola in 1192 was that Stryphnus, among other Byzantine officials, had levied extraordinary tariffs on Genoese ships (which may mean levies over the privileged four percent, although the tone of the complaint would indicate more), and perhaps this is what he did to Gafforio (Sanguineti and Bertolotto, "Documenti," 414).

82. *Codice diplomatico,* 3: 113–14, doc. 40.

83. Nicetas, *Historia,* 1: 482. Brand (*Byzantium,* 371, n. 10) thinks that a load of pepper entrusted to Gafforio by Lanfranco Leo referred to in the instructions to the Genoese ambassador of 1201 (Sanguineti and Bertolotto, "Documenti," 472) belongs to the period of negotiation when, so Brand thinks, Gafforio planned to resume his peaceful merchant career. It is also possible, however, that the expensive merchandise (Gafforio had to mortgage goods and ships to acquire it) is what Stryphnus had confiscated to start Gafforio's vengeful piracy.

84. The extent of Alexius' reprisals are known only through the instructions to the Genoese ambassador, Ottobono della Croce, in 1201 (Sanguineti and Bertolotto, "Documenti," 469–75) and Alexius' letter of March, 1199, to the commune (ibid., 464–66). There is disagreement among scholars as to the fate of the Genoese quarter, but della Croce's instructions indicate that in 1201 the Genoese were not in possession of their compound, for the consuls told their ambassador to pay special attention to the acquisition of the facility and of both wharves which "we used to have" ("quas habere solebamus," ibid., 470). Moreover, the wording of Alexius' letter to the Genoese government plainly stated that the Genoese were banned from Constantinople (ibid., 465).

85. Ibid., 467–68. Franz Dölger has dated the document to 1156 on paleographical evidence (cited by Brand, *Byzantium,* 214, n. 11). Although Dölger may be correct, the two facts that the document was found with others dating from Alexius III's reign and that only for the late twelfth century do we have other examples of a definite policy of the Byzantine

emperors to employ privateers make me hesitate to redate the document away from 1201. As early as 1197 Alexius had required the Pisans to expel their pirates from the empire and in 1199 the Pisan government spent money for escorting an imperial ship to Chios (Müller, *Documenti sulle relazioni delle città toscane,* 72 and 77).

86. Sanguineti and Bertolotto, "Documenti," 469–75.

87. Ibid., 475–99.

88. By far the most thoughtful consideration of the Fourth Crusade is the work of Donald E. Queller, *The Fourth Crusade: The Conquest of Constantinople,* 1201–1204 (Philadelphia, 1977), although I cannot subscribe to his theory of fortuitous accidents as explaining the diversion of the crusaders to Constantinople.

89. Letter of Hugh of St. Pol, in *Annales Colonienses maximi, Monumenta Germaniae historica, scriptores* (Hanover, 1861), 17: 813.

90. Nicetas, *Historia,* 1: 553–55; Geoffrey of Villehardouin, *La conquête de Constantinople,* edited and translated by Edmond Faral, 2 vols. (Paris, 1938–39), 1: 206–8, sections 203–4.

91. Ibid., 1: 210, section 205.

92. For the best account of the protracted Cretan affair and of Genoa's reaction to the Fourth Crusade in general, see Fotheringham, "Genoa and the Fourth Crusade," 37–57.

93. In the following chapters, several of these people will be studied in more detail.

94. Dione R. Clementi, "Some Unnoticed Aspects of the Emperor Henry VI's Conquest of the Norman Kingdom of Sicily," *Bulletin of the John Rylands Library* 26 (1953–54): 328–59.

95. Day, "Impact of the Third Crusade," passim.

96. Fotheringham, "Genoa and the Fourth Crusade," 37–57. One should also consult David Abulafia, "Henry Count of Malta and his Mediterranean Activities, 1203–1213," in *Medieval Malta: Studies on Malta before the Knights,* edited by Anthony T. Luttrell (London, 1975), 104–25.

97. See chaps. 1, p. 8, and 4, p. 130n26.

98. Deno J. Geanakoplos, *Emperor Michael Paleologus and the West, 1258–1282: A Study in Byzantine-Latin Relations* (Cambridge, Mass., 1959), 75–91, is the most available source of information on the Byzantine emperors' return to Constantinople.

# Chapter Three

༄༅༄

# Genoa's Eastern Partnership with the House of Montferrat

OTTO OF FREISING, the chronicler of Barbarossa's reign, said of Marquis William the Old of Montferrat that "he, almost alone of the barons of Italy, had been able to escape the dominion of the cities";[1] but in spite of the learned bishop's comment, the noble family of Montferrat, whose domains lay in the hills of Piedmont, some forty miles north by northwest of Genoa and included the towns of Asti and Turin, developed in the twelfth century a close relationship to the great Ligurian port city that was translated into the advancement of their respective ambitions in the East.[2] The story of Genoese-Montferrine cooperation, however, helps to explain both the Genoese presence in Byzantium and, more important, perhaps, the crusading electors' choice of Baldwin of Flanders as the first Latin emperor of Constantinople in 1204. To describe this connection between the house of Montferrat and Genoa, the story must go beyond the Byzantine Empire to crusader-held Syria and Palestine and to Liguria itself, where ample evidence exists to demonstrate a loose but persistent partnership that had both fortuitous and tragic consequences for both the feudal Montferrats and the commercial Genoese.

Although in the twelfth century the forty miles of mountainous terrain that separated Genoa from the lands of the Montferrats presented many obstacles, and the difference between the feudal outlook of the landed nobility and the business aspirations of the closely packed city folk could present an even more untraversible barrier, still, the Genoese and the Montferrats had interests that required cooperation between them. Much of the Piedmont was in the domain or under the sway of the Montferrats, and much of the noble house's wealth came from tolls and other duties imposed on merchants traveling in their territory on the way between the markets of France and the great western port of Genoa. While Genoese merchants had little difficulty sailing to commercial sites along the Mediterranean coast, the rugged terrain that rises directly behind Genoa and continues into the Alps and the larcenous nature of the feudal barons who inhabited that hinterland in the Middle Ages made so arduous the transportation of merchandise that Genoa could almost be termed a sea-locked city. In fact, the Genoese considered transportation north so risky that throughout most of the twelfth century they preferred to let northerners do the hauling.[3] The powerful marquises of Montferrat must have been some of the more intractable roadblocks to the flow of goods, for when the Genoese finally reached an agreement on the matter with Marquis Boniface II in 1232, the lord of Montferrat promised Genoa's merchants his protection on the road between Asti and Turin, but even then he reserved to himself the customary right to collect the wayfarers' toll, the *pedagium,* from traveling merchants.[4]

The political climate of northern Italy in the twelfth century gave the marquises of Montferrat cause to be concerned with the growing city of Genoa. Marquis William the Old, married to Barbarossa's niece, was a strong supporter of the German emperor, who had to take into consideration the strength of Genoa in his attempts to subdue Lombardy. Like the citizens of other Italian communes, the Genoese entered into that well-known phase of Italian urban development called the "conquest of the contado,"[5] in order to insure the security of their commerce and the maintenance of their political strength. Genoa expanded its control landward by subduing one by one the feudal lords whose turbulence menaced the city's progress. The Cerberus-like nature of the quarrels of the landed aristocracy required the Genoese to bring under their sway neighbors of recently vanquished feudatories until Genoese control covered the Ligurian littoral and the land extending into the interior from Monaco on the west to Portovenere on the east. By the middle of the twelfth century, then, the marquises of Montferrat must have viewed Genoa as the greatest threat to their feudal domination and even to their independence. It is to the credit of the marquises and the Genoese that in this potentially dangerous situation they preferred to develop a spirit of cooperation for their mutual benefit.

The Genoese had already developed a mechanism for coming to terms with their feudal neighbors by extracting from them oaths of loyalty to the *compagnia,* that is, to the commune. Beginning with the earliest example of a final accord between Genoa and a feudal baron, a document of 1135 involving Marquis Alderamo of Ponzone,[6] nobles, in return for Genoa's acknowledgment of their feudal rights (always reduced, of course) and for the city's promise of assistance against warlike neighbors, promised to reside in Genoa for a specified period of time each year, usually two or three months but longer in time of war; to abide by the decisions of the Genoese *compagnia* and to implement those policies in their own lands; and to serve with an armed retinue in the Genoese host during wartime. Other examples are numerous. In 1138 the counts of Lavagna made such an oath to the commune,[7] and in the next year, Ferraria, the mistress of the castle of Albissola, similarly bound herself to Genoa.[8] The lords of Lagneto and their adversaries, the lords of Nasci and Passano, took the oath in 1145,[9] in 1146 the counts of Ventimiglia,[10] and in 1148 the marquis of Savona made his promise.[11]

In the oath of Alderamo of Ponzone, it is specifically stated that he became a Genoese citizen by his submission, but the phrase is absent from later oaths. Nevertheless, there are cases in which noblemen did become Genoese citizens. The lords of Lavagna, Nasci, and Passano sired the noble Genoese families of Cavarunco, della Torre, Bianchi, and Fieschi, whose citizenship from the late twelfth century on cannot be disputed.[12] After Marquis Albert of Parodi had given his oath in 1145, the Genoese, in their promise of 1148 to help him escape from his captors, declared, "the commune ought to be bound to the marquis just as to a great and distinguished citizen."[13] Since the northern Italian barons understood their relations to other political entities in feudal terms, Marquis Albert, like the others, considered himself bound as a vassal to a new corporate lord (through the duties of knight service, obedience, and counsel), while the Genoese accorded him and his counterparts the rights and protection of its citizens (through residence in the city).

These oaths were not just empty promises but proved to be

effective instruments for subordinating the outlying nobility to Genoa. In 1150, for example, the Genoese consuls settled a dispute between the marquis of Savona and his dependants, the inhabitants of Noli.[14] So complete was Genoese control over the counts of Lavagna that in 1157 the city was able to force these feudatories to install a *compagnia* and consulate in their own town.[15] The oath clearly created a strong bond between the nobles and Genoa.

The squabbles of the outlying nobility eventually enabled the Genoese government to extract this same kind of oath from the marquises of Montferrat.[16] The background of the Montferrine oath was typically feudal. Albert, marquis of Parodi, under threat from his neighbors in return for Genoese help, had become a vassal of Genoa.[17] His action apparently did not protect him, for the people of Castelleto soon captured him and his castle. A Genoese force freed him, and peace was made.[18] In March 1146, the people of Gamundio, more of Albert's foes, recognized Genoese suzerainty over the luckless noble's other castles of Voltaggio, Fiaccone, Aimero, and half of Montalto.[19] Once again in 1148 the people of Castelleto captured Albert and his wife, Matilda. The Genoese, or perhaps the marquis' loyal vassals at Genoese instigation, freed the lord and formally bought the castle of Parodi from him for £700.[20] Albert's feudal lord and brother-in-law, the marquis of Montferrat, now entered into the dispute since he was probably displeased to see so many of his holdings under the control of the Genoese. It is not known whether the controversy came to blows, but in June 1150, an agreement was reached whereby the marquis relinquished his rights to Parodi and Montalto for £500 and a house in Genoa and promised to pay ten thousand marks if the matter of the castles arose again.[21]

In that same month in the Genoese cathedral of San Lorenzo before the people of the commune assembled in full parliament, the marquis of Montferrat also made his oath of loyalty to Genoa.[22] Important, of course, was Genoa's ability to force this powerful lord to the city to make his submission; of even more significance was the tenor of his oath, which closely corresponded to those of other Ligurian nobles who had submitted to Genoese authority. Marquis William swore to live in Genoa for part of the year, but in his case, because of the distance of the marquis' home from the city and because of his powerful feudal position, the exact terms of his residency were left to his discretion.[23] William also accepted the burden of military service, promising to serve in the Genoese host with ten knights without pay. He also promised to abide by the decisions of the consuls and to give the Genoese officials honest advice. As a recognition of the marquis' high standing, the novel stipulation was inserted in the agreement that he could attend governmental meetings whenever he was in Genoa.

Whether or not this oath bestowed Genoese citizenship on the marquis of Montferrat is questionable, but it is unlikely that the marquis, who was politically on the same level of the medieval heirarchy as the city of Genoa, if not on even a higher one, could have gained any real advantage from citizenship that he could not have acquired by alliance. Perhaps to medieval people it would even have seemed odd to consider such a powerful territorial lord as a communal citizen. Nevertheless, William of Montferrat's oath of 1150 established practically the same close relationship between himself and Genoa that local nobles had accepted. From that time on, the house of Montferrat and the city of Genoa would have a profound interest in each other's affairs.

The oath was not simply a stop-gap measure to be discarded by William after the temporary adversity had passed, for his involvement in Genoese affairs continued. In June 1162, the marquis acted as a witness to Frederick Barbarossa's treaty with Genoa.[24] William did not appear simply as an adherent in Barbarossa's entourage, but the documents concluding the Germano-Genoese alliance show how deeply Montferrat had penetrated the Genoese sphere and how concerned the city's officials were about the potential danger of so powerful a feudatory meddling in their business, in spite of Montferrat's twelve-year-old oath. The emperor promised to make William of Montferrat and some other powerful barons neighboring Genoa, along with the chiefs of the communal governments of Piacenza, Pavia, Asti, and Tortona, swear not to cause trouble for the city when its forces were serving under the imperial banner.[25] These very same people were the only Italians who appeared as signatories to the emperor's part of the treaty. Certainly the illustrious marquis signed the document only because the Genoese required of Frederick that Montferrat acknowledge the conditions of the alliance, and not because he happened to be in Frederick's retinue.

In spite of the Genoese-Montferrine settlement of 1150 regarding the castle of Parodi, the strategic fortress again became a source of conflict between the noble family and Genoa in 1166. After the city had purchased Parodi from its marquis in 1148, Genoa had stationed its own garrison there. Marquis Albert's sons, William and Renier, however, must have felt cheated of part of their inheritance,[26] for in late 1166 William induced his maternal uncle, William the Old of Montferrat, to help him regain the castle. Decrees of the Genoese consuls on November 15 and 20, 1166, confiscated the property and declared free the slaves belonging to the castellans of Parodi as a punishment for surrendering the fortress to the besiegers.[27] The Genoese complained to Barbarossa's powerful chancellor, Archbishop Rainald of Cologne, who summoned the brothers of Parodi and the marquises of Gavi to answer for their action. The nobles refused to obey the archbishop's command, and after several more fruitless attempts to call the marquises to his court, Rainald placed them under imperial ban on February 13, 1167, at Genoa and instructed the people of Pavia and several local nobles to help the Genoese recover the castle. The archbishop specifically forbade Marquis William of Montferrat from giving aid to his relatives against the Genoese.[28] A new settlement of the issue came only in 1171 when, almost as a mockery of the whole case, the marquises of Parodi made their customary oath of submission to the Genoese commune, as their father had done nearly twenty-five years before, and received possession of the castle from the city government.[29]

In this latter controversy over the castle of Parodi, matrimony emerged as a closer and more personal connection between the house of Montferrat and Genoa than mere geographical proximity or feudal relationships. Not only were the brothers of Parodi the nephews of Marquis William through their mother, but also one of William of Montferrat's daughters, Alasia, was married to Manfred, marquis of Saluzzo; and another, Beatrice, was probably married to Albert, marquis of Malaspina, against whom Genoa waged an intermittent struggle throughout the twelfth century. Later the woman was married to Henry of Carretto.[30] Manfred of Saluzzo was a brother and Henry of Carretto the son of Marquis Enrico Guercio of Loreto and Savona, a vassal of the Genoese commune.[31] Not only were both men deeply involved with Genoa, but Henry of Carretto's brother, Otto, had married into the noble Genoese house of Embriaco, was a commander of the Genoese contingent accompanying Henry VI to Sicily in 1194, and was elected as the city's *podestà* on the death of Uberto di Olivano in the same year.[32] These complex bonds of matrimony must certainly have forced the Montferrats to be much concerned with Genoese matters.

William of Montferrat was not indisposed to fulfilling the military obligations to Genoa contained in his oath. In 1172 the marquis of Malaspina, perhaps William's own son-in-law and a vassal of the Genoese archbishop, and his son, Muruel, a vassal of the commune, formed a rebellious conspiracy with the people of Lunisiana, Passano, and Lavagna. In December the malcontents attacked strategic positions on the outskirts of Genoa. To repel the invaders, Genoa called on its "neighboring marquises" for aid, and William the Old, along with the marquises of Savona, Lavagna, Gavi, Bosco, and Ponzone, came with their followers to the city's assistance. Once Malaspina had been forced to retreat, the combined Genoese host pursued him into the mountains, but the inclement winter weather caused such morale problems in the ranks of the marquises' contingents that a truce was arranged and the marquises went home after receiving their pay.[33]

Apparently the house of Montferrat's marriage alliances, the conditions of Italo-imperial politics, and the growing urban domination of the local aristocracy had made the Piedmontese family participants in the events in twelfth-century Liguria, primarily directed by Genoa. But the willingness of the Montferrats and the Genoese to assist each other in northern Italy was continued with an even more pronounced solidarity in the distant and exotic East, where the common background of the marquises and the Genoese seemed to unite them in cooperative efforts for the mutual good. Since the Genoese connection probably did not have a decisive influence on the popularity of William the Old's sons as husbands for eastern princesses, Montferrat's matchmaking can be attributed to other factors. William was the richest and most powerful northern Italian baron, he was a staunch supporter and an in-law of the German imperial house as well as of the French royal family, and he had four eligible sons who, like many of their contemporaries, seemed to yearn for the adventure that the East could offer. Nevertheless, Renier was offered the hand of a Greek princess when Manuel I Comnenus' pro-Genoese sympathies were at their highest,[34] and William "Longsword" married Sybilla, the sister of King Baldwin IV of Jerusalem in 1176 amid a flurry of Genoese hopes to have restored to them some of the privileges taken away by the dead King Amalric of Jerusalem.

The short-lived career of William Longsword in the Holy Land provides the first incontrovertible instance of Montferrine-Genoese collaboration. Genoese activity in the Kingdom of Jerusalem had been seriously curtailed when King Amalric sometime before 1167 had taken away some of Genoa's possessions, probably to compensate for the losses he had incurred in his unsuccessful invasions of Egypt in 1163, 1164, and 1167.[35] The proposed marriage between William and Sybilla gave the Genoese the expectation of regaining their property and rights through a friendly dominant influence at the crusader court. Consequently, on the eve of William's departure for the East in August 1176, he came to an agreement with the Genoese concerning his responsibilities to the city's interests.[36] The document reveals that Genoese and the Montferrats agreed on a common program in the East.

> In the name of the Lord, Amen. I, William marquis of Montferrat, agree and promise to you, the consuls of the commune of Genoa . . . that on behalf of the commune of Genoa I shall protect and maintain, as long as I shall live, all Genoese and the men of that district of Genoa and their goods and possessions in my whole land and district and domain that I have and . . . shall have henceforth on land and water. In all causes and discords which the Genoese will have henceforth, I shall offer them my counsel and aid in good faith to the end, and I will maintain them therein. Without fraud I shall assist the Genoese church and the commune of Genoa and the Genoese themselves to retain and to have quit, and if they should loose them, . . . to recover all the possessions and rights which they have and will have in the regions beyond the sea. And in no way will I be a party to a deed or plan that will diminish anything thereof to their disadvantage. But I shall effectively bring to bear on their behalf my counsel and aid to the end of the recovery of the possessions and rights across the sea which they shall sometime have or be able to demand by right, with the exception that I shall not make war therefor and with the exception of the county of Jaffa and its

appurtenances which the king specifically detains, so that I will give aid and counsel to the end that the Genoese themselves and their church and their commune either may recover those things or may obtain justice therefor, or at least that they may have agreement and concord thereof according to what will seem to me, without fraud, to pertain to the advantage and honor of the city of Genoa and of the king himself . . . [37]

The marquis, therefore, promised to do everything in his power, short of war, to help Genoa recover its possessions and to protect the city's rights to whatever it might win in the future. The county of Jaffa was excluded from the agreement because William was destined to receive it by his marriage to Sybilla and he did not want any dispute to arise that might threaten his possession of it.[38] Longsword would indeed have been a strong support to Genoese claims in Palestine, for as husband of the frail King Baldwin's sister, he stood a good chance to inherit the kingdom on the expected death of the king. Probably he came to the Holy Land to serve as regent for the kingdom.[39] Genoese hopes were dashed, however, when William contracted malaria soon after his marriage and died in June 1177, leaving Sybilla pregnant with the future King Baldwin V.[40] Genoa did not recover its lost property for the time being,[41] but William's agreement of 1176 established a pattern that would be followed repeatedly in the East, although the Genoese would have to wait ten more years before they could draw much profit from the momentous promise of 1176.

In the autumn of 1179, William the Old sent his youngest son, Renier, to Constantinople to marry Emperor Manuel's daughter, Maria Porphyrogenita. The young man was received in the Byzantine capital with much acclaim, and in February 1180, the nuptials were celebrated. Renier was given the loftly title of Caesar.[42] He was soon joined in Constantinople by his brother, Conrad, who had just blocked the German imperial advance into Tuscany and had captured Barbarossa's chancellor probably in fulfillment of the Montferrat part of the marriage bargain. After Manuel's death in September, Conrad, now despairing of winning his promised Byzantine reward for his Italian exploits, returned home to release his prize for a ransom of twelve thousand hyperpers and to let Renier face the coming storm alone.[43]

In September 1180, Emperor Manuel's death ended Renier's prospects of luxury at the Byzantine court and began the regency for twelve-year-old Alexius II. In the ensuing two years Byzantine politics became a three-sided affair. On one side of the court triangle, the regents, Marie of Antioch and Alexius the *protosebastos,* collaborated in matters both of politics and love to rule the empire and to oust everyone else from participation in its governance.[44] They sought the support of the Latins in the absence of an effective native following by giving westerners free rein in the empire's business life. On a second side of the struggle, Maria Porphyrogenita and Renier were also friendly to the Latins but deeply resented their exclusion from power. The princess had been disappointed by her brother's birth, which denied her the power that would come to Manuel's heir, and now she conspired with other disaffected courtiers to topple the regency. The third side was occupied by an anti-Latin faction that was opposed to the privileged position of the westerners. Andronicus Comnenus, an erstwhile cousin of the dead emperor and a political opportunist, quickly emerged as the champion of this group.

In 1181 hostility to the regency united the Porphyrogenite's followers with Andronicus' faction. Maria Porphyrogenita wrote to Andronicus, then serving an honorable exile as governor of Pontus, asking him to march with his troops in support of her proposed coup.[45] In late February 1181, the plot became known to the regents, who arrested some fifteen high-ranking conspirators. Maria Porphyrogenita and Renier fled to Hagia Sophia, where they obtained sanctuary from the sympathetic patriarch, Theodosius the Boradiote, and were besieged by imperial troops. By the second week of May, after an unsuccessful sortie led by Renier, who had collected some one hundred and fifty westerners, the rebels lacked sufficient strength to prevail over the regency. Maria fell on her brother's mercy, or rather on that of the regents, and obtained pardon for herself and her husband.[46]

The Genoese and Pisans contributed to the factionalism not only by their mere presence but also by their active support of one side or another. The Pisans distinguished themselves in their service to the regency. They were surely at least in part the object of the rumor circulating among the Byzantines that Alexius the *protosebastos* had promised specified Latins permission to loot

Constantinople and to reduce its population to servitude.[47] Probably the Genoese, with their traditional enmity toward the Pisans and their city's closeness to the Montferrats, gave assistance to Maria Porphyrogenita's faction. The band of westerners whom Renier led out of Hagia Sophia was very likely composed of a large number of Genoese who hoped to profit from the installation of a particularly pro-Genoese government.

With the reconciliation of Maria and Renier to the regents, the Latin question became the major dividing issue. The siege of Hagia Sophia had signaled Andronicus to march on the capital. After Andronicus had encamped at Chalcedon, a fleet sent by the regents under the megaduke Contostephanus to block the rebel's advance went over to his side.[48]

Although the treason of the regents' forces gave Andronicus a considerable advantage, only by engineering the famous Latin massacre was the rebel able to dislodge the formidable obstacle of Italian naval power from his path to the throne. The Genoese and the Pisans defended the regency government now to the very end, for they made up the "bravest and most aggressive" part of the Byzantine fleet blocking Andronicus' passage across the Propontis from Chalcedon.[49] Finally, the westerners who could foresee the probable outcome of events boarded forty-five Latin galleys and put to sea before the Byzantine populace could vent its growing animosity. Others put their belongings on ships still in the port. While these westerners waited to set sail, Andronicus sent a band of personally selected troops into the city, where the rebel's soldiers fell on the Latins with the assistance of the urban mob. The westerners who had been unable to escape by sea were slaughtered without regard to age, sex, or condition. The Byzantines' anger was particularly directed at the Latin clergy, whose members were barbarously put to death, including a papal legate whose severed head was irreverently tied to the tail of a cur. The buildings of the Latin sector were burned down, as was the hospital of Saint John, where the sick were put to the sword. More than four thousand survivors of the carnage were sold into slavery to the Turks. The few westerners who escaped both death and slavery headed for crusader-held Palestine, where they could continue their business in the oriental trade more safely. When the Italians who had earlier fled by ship heard of the massacre, they took vengeance for their slain friends and relatives by leaving a path of pillage and destruction all the way to the Mediterranean.[50]

In late April or May 1182, Andronicus triumphantly entered Constantinople and began to exterminate potential rivals. Alexius the *protosebastos* was imprisoned and blinded, and Marie of Antioch drowned. Maria Porphyrogenita and her husband, Renier of Montferrat, were poisoned by the new regent as payment both for their withdrawal of support and for their sympathies for the hated westerners. The next year Andronicus tired of his role as regent for the young emperor and had Alexius II put to death. He then donned the imperial purple himself, ushering in a period of both violent retribution against unsupportive Byzantine aristocrats and total exclusion of Latins from the empire.[51] The usurper's success thus interrupted for a few years Italian involvement in internal Byzantine politics. This first excursion of the house of Montferrat and its Genoese friends into the affairs of the Byzantine Empire had ended in tragic failure.

In 1185 the Byzantine court aristocracy, despairing over Andronicus' reign of terror and impatient with his ineffectiveness in dealing with the invasion of William II of Sicily, rebelled against the despised emperor and replaced him with Isaac Angelus, who was connected with the dynasty of the Comneni through his mother. Although Isaac represented a new dynasty, he returned to the pro-Latinism of Manuel's court. Not surprisingly, the Montferrats once again won an opportunity to make a marriage connection with Byzantium. William of Montferrat's son, Conrad, was invited to Constantinople to become the husband of Isaac's sister, Theodora.[52] Soon after the Lombard nobleman's arrival in Byzantium in early 1187, the weak emperor called upon this western strongman to defend him from rebellion. While the marriage was being celebrated, Alexius Branas, a Byzantine general who already had revolted once against Isaac but had been pardoned and given the governorship of Adrianople, proclaimed himself emperor and began his march on Constantinople.[53] Isaac now proved himself quite unable to cope with the dangerous situation. In his irresolution he entrusted his fortune to the prayers of monks and the defense of his capital to Conrad. The western baron accepted the challenge, and with a core of two hundred and fifty western horsemen and five hundred foot soldiers, he organized the Byzantine forces for the coming encounter. Conrad's hastily assembled army routed the rebel force and killed Branas just outside the walls of the great city, saving Isaac's throne.[54]

Ungratefully, the emperor refused to reward Conrad for his immense services, perhaps feeling that Conrad was only fulfilling the obligation incurred by his recent marriage. Probably the emperor's stinginess was motivated by the rioting between the Byzantine populace and the Latin residents of the city in the days following Conrad's victory.[55] Whether one discounts the charges of the Genoese annalist that Isaac, fearing Conrad's power, began plotting against him,[56] or one only accepts that Conrad was wholly dissatisfied with the lack of recompense, it was necessary for him to leave Byzantine territory. On the advice of his Genoese confidant, Ansaldo Bonovicino, the marquis set out in a Genoese ship belonging to Baldovino Erminio to find out what his adventuresome spirit could win in the Holy Land.[57]

Throughout Conrad's brief experience in Constantinople, some Genoese helped him on every occasion as indicated by the mention of Ansaldo Bonovicino's counsel and of the Genoese ship that took Conrad from Constantinople. Bonovicino must indeed have been close to the marquis, for the former followed the latter to the Holy Land and was influential enough to become the castellan of Tyre[58] and to receive special attention for his fiefs in Palestine in Henry of Champagne's confirmation of 1195 of Genoese privileges in the Holy Land.[59] In the charter memorializing this confirmation one finds that Ansaldo's wife was Ellena, the daughter of Roglerio d'Isolis, thus connecting Bonovicino with one of the powerful viscountal families of Genoa. The example of Bonovicino leads readily to the likelihood of the presence of other Genoese in Conrad's entourage. When the marquis enlisted additional fighting men from the Italians in Constantinople for his stand against Branas, he surely must have looked to the Genoese in the city, many of whom, as it will be seen, came with the diplomatic mission of Pevere and Mallone at the end of 1186.[60] It cannot be assumed, moreover, that there were many other Italians in Constantinople, for the Venetians were still in the process of recovering their possessions in Byzantium and the Pisans would not return in any large numbers until they had regained their concession in 1192.[61] Nicetas' designation of Conrad's recruits as "Latins" indicates the multi-city composition of westerners in Constantinople, but with the possible exception of the Venetians, only a large number of Genoese in Constantinople in early 1187 can be assumed.[62]

A very clear picture of the cooperation between Montferrat and Genoa can be seen in the Christian reconquest of crusading territory following Saladin's invasion of 1187. When Conrad and his Genoese compatriots arrived off Acre in July, the sight of a Moslem patrol boat coming from the city, which had fallen only a few days before, caused the marquis to change course for Tyre.[63] The would-be crusaders found Tyre hard-pressed by Saladin's forces. As at Constantinople, Conrad and the Genoese took on themselves the defense of the city. Conrad's success in repelling the infidel made him the acknowledged leader of the residual crusading forces that were to begin the arduous task of reconquest. The Latin barons showed a well-deserved generosity to their Genoese helpers by granting Genoa the right to carry on business and to have a facility at Tyre, from which they previously had been excluded.[64]

The crusading host was severely split by factionalism, and the arrival of large forces from Europe on the Third Crusade only intensified the rivalry, which the Genoese and the Pisans hoped to use to their own advantage. The capable and successful Conrad of Montferrat attracted a large following that supported his ambition of becoming the king of a reestablished Christian state. Conrad's rival was Guy of Lusignan, the titular king of Jerusalem whose worthlessness had been demonstrated by his blundering loss of the kingdom's army at the battle of Hattin and by his subsequent capture by Saladin. After Guy had been released through the efforts of Conrad himself, the king refused to relinquish the crown that he owed to his wife, Sybilla, even after her death in 1190 and Conrad's marriage to Sybilla's sister, Isabel. Conrad found a champion in King Philip Augustus of France, a relative and the son of the probable proposer of William Longsword as the groom of Sybilla of Jerusalem back in 1176.[65] King Guy obtained the support of King Richard of England, who was the lord of Guy's family for its French fiefs.[66] As for the Italians, the Genoese remained faithful to Conrad, a loyalty that was strengthened by Genoa's transportation contract with Philip.[67] Genoa's Pisan rivals predictably chose Guy's cause. The Italian partisanship was so intense that on at least one occasion in 1191 open fighting broke out between the

Genoese and Pisan contingents and continued for three days before Richard was finally able to restore peace.[68]

In 1190, after Guy's claim to the kingdom had died with his wife and Conrad considered himself legally able to grant charters, Montferrat proved his good faith to his Genoese partners. The marquis granted them a compound in Tyre with a mill, bath, ovens, an undetermined amount of land around Tyre, one-third of the customs revenues, and a free court competent in all but capital offenses.[69] To complete his gift at Tyre, Conrad persuaded the archbishop of the city to allow the Genoese their own chapel and chaplain subject to the prelate's jurisdiction.[70] At the height of his power in 1192, Conrad confirmed to the Genoese his earlier gifts and their pre-Saladinic rights and properties in the Kingdom of Jerusalem as a whole. In addition, Conrad gave the Genoese a compound in Ascalon, and in both Ascalon and Acre a third of the import revenues and a free court.[71] Guy, who had lost the support of the crusading baronage, could do very little except confirm Conrad's generosity.[72] All the concessions were reconfirmed by Henry of Champagne, who assumed power in the kingdom as a compromise candidate after Conrad's untimely assassination in 1192.[73] Thus the long cooperation between Genoa and the house of Montferrat saw its reward when the Genoese gained primacy in the trade of the crusading states and Conrad nearly won a kingdom, had not an assassin's dagger cut short his ambitions.

The removal of the Montferrats from the East ended for the time being the collaboration for profit and power in that part of the world, but back in Italy, William the Old's last surviving son, Boniface, continued the family's involvement in Genoese affairs. In 1191 the marquis had already shown his favor to the Genoese by prosecuting before the German emperor, Henry VI, the marquises of Incisa, who had waylaid some Genoese ambassadors traveling through their lands in 1189 on the way to kings Richard and Philip to enlist their aid for the projected crusade.[74] In 1193 Marquis William of Parodi, whose loyalty to Genoa had been settled twenty years before, arbitrated a dispute between the city of Asti and the marquises of Montferrat and Incisa, who apparently had set aside their differences of two years before.[75] In spite of Montferrat's friendliness to Genoa, the Genoese alliance of 1191 with the German emperor to invade Sicily included a clause—

similar to the one in an earlier treaty with Frederick Barbarossa, thirty years before—expressly forbidding Boniface and certain other local nobles to harm Genoa while the city's armed forces were engaged with Henry.[76] Since the provision of 1191 occurs in Henry's confirmation of his father's concession, however, its inclusion in practically the same words implies that it was included mechanically and may have had little real meaning by 1191. Boniface was a signatory to Henry VI's confirmation of Emperor Conrad II's privileges to Genoa in 1194,[77] and in the same year the marquis of Montferrat participated in Henry VI's invasion of southern Italy, accompanying Henry's seneschal, Markward of Anweiler, and the Genoese *podestà*, Uberto di Olevano, who captured the city of Gaeta.[78] After the Genoese *podestà* had been killed in fighting that had broken out between Henry's Genoese and Pisan contingents, Boniface was present in Uberto's funeral procession and barely missed being killed by a Pisan ambush lying in wait for the mourners in Messina.[79] It is interesting in this regard that the Genoese elected as their new *podestà* Otto of Carretto, Boniface's in-law.[80]

There is no further record of any relations between Montferrat and Genoa until 1202 when the marquis served as mediator in an unsuccessful attempt to end the Genoese-Pisan war.[81] Probably the marquis was acting on this occasion with an eye to the projected crusade and the hope of enlisting the Genoese support that had nearly won his brother a kingdom ten years before. Boniface had already taken the cross in 1201 and had been accepted by the leaders of the future host on the death of Theobald of Champagne as the overall commander of the Fourth Crusade.[82] Although the Genoese, whom the crusader envoys had visited after concluding the contract with Venice for the army's transportation, may have been the ones who indicated to the crusaders Boniface's interest in going on holy war, there is very little evidence of Genoese participation in the crusade at all.[83]

Venetian enthusiasm for the crusade once the host assembled in Venice was intensified by its concern for the spoils Genoa might possibly win in a crusade led by a man whose family had for fifty years been so intimately linked with Genoese advancement in the East. After the conquest of Constantinople the electors of a new emperor, six crusaders and six Venetians, denied Boniface the throne that he had expected to receive on account of his strong

Genoese connections.[84] Although Boniface's support of the foolish Alexius IV, who got the crusaders into their predicament in the first place, weighed heavily on the minds of the electors, the impact of Montferrat's past cooperation with the Genoese cannot be underestimated. Indeed, the Venetian electors must have been all the more fearful of Genoese intentions if one accepts as true a variant manuscript tradition of the Genoese annals that tells of a Genoese expedition that took the city of Zara away from the Venetians and returned it to the king of Hungary while the crusading army was in Constantinople.[85] Perhaps the Venetian fear over Boniface's connections with the Genoese was unfounded, however, for when Boniface was looking for a buyer for the island of Crete, part of his spoils of victory, he was not averse to passing over the Genoese offer and accepting the more lucrative price that the Venetians were willing to pay.[86] The marquis probably could see no reason to be generous to Genoa, which had not given him the same crusading aid that it had so willingly furnished his brother in the Third Crusade.

Boniface seems not to have appreciated the neutral stand that Genoa took in the crusade, perhaps out of respect for the city's long friendship with the Montferrats, rather than coming to the defense of the Byzantines. The Fourth Crusade, it must be remembered, was the first time since 1155 that Genoa failed to honor its treaty obligations to the Byzantine Empire by not bringing its naval might to the defense of the empire in a moment of crisis. The Genoese-Montferrine collaboration in the East was beginning to break down. Nevertheless, the marquis allowed the Genoese to trade in the kingdom of Thessalonica, and in 1206 four Genoese galleys transported Agnes of Montferrat eastward to be married to Emperor Henry of Constantinople.[87] The death of Boniface in Greece in 1207 brought to a close the era of mutual aid for advancement in the East between the house of Montferrat and the commune of Genoa.

The thirty-year-long partnership between Genoa and Montferrat in the East had not been very successful. The first instance of collaboration, involving William Longsword in 1176, ended with William's premature death and Genoa's failure to recover its lost privileges in the Kingdom of Jerusalem. Renier's episode in Constantinople seemed profitable at first, but it suddenly turned into tragedy when the nobleman was poisoned and the Genoese were expelled from the empire altogether. Only Conrad of Montferrat's adventures seemed successful. Isaac II kept his throne, and Genoa set the groundwork for its return to Byzantium. The adventure of the Third Crusade nearly brought Conrad a kingdom, and it gave Genoa commercial primacy in the Latin Orient. Boniface separated himself from Genoa by going on the Fourth Crusade, but his family's past favor to the city played a substantial part in denying him the throne of the new crusading empire. Boniface proved too weak and too disrespectful of his family's traditional closeness to Genoa to share much of his spoils from the Fourth Crusade with his house's staunch supporters. On the whole, Genoese friendship with Montferrat had only involved the city's citizens in futile political intrigue and in its dangerous ramifications.

## Notes

1. "Pene solus ex Italiae baronibus civitatum effugere potuit imperium" (*Gesta Friderici I imperatoris,* edited by Roger Wilmans, *Monumenta Germaniae historica, scriptores,* 20: 397.

2. Although the connection between Genoa and the house of Montferrat has been acknowledged by some historians and ignored by others, there has not been a thorough study of this relationship. Most remarkably, the biographer of the house of Montferrat, Leopoldo Usseglio, seems to have been unaware of his subject's Genoese connection (*I marchesi di Monferrato in Italia ed in Oriente durante i secoli XII e XIII,* 2 vols. [Turin: 1926]). Brand only mentions Genoa's "friendship for the Montferrat family" (*Byzantium,* 165). Edgar H. McNeal and Robert Lee Wolff similarly just mention Montferrat's ties to Genoa ("The Fourth Crusade," in *History of the Crusades,* edited by Setton, 2: 165). Wolff, however, does attribute Boniface's failure to be elected Latin emperor of Constantinople to Venetian concern with Genoa ("The Latin Empire of Constantinople," in *History of the Crusades,* edited by Setton, 2: 189). The *locus classicus* for Montferrine-Genoese relations and their impact on the Fourth Crusade is Fotheringham, "Genoa and the Fourth Crusade," 35–36. He said very little about the matter as it existed before the Third Crusade, but he stressed the importance of Boniface of Montferrat's Genoese connection in the marquis' unsuccessful bid to become Latin emperor.

3. Robert L. Reynolds, "Genoese Trade in the Late Twelfth Century,

Particularly in Cloth from the Fairs of Champagne," *Journal of Economic and Business History* 3 (1931): 364–66.

4. *Liber iurium,* col. 911.

5. There is no point here in belaboring the extensive bibliography concerning this twelfth-century phenomenon. The basic outline can be found in Charles W. Previte-Orton, "The Italian Cities till c. 1200," in *The Cambridge Mediaeval History,* edited by Bury (Cambridge, 1926), 5:224–26. A good survey of the historiography on the subject is in the introduction to Bach, *Gênes.* For Genoa's conquest specifically, see Nilo Calvini, *Relazioni medioevali tra Genova e la Liguria Occidentale (Secoli X-XIII)* (Bordighera, 1950).

6. *Codice diplomatico,* 1: 90–92, doc. 73.

7. Ibid., 107–8, docs. 87 and 88.

8. Ibid., 120–21, doc. 101.

9. Ibid., , I, 193-195, docs. 154-55; 188–90, doc. 149; 193, doc. 153; and 195, doc. 156.

10. Ibid., 201–02, doc. 162.

11. Giulio de'Conti di San Quintino, "Osservazioni critiche sopra alcuni particolari della storia del Piemonte e della Liguria nei secoli XI e XII," *Memorie dell'Accademia delle Scienze in Torino,* 2d ser. 13 (1853): 182, doc. 26.

12. For the origins of these families, see *Codice diplomatico,* 1: 188–89, n. 1.

13. "Comune Ianue debet teneri adversum marchionem tamquam magno et honorabili civi" (*Codice diplomatico,* 1: 234, doc. 187).

14. Ibid., 264–65, doc. 213.

15. Ibid., 359–60, doc. 286.

16. Ibid., 263–64, doc. 212.

17. Ibid., 196–97, doc. 157.

18. *Liber iurium,* col. 107.

19. *Codice diplomatico,* 1: 198–200, doc. 160. Imperiale reported that a note in the manuscript margin identified Gamundio as the place "qui modo dicitur Alexandria" (ibid., 1: 198, n. 2.

20. Ibid., 1: 232–36, docs. 186–89; *Annali genovesi,* 1: 36.

21. *Codice diplomatico,* 1: 262–63, doc. 211.

22. Ibid., 1: 264, doc. 212.

23. This liberality on the part of the Genoese may answer why Otto of Freising was still able to comment on William's independence from municipal authority.

24. *Codice diplomatico,* 1: 404, doc. 308.

25. Ibid., 1: 400, doc. 308. This same clause, with the addition of the marquises of Gavi and Lavagna (already Genoese citizens), occurs in

Frederick's similar pact with Pisa (*Constitutiones imperatorum,* 1: 282–84). This stipulation must mean not that Genoa had anything to fear from the marquis but that the Italian cities generally required assurance against the unpredictable bellicosity of the northern Italian feudatories. Given the wars of the Lombard League raging at the time and the tragic fate of Milan, recently destroyed by Barbarossa, one can easily sympathize with municipal anxiety.

26. As part of the agreement of 1145, Genoa promised Marquis Albert possession of the castle for himself and his heirs (*Codice diplomatico,* 1: 197, doc. 158). Circumstances, however, required Albert to sell the castle to Genoa in 1148, so that any claim Albert's sons may have made to Parodi nearly twenty years later must have been extremely dubious, especially to the Genoese.

27. Ibid., 2: 58–59, doc. 20. For the family relationships, see "Alberi genealogici compilati dall'annalista Iacopo D'Oria," edited by Cornelio Desimoni, *Atti della Società Ligure di Storia Patria* 28 (1896–98): 308, table 6, nn. 2 and 3.

28. *Codice diplomatico,* 2: 63–65, doc. 24.

29. Ibid., 135–37, docs. 61–63.

30. Cornelio Desimoni, "Due documenti di un marchese Arduino crociato nel 1184–85," *Giornale ligustico di archeologia, storia, e belle arti* 5 (1878): 342–43.

31. Ibid., 344.

32. *Annali genovesi,* 2: 31.

33. Ibid., 1: 255–57.

34. The marriage took place in 1179, the same year that a Genoese fleet escorted Agnes of France to Constantinople to marry Manuel's heir, Alexius. On the diplomatic considerations surrounding the union, by which Manuel seems to have successfully pried the house of Montferrat from its longstanding adherence to Barbarossa, see Brand, *Byzantium,* 18–20.

35. For Genoa's problems in the Holy Land, including Amalric's confiscations, see above, chap. 1.

36. *Codice diplomatico,* 2: 235–36, doc. 105. The custom of the time was to call both the nobleman himself and his sons by the title. The document does not specify which William of Montferrat is meant, but it is likely that the Genoese would have been more concerned at the moment with Longsword's vow of support than his father's. Therefore, the younger William is the one who made the agreement.

37. The document was first published by Cornelio Desimoni in *Giornale ligustico di archeologia, storia, e belle arti* 13 (1886): 355. The document states: "In nomine Domini amen. Ego Wilielmus marchio Montisferrati

convenio et promitto vobis consulibus Ianue ... pro comuni Ianue quod salvebo et manutenebo, quamdiu vixero, universos Ianuenses et homine de districtu, atque posse quod habeo et ... de cetero habebo in terra et in aqua. ego in causis atque discordiis omnibus, quas deinceps Ianuenses habebunt, pro bonam fidem (sic) eis ad finem consilium et auxilium prestabo et eos inde manutenebo. ego sine fraude adiuvabo ecclesiam Ianuensem et comune Ianue atque ipsos Ianuenses retinere et quiete habere, et si, quod absit, perdent, recuperare omnes possessiones et iura, que quasve habent et habebunt in untramarinis partibus. et nullo modo ero in facto aut consilio quod inde que aliquando habuerint ultra mare vel de iure poterunt postulare, eis per bonam fidem auxilium et consilium efficaciter impendam usque in finem, excepto quod guerram inde non faciam, et excepto de comitatu Iope et pertinentiis eius omnino et de his que ipse rex specialiter detinet, ita quod opem et consilium dabo, ut ipsi Ianuenses et eorum Ecclesia atque Comune vel ea recuperent vel inde iusticiam consequuntur aut saltem convenientiam et concordiam inde habeant secundum quod ad commodum et honorem civitatis Ianue et ipsius regis michi sine fraude visum fuerit pertinere. hec omnia per bonam fidem, omni fraude et malitia remota, ego Wuilielmus marchio observare et adimplere iuro et in contrarium, me sciente, non faciam ... "

38. Marshall W. Baldwin, "The Decline and Fall of Jerusalem, 1174–1189," in *History of the Crusades*, edited by Setton, 2: 593.

39. Ibid.

40. Ibid.

41. Urban III was still trying to persuade the king and lords of Jerusalem to restore the Genoese possessions in 1186. See above, chap. 1.

42. Nicetas, *Historia*, 1: 170; Brand, *Byzantium*, 19; Usseglio, *I marchesi di Monferrato*, 2: 60. Most recently, Walter Haberstumpf has done a study of Renier's Byzantine adventure: "Ranieri di Monferrato: richerche sui rapporti fra Bisanzio e gli aleramici nella seconda meta del XII secolo," *Bolletino storico-bibliografico subalpina* 81 (1983): 603–39. Although the article is otherwise an excellent one, it unfortunately does not deal at all with the connection of the Genoese with Ranier nor his family.

43. Nicetas, *Historia*, 1: 200-1; Roger of Howdon, *Gesta Henrici Secundi Benedicti Abbatis: the Chronicles of the Reigns of Henry II and Richard I, AD 1169-1192*, edited by William Stubbs, *Rerum Britannicarum Mediae Aevi scriptores*, 49, Pts. 1 and 2), Pt. 1: 243-44 and 250; Brand, *Byzantium*, 19-20; Usseglio, *I marchesi di Monferrato*, 1: 417-26.

44. Nicetas, *Historia*, 1: 223-25 and 230-31. A good account of the last Comneni is Brand, *Byzantium*, 31-75.

45. Nicetas, *Historia*, 1: 231. Usseglio takes for granted Maria's exclu-

sion (*I marchesi di Monferrato*, 2: 60), but Brand suggests that she was originally included in the council (*Byzantium*, 29.)

46. Nicetas, *Historia*, 1: 232-41; William of Tyre, *Historia*, Pt. 2: 1070.

47. *Gli annales di Bernardo Maragone*, edited by M. L. Gentile, *Rerum italicarum scriptores, editio altera*, 6, Pt. 2. 71; Eustathius, *Thessalonica*, 389.

48. Nicetas, *Historia*, 1: 245-47 and 258-60.

49. Ibid., 247.

50. William of Tyre, *Historia*, Pt. 2: 1083-86; Maragone, *Annales pisani*, 73.

51. Nicetas, *Historia*, 1: 267-70 and 272-74.

52. Ibid., 382-83.

53. Ibid., 376-81.

54. Ibid., 382-87; Usseglio, *I marchesi di Monferrato*, 2: 81-82; Brand, *Byzantium*, 81-82.

55. Nicetas, *Historia*, 1: 391-93.

56. *Regni Iherosolymitani brevis historia*, in *Annali genovesi*, 1: 144. The undoubtedly confused chronicler believed that Conrad left Constantinople to escape Isaac's wrath for killing Branas.

57. Ibid.

58. *Codice diplomatico*, 2: 371, doc. 194.

59. Ibid., 114-15, doc. 40.

60. See above, chap. 2.

61. See above, chap. 2.

62. Nicetas, *Historia*, 1: 384.

63. *L'estoire de Eracles Empereur et la conquête de la terre d'Outremer*, in *Recueil des historiens des croisades, historiens occidentaux*, 2: 74-75.

64. *Codice diplomatico*, 2: 318-20, doc. 170.

65. On Louis VII's role in Longsword's marriage, see Runciman, *History of the Crusades*, 2: 411.

66. One need only bring to mind the well-known predicament in which King John was to find himself ten years later when he married Isabel of Angoulême, who had been betrothed to Hugh of Lusignan (Austin Lane Poole, *From Domesday Book to Magna Carta*, 1087-1216, 2d ed. [Oxford, 1955], 380-81).

67. *Codice diplomatico*, 364-68, docs. 191 and 192.

68. Richard of Devizes, *Itinerarium peregrinorum et gesta regis Ricardi*, edited by William Stubbs (*Rerum Britannicarum Medii Aevi Scriptores*, XXXVIII), 321-23.

69. *Codice diplomatico*, 2: 369-72, doc. 194.

70. Ibid., 372-74, doc. 195.

71. Ibid., 3: 48–50, doc. 19.
72. Ibid., 22–23, doc. 8.
73. The confirmation itself was made in 1195. Ibid., 112–15, doc. 40.
74. *Annali genovesi,* 2: 30, and n. 2.
75. Cornelio Desimoni, "Sulle marche d'Italia e sulle lora diramazioni in marchesati," *Atti della Società Ligure di Storia Patria* 28 (1896–98): 327.
76. *Codice diplomatico,* 3: 8, doc. 2.
77. Ibid., 108–10, doc. 37.
78. *Annali genovesi,* 2: 46–47.
79. Ibid., 50.
80. Ibid., 51. and nn. 30 and 31.
81. *Annali genovesi,* II, 83.
82. Geoffrey of Villehardouin, *Conquête,* 1: 40–46, secs. 40–45.
83. McNeal and Wolff, "The Fourth Crusade," 165.
84. Fotheringham, "Genoa and the Fourth Crusade," 35–36.
85. *Annali genovesi,* 2: 89, n. 1.
86. Fotheringham, "Genoa and the Fourth Crusade," 38–41.
87. Balard, "Les Génois en Romanie," 472–73.

*Chapter Four*

✣✣✣

# Byzantium in the Growth
# of Genoese Factions
# to 1164

THE MONTFERRATS VIEWED THE EAST as a vast arena where they could win the honor and glory that their adventuresome spirits demanded, but for most Genoese the Levant, and the Byzantine Empire in particular, offered the more tangible expectations of commercial opportunity and financial profit. Genoa's enormous mercantile development in the twelfth century was neither a spontaneous nor an inevitable historical phenomenon. The city's rise to a position of consequence in the Mediterranean resulted largely from the policies promoted by one political faction which had enemies devoted to its destruction by whatever means available.[1] Although Genoa's twelfth-century relations with the Byzantine Empire have been considered in the context of high level European and Mediterranean diplomacy, the particular course that those relations took can be explained further in terms of the only partially investigated political conditions within Genoa itself.

Genoa's relations with Byzantium would play a large role in the emergence of factionalism within the Ligurian city, and vice-versa, internal politics in Genoa would sometimes profoundly affect the diplomatic situation. One powerful Genoese, Ingo della Volta, and his associates—all deeply involved in the Syrian and Sicilian trade—would attempt to add Byzantine commerce to their business, and this conglomeration of trade interests would give substantial economic strength to the group's political position at home. This group's aggressive drive for power and profit alienated other notable people in Genoa, people who reacted for a variety of reasons by allying into an opposition that would gain sufficient cohesiveness in the early 1160's to be called a faction. By 1164 della Volta and his faction had overextended their power, and Ingo's ambition of controlling Genoa's politics and trade collapsed because he was unable to walk the tightrope among Frederick Barbarossa, the kings of Sicily, and Manuel I Comnenus and still be able to stifle internal opposition. In that year Genoa would experience the first round of civil strife that would characterize the city's history for years. Events in far-off Constantinople would play a significant role in della Volta's rise and in his eventual fall.

The city of Genoa offers a rather unusual conception of government because the communal organization had no revered or mystical rationale that could justify its existence or sustain its continuance. Only a very sketchy record of Genoa's history before 1100 exists, and even for the twelfth century many aspects of Genoa's constitutional structure are unknown. There is even much scholarly debate concerning the origins and nature of the early communal government, or the *compagnia,* as the Genoese themselves called it.[2] In the eleventh century Genoa, like many other northern Italian cities, was ruled by its bishop as a deputy of the archbishop of Milan in the imperial administrative structure by which, beginning with Otto the Great in the tenth century, more trustworthy ecclesiastics replaced the older and less amenable Carolingian system of counts. In that former system of government, a viscount had controlled Genoa, and indeed, in the twelfth century the leading families of the city were descended from a Viscount Ido of the tenth century. The episcopal control of the city became complete in 1052 when the local feudatories swore fealty to Bishop Oberto and became his direct vassals.[3] The episcopal court from then on served as the principal source of justice for the city, and the bishop as the chief organizer of defense.

The bishop presiding over his court was, of course, surrounded by his vassals.[4] Principal among these were the representatives of the families descended from Viscount Ido. By 1100 this ancient noble's progeny had separated into three branches, the Maneciano, the d'Isolis, and the Carmadino. Families of the Carmadino branch (Carmadino, Pevere, Avvocato, Lusio, and Usodimare) provided the major assistants to the bishop, with one of these families, the

Avvocato, adopting as its surname the title of the position it held in the bishop's administration. Along with these dominant "viscountal" families were other feudal families such as the della Volta, Mallone, Vento, della Corte, and several others. These people probably played a lesser role in general in the city's administration, but from their numbers would eventually come most of the commune's leaders in the second half of the twelfth century. All these families that attended the bishop's court were called noble by the Genoese, but it must be remembered that unlike the nobility of northern Europe, these nobles were forced to live in Genoa or its immediate environs for at least a few months a year while maintaining their connections with the rural outreaches of the city.

The political situation in Genoa was changed dramatically in 1099 when the *compagnia* was formed,[5] the nature of which has been disputed. In the eleventh century various neighborhoods of Genoa were organized into associations to maintain defense of particular sectors of the city's walls. These associations, called *companie,* assumed a wider military function in that the city's forces were organized according to them, and they became standard units of municipal administration. Although the citywide *compagnia* founded in 1099 might be seen as sort of a super government set up over these local *companie,* which provided representatives to the larger organization,[6] there is no evidence for either a revolution which overthrew the bishop's power, as happened in many other developing cities of the time, or a reason for such a considerable constitutional change because citywide coordination of activity was already managed by what appears to have been the accepted episcopal and feudal authority.

Probably, however, the *compagnia* originated as a consortium of businessmen, especially of aristocratic merchants, founded to finance a private expedition to aid the forces of the First Crusade.[7] These people simply adopted the name of the older type of organization with which they were most familiar. Our one source of information for the foundation of the *compagnia,* the annalist Caffaro, says simply, "At the time of the fleet to Caesaria, or a little before, in the city of the Genoese a *compagnia* of three years and six consuls was begun."[8] Caffaro immediately continues by describing the exploits of the Genoese expedition to the Holy Land. In the annalist's mind, the founding of the *compagnia* and the naval expedition were closely linked. So successful were the results of this organization that in 1102, "a *compagnia* of four years and four consuls was begun,"[9] and again in 1106, "when the aforesaid four years were up, there was begun another *compagnia* in a similar fashion of four years and four consuls."[10] Thus, an ad hoc association did not replace the older government of the bishop, but simply grew up beside it and became a corporate advocate for the bishop. As the twelfth century progressed, this paragovernmental organization gained in strength until it was able to usurp all of the political and judicial responsibilities of feudal and ecclesiastical authorities. The history set forth in the Genoese Annals, then, is no more than an account of the ways in which this *compagnia* struggled to gain legitimacy and sought to advance its original objective of profit obtained from broadening the city's market base in the Mediterranean world. The association's success was due to its command of all such elements of power as capital, manpower, feudal rights, prestige, and judicial competence, much of which it usurped from the bishop through excercising its championship of the prelate. The reasons for the metamorphosis of this profit-oriented consortium into Genoa's government can be uncovered only after additional research has been done, but judging from the subsequent Genoese experience, these causes probably lie in a power struggle between the senior and cadet lines of the viscountal nobility who had serviced the bishop.

The fledgling *compagnia* was always respectful of the bishop, whose advocate it had become. The concessions in the Holy Land were specifically granted to the city's prelate. Nevertheless, the bishop's powers were being pushed aside. The bishop had always been a loyal adherent of the commune, and his favor was enhanced greatly when the new government in 1133 obtained the promotion of the see to an archbishopric.[11] The elevation undercut the traditional political domination exercised by the archbishop of Milan through his feudal deputies in Genoa and made the Genoese prelate the equal of the archbishop of Pisa, Genoa's primary rival. The reconciliation of the Genoese church to the new order of government was completed in 1163 when the leaders of the commune succeeded in electing as the new archbishop Ugo della Volta, a member of the leading communal family.[12]

Whatever the origins of the *compagnia,* from the time of its inception it assumed governmental responsibilities. It was run by a board of consuls, at first six men for three years, then four who served four-year terms until 1118, when the office became biennial and finally annual after 1122. The number of consuls varied between three and eight throughout the twelfth century. By 1130 there appeared another group of officials, called "consuls of the pleas," who were responsible for justice in the city. Later in the century, other municipal officials were established, such as the offices of chancellor, treasurer, and one official called the *cintrago,* who was sort of a constable and spokesman for the people as a whole.[13] These officials were elected indirectly by at least two electoral boards, and fleeting references by mid-century to the "parliament" of Genoa tell us nothing more than that the institution existed. Behind the administration was a *consiglio* that directed foreign affairs, public finance, and constitutional structure.

The viscountal clans of Maneciano (Spinola, Embriaco, di Castro, and Brusco) and Carmadino were the dominant political groups in Genoa in the first half of the twelfth century. The early *compagnia* and the government that derived from it were controlled by members of the Maneciano branch and their supporters. One of the first consuls was Amico Brusco, while the two commanders of the Genoese fleet created by the *compagnia* were Guglielmo Embriaco and Primo di Castro. All three of these men were sons of Guido Spinola, the head of the Maneciano branch. Another son, also named Guido Spinola, served in the consulate of 1102 to 1106. Other families associated in the first consulate were Piazzalunga, Medolico, della Volta, and di Rustico. These men and their friends formed the "expansionist" faction. The basic policy of this group was to use the resources of Genoa to expand commercial influence, and its own profit, throughout the Mediterranean.[14]

The Carmadino families, on the other hand, opposed their expansionist cousins and would support a conservative, sometimes even a reactionary political program based on maintaining the old German imperial system from which they derived their feudal power in Genoa. Indeed, the low level of participation in the communal government on the part of the Carmadino families may reflect either a hostility to the upstart organization or simply their exclusion from it. Of the one hundred and fifty communal consulships between 1099 and 1149, only fifteen were held by members of the Carmadino clan, and twelve of these by only two men, Guglielmo and Lanfranco Pevere. Although other consulships may have been held by Carmadino supporters who no longer can be connected with the clan, nevertheless, most of the other one hundred and thirty-five consulships were held by members of the Maneciano families and their documentable supporters.[15] Carmadino opposition, nevertheless, was directed not so much against the policies of their antagonists as against the personalities themselves, who had deprived them of their former positions of dominance under the episcopal regime. Throughout the first half of the twelfth century these Carmadino families in general remaining aloof, probably with some contempt watched the commune grow in power and waited for their opportunity to regain municipal control.

Within this political context of the first half of the twelfth century, only one instance of turmoil exists: the conspiracy, or "rassa," against Filippo di Lamberto in 1147. Very little can be said about this incident, because there are only a few scattered references to it: three documents in which the consuls and the archbishop judged against di Lamberto and then reversed their decision,[16] a vague allusion in the brief chronicle of the Genoese campaign against Spanish Almeria and Tortosa,[17] and a passage in the oath to the *compagnia* of 1157 by which the consuls swore to uphold di Lamberto's son's right of political participation.[18] Di Lamberto, whose family connections are unknown, became consul for the third time in 1147 and was instrumental in involving Genoa in the Spanish campaigns.[19] While he was consul, he was accused of some malfeasance in office, probably connected with the Spanish business, although such behavior may be dated to the 1130's when Alberto Vento unsuccessfully claimed from the commune compensation for losses he had sustained in Genoa's war against King Roger of Sicily.[20] In 1147, at any rate, the consuls, afforced by the archbishop since di Lamberto himself was a consul, banned di Lamberto from any future participation in Genoese politics. On the testimony of some men who cleared di Lamberto, however, the decision was reversed, di Lamberto's civic rights were restored, and the members of the conspiracy were ordered to pay di Lamberto one hundred pounds as compensation. The members of the conspiracy were Gionata Crispino, Corso (Sigismundi?), Corrado Porcello, Negranzo, Guglielmo Strallando, Albertono Rizo, Nuvelone (d'Albericis?),

Bernizone, Navarro, Lamberto Porco, Bonsegnior Rufo, and Oglerio di Ranfredo.[21] Interestingly, di Lamberto was cleared by the oaths of Ogerio di Guidone (one of his consular colleagues), Ansaldo Mallone, Ido Porcello, and Ansaldo di Nigro.[22] This whole incident was handled in the courts and probably not in the streets. Because of the individuals involved this conspiracy was a private matter and not a power move of political groups, especially since members of the Porcello family were on both sides. Violent conflict among Genoa's political factions would not become a threat to civic peace until later in the century.

The patient conservative Carmadino group got its chance to run the city government in 1150, after the expansionists' foreign policy had backfired and had thrown them into disgrace. In 1150 the Carmadino group came to power in the wake of the city's ill-fated expedition to aid the forces of the *Reconquista,* a misadventure that had plunged Genoa into enormous debt.[23] The conservative attitude of the Carmadino group was evident because of the policies of its members. Now the city government intensified the long-standing practice of incorporating the outlying feudality into the communal system by extracting from them oaths of submission and loyalty to the Genoese government. This move enlarged the conservative element in the Genoese body politic and bolstered Carmadino interest in the feudal concerns of the rural nobility. Shockingly, the Genoese government also began what can accurately be called a policy of feudalizing the communal administration through the extensive use of the *compera* and investiture. The *compera* was the practice of leasing to consortia of businessmen for specified periods of time certain municipal revenue producers in return for a fixed fee. The earliest *compera* for Genoa can be dated to 1141,[24] but from 1150 to 1153 the city government granted its monopolies over minting, banking operations, salt, and the collection of various import and excise duties to consortia of businessmen. Investiture, so-called because the pertinent documents use the Latin word, *investire,* to express the transfer of property and authority, was a method of relieving the government of the administrative and financial burden or ruling over its growing possessions by granting to particular individuals the management and perquisites of property that had come into Genoese hands. Again, this practice had been used before 1149, mainly in investing individuals, often the original holders, with castles in the outlying areas. Now not only were people given castles, but also the newly won Genoese properties in Tortosa were sold to a consortium of businessmen, and the city's properties in the crusading states were entrusted to three members of the Embriaco family. This feudal attitude of the city's new regime was denuding Genoa of its long-term sources of revenue in return for quick, stop-gap sums of cash to help liquidate the huge debt. Unfortunately for the Carmadino people and for the Genoese as a whole, the policy was only making the financial woes of the city worse, and in 1154 the Carmadino element would be forced out of office.[25]

Probably the differences between the personnel who had led the commune before 1150 and the men who were in power from 1150 to 1153 have been overstated. "None of the political leaders of the years preceding 1149 appears in the consular lists between 1150 and 1154";[26] but of these latter consuls, several had been leaders previously. Ansaldo Mallone had been consul in 1136, 1138, 1142, 1146, and 1148; Guglielmo Lusio in 1137 and 1145; Rodoano di Piazzalunga's relatives had served in the original consulate and in 1106–9, 1123, 1131, and 1144; Lanfranco Pevere had been a consul in 1136, 1138, 1141, 1143, 1146, and 1148, while his father, Guglielmo, had served in 1125, 1128, 1131, and 1139; Rubaldo Bisaccia had been a consul in 1149 and his brother, Enrico Guercio,[27] in 1137 and 1148; the father of the Spinola brothers, Ansaldo and Oberto, had been in the early consulates of 1102–3, 1110–13, and 1120–21.[28]

Also the early power of the della Volta family has been exaggerated.[29] Although members of the family had been consuls on the original board and in 1123, 1127, 1130, 1132, 1139, 1141, and 1143, the families who would later be most closely connected with the della Volta group, Vento and Mallone, had held but seven consulships (Guglielmo Vento only one, 1143; Ansaldo Mallone five; Bonsegnior Mallone, one in 1143), while Ansaldo Mallone himself was a consul in 1150. Thus the later factional lines of Genoese politics were very blurred in the period before 1149 and may have been nonexistent altogether. In the early period Ingo della Volta and his associates were strong supporters of the old viscountal house of Maneciano but played a subordinate role to other men. The relative unimportance on the political scene of

Ingo della Volta and his friends at this early time is suggested by the fact that during the years of Carmadino ascendency, some of the major beneficiaries of the policy of leasing out the commune's revenue producers were the houses of della Volta, Embriaco, Mallone, and Vento. In fact, it is almost impossible to divide the Genoese political and business aristocracy of the 1150's into factions, for alleged rival families intermarried. For example, the powerful Carmadino politician, Lanfranco Pevere, married one of his daughters to Guglielmo Vento and another to Rubeo della Volta, the son of Ingo himself.[30]

Nevertheless, in the years between 1150 and 1153 Carmadino influence in the consulship was strong, perhaps strong enough to predominate, although only Guglielmo Lusio and Lanfranco Pevere were connected by blood to the clan. The repeated appearance of Piazzalunga (1150 and 1152), and Guercio (Bisaccia in 1152 and Enrico in 1153) show that these families supported the Carmadino policy. Perhaps connections of the Rufo family with the conservatives later in the century may mean that Otto Rufo (consul in 1151) could be placed with the group in power.[31] Ansaldo Spinola, consul in 1152, alone stands as a representative of his clan's interests during these years of conservativism.

The fiscal policies of the conservatives brought on a severe economic recession for Genoa, and by 1154 the out-of-office expansionists, increasingly represented by a group of men led by Ingo della Volta, had gained sufficient strength to reassert its control over the city's government. The annalist Caffaro, who by his own testimony was inspired to resume writing his annals by the political changes of 1154,[32] quaintly, perceptively, and effusively described the new consuls' actions:

> When they had been elected, these consuls, since they realized that the city was asleep and was suffering from lethargy and was like a ship wandering across the sea without a pilot, were unwilling to swear the consulate. But because they were admonished by the archbishop for the remission of their sins and were prompted by the people, they at last swore to the consulate for the honor of the city. After they had sworn, upon immediately giving much consideration as to how they might rescue the city from its slumber, the consuls soon, at the beginning of their consulate, began to build

galleys, which the city lacked, for the city's protection, and they began to pay to the city's creditors money in a number of pounds beyond fifteen thousand. Wherefore the citizens who had been sleeping roused themselves a little from their slumber and said that they would obey all their commands.[33]

These new consuls immediately ended the feudalizing of the commune's revenues and even swore never to do it again,[34] and they embarked on a grand policy of developing privileged trade in the Mediterranean for their city. Thus, in 1155 a promise was accepted from the Byzantines to give Genoa a compound and trading privileges in Constantinople; in 1156 a commercial treaty was struck with King William I of Sicily; and by 1160 Genoese ambassadors had gone to Moslem-controlled Valencia, to Almohad Morocco, and to the coastal cities of the French Riviera to establish privileged trade.[35]

The della Volta faction actually emerged from the financial regrouping of the 1150's, in theory with five families—the della Volta, Burone, Mallone, Usodimare, and Vento—all connected by blood, marriage, and business—who gained in the decade 1154 to 1164 a near monopoly on Genoa's trade with crusader-held Syria and, building on that economic base, came to control politics in Genoa itself.[36] The personnel making up the della Volta faction must be modified, however. Ingo della Volta was at the center of it, assisted by his sons, Marchese della Volta, Guglielmo Cassicio, and Ingo di Flessia, with others still too young perhaps to play a large role. Guglielmo Burone was Ingo's brother, so that his family was really part of the della Volta family.[37] Mallone and Vento were clearly connected with della Volta. The Mallone family, connected especially through the long and close business relationship of Burone and Ido Mallone,[38] would take a leading part in the faction's activities. Two brothers of the Vento family, Guglielmo and Ogerio, and their sons, Ogerio, Guglielmo, and Simon, supported the faction throughout the twelfth century. These two families were also among the leaders in families having associations in notarial contracts with the della Volta family members.[39] The closeness of the association between the della Volta group and the family of Usodimare is questionable. The latter was part of the Carmadino clan, and its leader, Baldizone, rarely appeared in notarial entries with della Volta people. Indeed, in two documents Baldizone and Ingo della Volta were acting in their official capacities as consuls of the commune,[40] and in the only other one in which they appear together, they were witnesses to the settlement of a dispute between Pietro Clerico on one side and Ingo's brother, Guglielmo Burone, and Marino di Castro on the other.[41]

Two families who should be added to the faction are those of Doria and Embriaco. The Doria family was at least in legend related to the della Volta by blood, seeing its origin in an Oria della Volta who lived around the time of the First Crusade.[42] In 1161 the Doria and della Volta families were next-door neighbors, with Ingo living on one side of his son, Marchese, and Simon Doria living on the other.[43] Ansaldo Doria and his sons, Guglielmo, Enrico, and Simon, were also closely associated in business with the Vento family, and perhaps Ansaldo's second wife was a Doria woman. The Embriaco family, most of whom emigrated to Syria after the First Crusade, conducted business for the della Volta family there and later in the century members of the family, beginning with Nicola Embriaco, were closely associated with della Volta people politically.[44]

Ingo della Volta also allied his family with the two most powerful families of the Maneciano clan. He married one of his daughters, Sibillia, to the powerful Oberto Spinola, the head of the senior family in the clan.[45] Ingo's other daughter, Adalasia, was married to Fulco di Castro. Although Fulco's exact relationship to the great di Castro house cannot be determined, by 1164 he was considered one of the leaders of the della Volta faction, and in the later twelfth century he became the foremost citizen of Genoa, culminating his career in his election to the office of *podestà* in 1205.[46]

Other families, like that of the annalist Caffaro, surely sympathized with della Volta and may have considered themselves allied with him, but sufficient proofs of their connections no longer exist. Many lesser men in Genoa, those who concentrated on business and took little or no part in politics, worked to build not only their own small fortunes but also the financial and political interests of the powerful della Volta families. These men, whose lives were largely spent as factors, or traveling agents, for della Volta investments, were sometimes rewarded for their services, as Rogerio Nocenzio, who married a della Volta woman,[47] or Pulpario, who became the in-law of Guglielmo Vento.[48] Although this network is now traceable only in a very few instances, these cases do strongly suggest that at least a vague patronage system existed in twelfth-century Genoa as it did in the institutions of vassalage and seignorialism in the rural medieval world. Thus, the chief families of the della Volta group, who themselves were vassals of the archbishop,[49] transferred to their business associations the relational attitudes with which they were familiar in the older system.[50] The leaders of the della Volta group would prove to be quite adept at using this business system for the advancement of the various ambitions of everyone involved in it.

Common business interests and the wish to see Genoa take a more aggressive approach to expanding its overseas commerce brought together the families making up the della Volta faction. The dramatic political change in 1154 brought about the ascendency in Genoa of the della Volta group and its friends, but even during the years of conservative rule, the della Volta people took advantage of opportunities to profit from governmental policy. Members of the della Volta group were heavily involved as the recipients of the commune's generosity. The four families of della Volta, di Castro, Doria, and Vento invested £795 in the various leases from the commune. The Embriaco family, already entrenched in the Holy Land, were invested with the city's possessions in Jubail, Lattakian, Antioch, and Acre, thus giving the family overwhelming responsibility and control over Genoese activity in the crusading states. Ansaldo Mallone was one of the participants in the investiture of the commune's newly acquired possessions in Tortosa. While many other men, including Lanfranco Pevere, invested in the commune's plight, only the Guercio bloc (Guercio, Detesalve, and Malocello) contributed a sum (£427 1/2) that could rival the della Volta group's outlay. Clearly the della Volta people intended to profit from the situation.

The profits made by the della Volta people cannot be estimated. The investiture of the Embriachi in Syria definitely served as the basis for their later political influence in Genoa, but the Mallone family probably did not realize much profit for its involvement with Tortosa since in 1153 it was sold to the count of Barcelona.[51] The decision of the consuls in 1154 to end the leases on communal revenues surely cut short whatever money the leaseholders hoped to acquire from their investments. Still, these men must have seen some return both for the years the leases were in operation and in whatever money they received when the government bought them back.[52] Although the participation of the della Volta bloc in this conservative policy may have brought the families together, by 1154 they realized that the policies of the government were wrecking their city. The conservative interlude plainly demonstrated to della Volta and his friends that the strength of Genoa and their own long-range financial futures should be based on expanding commerce throughout the Mediterranean and not in maintaining the old ways of conducting business. In fact, the della Volta people turned their backs on the past and boldly attempted to alter the system for their city's benefit. Their goal required permanent control of Genoa's government and the exclusion from it of those factions who were opposed to changing the system.

Opposition to the della Volta program slowly emerged from 1154 to 1164. So gradual was the development of this second faction that only in the 1180's did it have sufficient cohesion to be identified by the annalists and perhaps by the Genoese themselves. In this "della Volta decade," however, certain powerful individuals in Genoa realized that the della Volta group was harmful to their personal interests and to their general conception of Genoa's place in the larger political world of the medieval Mediterranean community.

This second faction may be identified as the della Corte faction, following the practice of the annalists in the late twelfth century, who applied to it the name of one of the leading families belonging to it. The group has largely been ignored because it has suffered almost a complete *damnatio memoriae* in the surviving sources.[53] From 1183 on there is a vague record in the Genoese Annals of a group called "illi de Curia," who were opposed to the della Volta faction.[54] The identity of this faction depends on what is meant by "de Curia."

One identification of "illi de Curia" is that it refers to a group of people opposed to the della Volta faction who customarily met at the house of their leader, Lanfranco Pevere.[55] This view is based on the mention of a *curia,* or courtyard in front of Pevere's house in a document in Giovanni Scriba's register.[56] But, there is nothing unique in Pevere's possession of a *curia,* since notarial entries contain references to other *curiae* as well, including the *curia* of the

Embriachi, of the Gontardi, and even of the della Corte family itself.[57] The term, "de Curia," as it was used in the notaries, did not apply to one particular place or family unless it was used as a surname like "de Volta," "de Porta," or many others. Also, mention of Pevere's *curia* does not establish the custom of political gatherings there especially some twenty and thirty years later when the "de Curia" faction was identified by the annalists. In fact, in the 1160's, when the notarial reference was made to Pevere's *curia*, Lanfranco Pevere the Elder cannot be shown to have opposed della Volta because he entered into various business arrangements with della Volta people (although not with Ingo himself),[58] married two daughters to men in the inner circle of the della Volta group,[59] and participated actively through ambassadorial missions in the expansionist program of the commune. His son, Lanfranco Pevere the Younger, would in the 1180's be a very influential member of the "de Curia" faction and in 1190 would be assassinated by della Volta adherents,[60] but nowhere was he credited with being the leader of the faction.

Another meaning of "de Curia" places it within a Guelf-Ghibelline context, where the term is identified with those families who sided with an imperialist archbishop against the Guelf business interests of the city.[61] However, in the twelfth century, Genoese prelates also sided with the business interests of the city. At the very beginning of the commune, Bishop Airaldo was finally consecrated only with the support of the newly formed *compagnia* in 1099.[62] Later, Bishop Syro, during whose reign the see was elevated to an archbishopric, was a member of the business-minded Porcello family,[63] and in 1163 the new archbishop elected was Ugo della Volta, the brother of Ingo della Volta.[64] Moreover, the della Volta people often cooperated with Frederick Barbarossa and Henry VI from Genoa's treaty with Barbarossa in 1162, engineered by Ingo della Volta himself, to the city's support of Henry VI's invasion of Sicily in 1194. Finally, the leading Ghibelline families were precisely the della Volta adherents.[65] Imperial considerations were to play a large role in the factional divisions of twelfth-century Genoa, but the actual scenario was far different from that portrayed by the episcopal identification of "illi de Curia."

Probably, "illi de Curia" refers to the faction led by the della Corte family. Although the surviving references to the family are few, nevertheless, they are sufficient to prove the existence of the della Corte family,[66] or as it appears in Latin, "de Curia," or "de Curte."[67] It was conventional in the *Annals* to refer to della Volta partisans as "illi de Volta." For reasons of symmetry, it was only natural that this convention be extended to designate the opposition group by using the surname of its leading family, the della Corte. The practice was used even earlier in the archepiscopal records, where in the 1143 list of the archbishop's vassals, the members of the two families are designated as "isti de Volta," and "isti de Curte."[68]

Only a few members of this della Corte family can be identified, and a construction of a genealogical chart for the family is impossible. The earliest mention of the della Corte family comes from the Genoese *Annals,* which mention a Guglielmo Rufo della Corte in command of a Genoese flotilla in 1122.[69] This early connection of the della Corte family with the Rufo or Rubeo family will be important for understanding the later factional divisions of Genoa. The connection is corroborated later in the century when one of the consuls of the pleas for 1152 was called in the *Annals* Corrado Rufo, but in the archbishop's register he appears in judgments handed down by the consuls of the pleas for 1152 as Corrado della Corte.[70] In the same register of the archbishop's court the brothers Rubaldo and Guglielmo della Corte are mentioned in 1143 as holding land in the Bisagno region of Genoa from the prelate.[71] Interestingly, the brothers held the land in partnership with the della Volta brothers, Ingo, Giordano, Alberto, and Guglielmo Burone. Another close connection with the della Volta family is hinted at, at least, in the name, Rubeo, which Ingo chose for one of his sons, perhaps in honor of his wife's family. By the 1150's the della Corte family was headed by Amigo ("Amigonis") who had two brothers, Raimondo and Rubaldo, who would serve as a consul of the pleas in 1184,[72] if this Rubaldo della Corte was not of the next generation. Adalardo, Ansaldo, and Martino della Corte are also mentioned in notarial entries, and an Ogerio della Corte is mentioned not only in Giovanni Scriba's register but also in the list of Genoese who swore to uphold their city's treaty with Pisa in 1188.[73]

Only two incidents connect the della Corte family (as opposed to the "de Curia" faction) with opposition to the della Volta faction. The first occurred in 1164, when the consuls of the commune, attempting to quell the civil disorder that had erupted that year, determined to punish the leaders of the two warring factions by tearing down their towers. Thus, the consuls supervised the razing both of Ingo della Volta's tower and of Amigo's.[74] This name, unlike the more familiar second-declension name, "Amicus," was rare in twelfth-century Genoa. Indeed, the indices of the editions of the sources—notarial records, the Genoese *Annals,* the *Codice diplomatico,* and the archiepiscopal records—reveal only two men named Amigo who could qualify as leaders of a political group powerful enough to oppose the della Volta faction: Amigo di Castro and Amigo della Corte. The former was unlikely to do so because the della Volta and di Castro families were closely associated in business,[75] and because the champion of the della Volta who instigated the trouble in 1164 was Fulco di Castro, Ingo della Volta's son-in-law.[76]

The second incident of della Corte opposition took place thirty years later in 1194 when a group of people frustrated with the della Volta–run government actually seceded and established their own government. One of these secessionist consuls was Rubaldo della Corte.[77] Not only does this fact demonstrate the man's opposition to della Volta, but also the respect he enjoyed among the members of the opposition.

These two pieces of evidence, one at the beginning of the factional strife and the other during its peak in the 1190's, when connected with the annalists' labeling of the faction as "illi de Curia" in the intervening period, prove the existence of a "della Corte" faction, not as strong as the della Volta, but dedicated to blocking the della Volta program and to removing it from power.

How did the della Corte family and the Carmadino lineage, led in the 1160's by Rolando Avvocato, Lanfranco Pevere, and Baldizone Usodimare, coalesce to form a faction hostile to the della Volta camp? Just as the della Volta family emerged from the political changes of the 1150's to lead the expansionists, which included the old Maneciano families, so would the della Corte family take over the leadership of the old Carmadino group with its conservative attitudes. The family's refusal to serve in communal office in the first half of the century with rare exceptions suggests that it may have sympathized with the old guard Carmadino families before the Genoese aristocracy divided itself into factions. The della Corte family had some association with the Avvocato family since in 1160 Rolando Avvocato owned land next to the house of Amigo della Corte, while in the next year Rolando would stand surety for a loan made by Amigo della Corte.[78] By 1164, whatever earlier association there had been had become political as well, since the consuls thought the best way to end Rolando Avvocato's violence was to tear down Amigo della Corte's tower. In 1154 the Carmadino families surely must have resented the waning of their eleventh-century feudal power with the rise of the commune and their embarrassment from the fiasco they made of their one opportunity to control municipal policy in the early 1150's. But not even these considerations were sufficient to prevent members of the clan from associating with leading expansionists or even from marrying into their families, as the marriages of the daughters of Lanfranco Pevere to Rubeo della Volta and to Guglielmo Vento the Younger point out. Nevertheless, particular events that took place between 1154 and 1164 would, for different reasons, alienate both the Carmadino and the della Corte families from the new municipal power structure, represented by della Volta, and they found that they could unite their disparate interests to topple their mutual foes.

Probably the most important factor contributing to the alienation of the della Corte family from the della Volta program was its failure to dominate the new trade that the Genoese hoped would be generated by the establishment of a commercial link with the Byzantine Empire in 1155. Several powerful families would become involved in vying for such dominance. The Guercio family was most closely tied to the Byzantines and most enthusiastically pushed the development of Genoa's involvement with Byzantium. In the early stages, the della Corte family actively supported the ambitions of the Guercio group and participated in these efforts to forge a commercial link. By 1160, however, the della Corte help had proven ineffective in bringing the promise of 1155 to fruition, and the della Volta combine, with its economic and political power, succeeded in obtaining a quarter in Constantinople for Genoa and, consequently, in excluding the della Corte people from participation in the trade.

The four consuls of 1154, who initiated Genoa's radical change in foreign and commercial policies, were clearly della Volta people.

Oglerio di Guidone appeared in several notarial entries with della Volta adherents;[79] Oberto Spinola was Ingo's son-in-law; and Ansaldo Doria was a della Volta relative and business associate. Only Lanfranco Pevere's loyalty could be questioned, but at this time he was associated with the della Volta group and was acceptable to Ingo, at least. This consular board's primary objective was to establish a sound financial basis for the government. The practice of leasing government revenue producers was stopped, and the consuls even swore to desist from issuing new leases. More important, these della Volta consuls understood that the government would be financially secure only if it rested on a strong economic base. With this in mind, the consuls initiated, and their successors continued, the construction of a Mediterranean-wide network of privileged trade out of which would develop Genoa's later medieval commercial empire.

The della Volta combine was not so successful in controlling the consular board for the crucial year of 1155. This group of consuls was composed of men who were neither politically powerful nor closely tied to the della Volta families. Guglielmo Porco, of the same family as the archbishop, was more closely associated with the Guercio family.[80] Oberto Cancellario, the city's chancellor since 1144, had served previously as a consul of the pleas in both the conservative consulates of the early 1150's and in the expansionist regimes earlier, so that he was perhaps "above politics."[81] As for Giovanni Malocello, he was associated in notarial entries with both expansionists and conservatives alike, but his only previous office had been a term as consul of the pleas in 1153 when the conservatives were in power.[82] Malocello's family may have leaned toward the della Corte coterie. He and his relative, Guglielmo Malocello, were witnesses to the della Corte's brothers' sea loan of 1156 to Boleto,[83] and Adalardo della Corte's loan to Rubaldo Bisaccia in 1160 was transacted in the house of Guglielmo Malocello, whose son acted as guarantor for repayment of the loan.[84] The Malocelli appeared to be much closer to the Guercii and to have followed them through their factional switches.[85] (Indeed, an indication of the weakness of partisanship in this early period is a notarial document from August, 1160, in which Guglielmo Malocello was a co-purchaser with Ansaldo Doria of a house that belonged to Rolando Avvocato.[86]) The fourth consul, Guglielmo Lusio, was a first cousin of the Avvocati and had served in 1150 and 1153 as a consul of the commune, more than likely supporting the conservative program.[87] If the influence of any one bloc predominated on this consular board, it was that of Guercio.

It is the strength of the Guercio and conservative influences on this particular board of consuls that explains why Genoa in 1155 was receptive to making an agreement with the Byzantines. The Guercii (represented by Porco and Malocello), already with an interest in Byzantium, had combined with the conservatives as a continuation of their association in the governments of 1149 to 1153, to draw Genoa closer to Byzantium. While the advantage of such a coalition is evident for the Guercii, the conservatives too stood to gain from a pro-Byzantine policy. One of the major programs of the government from 1149 to 1153 was to accelerate Genoa's assertion of hegemony over the neighboring nobility. The most obvious rival for Genoa's quest for leadership in Liguria was, of course, Frederick Barbarossa, the actual suzerain of the nobles and the person to whom they would turn for help against Genoese aggressions. In 1154 the new German emperor had invaded Lombardy to put some force behind his pretensions of Italian overlordship,[88] and his intrusion into northern Italian affairs in 1155 so frightened the Genoese consuls that they began construction of new city walls.[89] In light of Barbarossa's visible plans for Italian domination the conservative faction for whom independent action in feudal Liguria was so important saw the overture of the Byzantines as a possible counterpoise to Barbarossa's threats against its fast-developing power in the feudal hinterland. These people would realize only a few years later that Barbarossa was not their foe, but in reality, he was the one authority that could maintain the traditional order of things on which their influence in the Genoese community rested.

The della Corte family gladly gave its assistance to the Guercio bloc in its grand design to move Genoa closer to Byzantium. The della Corte people had learned from the disasterous experience of the early 1150's that the way to Genoa's future lay with foreign trade, and the opening of commerce with Constantinople could dramatically improve their reputation with the large nonaligned Genoese business community and give them substantial financial support for their own political aspirations. So much did the della

Corte family see itself as a major participant, if not the director, of Genoa's new Byzantine policy that in 1156 Amigo della Corte and his two brothers journeyed to Manuel's court.[90] The purpose of the visit is no longer known, and because Caffaro makes no mention of a diplomatic mission, the della Corte trip was probably not official. Nevertheless, the della Corte brothers must have intended to persuade Manuel both to fulfill the promise of commercial concessions made a few months before and perhaps to give them a special advantage in the operation of the new trade.

At first, the della Volta people applauded the opening of Constantinople, but they soon saw the problems that a Byzantine connection posed to their own interests. Guglielmo Burone could not pass up the opportunity to make some money, and he sent Ido Mallone off with the della Corte expedition to trade £392¾.[91] In August, 1156, Ingo della Volta himself put up £200 to Nicola Berfogio's £100 for a voyage to Adalia, a city within the confines of the Byzantine Empire.[92] These investments indicate that from the very beginning the della Volta group intended to profit from their city's new acquaintance with Byzantine wealth, but soon the della Volta leaders must have realized that the flirtation with Byzantium could very easily discredit them in the eyes of William I of Sicily and could bring on the disruption of della Volta's profitable Sicilian connection.[93] An even greater blow would perhaps be dealt to della Volta's economic strength by the damage that might be done, given Sicily's geographic position, to the trade with the crusading states. A trading voyage sponsored in part by the della Volta group went to Sicily in May of 1156, and probably on the merchants' arrival in the island kingdom they discovered the king's displeasure with the past year's agreement with the Byzantines.[94] The della Volta people reacted decisively to the new threat posed to their profitable business. Already at the end of 1155 they had regained control over the consulate for the next year, with Guglielmo Burone, Ogerio Vento, and Enrico Doria serving as three of the four consuls. This Genoese government sent the heads of two della Volta families, Guglielmo Vento and Ansaldo Doria, to Sicily to negotiate a treaty with King William.[95] The embassy concluded a commercial treaty in November 1156, which accorded to Genoese merchants for the first time various privileges in the island kingdom.[96]

Probably Amigo della Corte and his brothers, along with members of the Guercio family, were upset with the diplomatic maneuver of the della Volta government in their absence. Their Byzantine project had collapsed, because Manuel would not deal with people who had just proven themselves so friendly to his archenemy, the king of Sicily. The della Corte family were further alienated as it became apparent that the della Volta leaders were not opposed to Byzantine trade so long as they could control its effects in other areas. After all, both Ingo della Volta and Guglielmo Burone had invested in the nascent Byzantine trade. In the next few years the Guercio family would see that only the della Volta group had the power to make the Byzantine trade a reality for Genoa, and they grew closer to the della Volta faction and turned their backs on their former supporters, the della Corte family.

Della Volta domination of the commune continued into 1157, and the faction now felt secure enough to try its hand at negotiating with the Byzantines. Three of the four consuls, Rogerono di Ita (di Castro),[97] Guglielmo Vento, and Oberto Spinola, were very much in Ingo's camp. They sent Amico di Murta to Constantinople to negotiate with the Byzantine Emperor. The ambassador, however, quickly found that Manuel had no desire to talk to him.[98] Genoa's conclusion of an agreement with Sicily had undone the very purpose of the Byzantines' initial advances to Genoa, and the emperor surely did not trust the representative of a government now run so completely by politician-businessmen who were so deeply involved in the Sicilian trade.[99] In their turn, the della Volta people had failed to deliver the Byzantine trade to their city, and for the next two years there would be no further effort to renew relations with Constantinople. As a reflection of the diplomatic failure, Marchese della Volta, in a contract from 1157 with Guglielmo Trallando for a voyage to Alexandria, forbade his factor from going to Romania unless Trallando first shipped home Marchese's goods and bore the expenses of the extended voyage himself.[100]

The potential profits that a commercial link to the Byzantines held could not be disregarded by the business-minded Genoese who gave the della Volta faction their support. After Manuel's Sicilian campaign had been crushed by his army's defeat at Brindisi in 1158,[101] the humbled emperor could no longer flippantly refuse friendly offers. The Genoese found in Enrico Guercio the ideal negotiator who would be acceptable both to Manuel and to the factions in Genoa. Guercio was a respected statesman who, along with his brother, Rubaldo Bisaccia, had held communal consulships under both expansionists and conservative regimes. Moreover, his other brother, Baldovino Guercio, enjoyed the confidence of the Byzantine emperor. The combination of della Volta and Guercio families had at last in 1160 resulted in the acquisition of a privileged trading facility for the Genoese in Constantinople.

While Guercio's embassy was a success, it also signified the last cooperative effort of the della Volta and della Corte groups, stimulated perhaps by the Guercii and other nonaligned families to insure the achievement of their Byzantine goal. The Guercio brothers accepted money from both the della Corte and the della Volta families to pay for their voyage. In May 1160 Adalardo della Corte lent Bisaccia £200 for his expedition east.[102] On the other side, Marchese della Volta, shrugging off his former hesitancy about investing in Constantinople, lent Rubaldo Bisaccia £100 as a sea loan to insure the latter's three galleys on their trip.[103] At the beginning of June Marchese also entered into a contract with Musso Scalzagegia for a total of £144 7½s to finance Musso's venture to Constantinople and Alexandria.[104] On June 3 Marchese witnessed a contract in which his uncle, Guglielmo Burone, along with Simon Doria and Guglielmo della Volta (Cassicio), each lent Guidoto di Bonobello £50 to go on Bisaccia's galleys, while Guglielmo della Volta separately put up £21 to Guidoto's £10½.[105] Three days later Ingo della Volta and Guglielmo Burone made a complicated deal with Guglielmo Piperata della Volta by which the brothers lent Piperata £100 so that he could pay his share of a *societas* with Guglielmo Malocello (who contributed £200) and they lent Piperata's son £100, all of which money Piperata and his son were to take to Constantinople on Bisaccia's galleys.[106] At the end of August, probably just a few weeks before the departure of the embassy, Burone showed his continued enthusiasm for the venture by investing another £100 with Otto Giudice di Castro to send di Castro's grandson to trade in Constantinople and other Mediterranean ports of call.[107] The della Volta family, for this one voyage, had invested at least £617. 10s, a very considerable sum.

The financial contributions to Guercio's embassy indicated that both della Corte and della Volta people intended to profit from the opening of the market in Constantinople; but in reality, the della Volta group took over the trade by using its immense economic resources and connections. There are no more contracts showing the involvement of della Corte members in Byzantine commerce, but there is ample evidence of growing della Volta interest in the trade. In one contract, Filippo Aradello and Pietro di Bernardo formed a *societas* worth £45. 22 1/2s for a venture to Romania.[108] Aradello was definitely associated with the della Volta family, for his name appears in three entries with members of the family and in another three with Guglielmo Vento, who was one of the della Volta business group.[109] Toward the close of the summer of 1161 Ingo witnessed a contract for a *societas* of £170 made between Stabilis, a foreigner resident in Genoa, and Donadeo for a trip to Constantinople.[110] On September 9, Guglielmo Burone arranged a complicated *societas* with his trusty factor, Ido Mallone, and two other Genoese financiers, repeating a similar arrangement among the four in the previous year.[111] Burone and Mallone contributed £300, Guglielmo Ciriolo £200, and Ugo d'Elia £80 to the capital that d'Elia would take to undesignated ports of call. This particular *societas* gains considerably in interest when one looks at the list of Genoese losses suffered in 1162 that make up a part of Grimaldi's instructions of 1174.[112] Ugo's expedition took him to Constantinople, where he lost the money entrusted to him. The sum claimed in 1175 was 1,500 hyperpers, which at the then current exchange rate of three hyperpers to one Genoese pound corresponded exactly to the £500 invested by Burone, Mallone, and Ciriolo, while an additional 240 hyperpers were claimed, equaling d'Elia's own contribution of £80.[113] Grimaldi's list also reflects three investments made by Ingo della Volta. In one of the items, Ingo claimed to have lost 700 hyperpers that he had in a *societas* with a certain Gioele.[114] Since both Ingo della Volta and Gioele di Bonico were witnesses to two contracts that Giovanni Scriba recorded on September 8, 1161, including Stabilis' deal with Donadeo for trading in Constantinople, it is likely that Ingo and Gioele made their partnership about the same time, although the contract itself is lost.[115] In another entry of Grimaldi's list Ingo and Pietro Capra claimed nineteen hyperpers lost at Constantinople.[116] This claim may represent a trading voyage begun in October 1160, when Ingo and Pietro made a contract for a *societas* of £225 and an additional £10 of Capra's own.[117] Grimaldi's list also contains an item for a loss of 278 hyperpers in a partnership that Ingo had with Opizo Amici Clerici.[118] Like the matter involving Ingo and Pietro Capra, this claim may represent the tail end of a *societas* made in August 1160, between Ingo and Opizo for an extended trading voyage including Bougie, Alexandria, and Syria.[119]

The contracts between Ingo and his factors and the one involving Guglielmo Burone and his partners prove that some of the many business arrangements recorded in Giovanni Scriba's cartulary included Constantinople as a port of call, although it was not so designated. Thus, the Genoese trade with the Byzantines, and the della Volta contribution to it, was larger than is reflected in statistics based on Giovanni Scriba's cartulary. In fact, very few of the business agreements described in Grimaldi's instructions appear in Giovanni Scriba's register, which reflects little trade at all with Constantinople. However, three hundred or so Genoese merchants in Constantinople at the time of the Pisan attack in the late spring of 1162 acted on contracts that do not appear in Giovanni Scriba's cartulary.[120] In Grimaldi's list of 1174, members of the della Volta group and other merchants who can be definitely associated with the core families figure prominently.[121] Conversely, hardly anyone in the list can be connected to the della Corte family although, granted, this may be simply because there is so little information about the della Corte associations.

One person possibly connected with the della Corte family was in Constantinople during the Pisan sack: he was the son of Otto Rufo, the former consul. Caffaro the annalist reported that the son was killed, and this is the only person he listed as dying in the battle; the Pisans captured and executed him.[122] Even the son's first name is unknown. If, as noted before, the della Corte family was a branch of the Rufo family, or somehow closely related, then indeed the della Corte people may have strongly resented the loss of a relative and may have blamed it on the della Volta combine, whose project the whole Byzantine affair had now become.

The course of Genoese relations with the Byzantine Empire in 1162 gave the della Corte family ample reason to dislike the della Volta people and their methods, and other Genoese who had their own scores to settle with the della Volta regime aligned themselves with the della Corte family. One welcome ally was Rolando Avvocato, a member of the old feudal viscountal nobility. For years

Rolando had held from the archbishop of Milan seignorial rights over the Genoese district of Recco. Rolando's privilege must have certainly seemed to be an anachronism to many Genoese by the middle of the century, and at least from 1147 the inhabitants of Recco had petitioned the Genoese government to stop what they considered to be Rolando's extortions of them. Avvocato had disregarded the consuls' request that he desist in 1147, but in 1162, the Genoese consuls absolved the people of Recco from their obligations to Rolando. One of the consuls who issued the unfavorable judgment was Ingo della Volta's son, Marchese, and another was Oberto Spinola, Ingo's son-in-law. One can only imagine Rolando's indignation at the consuls' decision, which he must have regarded as another example of della Volta disregard for custom and meddling in matters that were none of their concern.[123]

The della Corte people and Rolando Avvocato now must have felt a certain degree of comradery in their dissatisfaction with the della Volta group, but the issue that would finally bring them together and would add to their bloc the politically active Lanfranco Pevere, Avvocato's cousin, was the Genoese treaty made with Frederick Barbarossa in 1162. This treaty, engineered by Ingo della Volta himself and his consular colleague, Nuvelone d'Albericis, has been hailed as the beginning of Genoese independence.[124] That is an overstatement, because the treaty actually made Genoa a corporate vassal of the German emperor, but the granting of the immunities of dominion over the Riviera from Monaco to Portovenere, and the rights of electing their own magistrates, of administering justice, of collecting taxes, and of following an independent foreign policy certainly gave the Genoese considerable freedom from imperial control.[125] The administrative separation of Genoa from the empire effected by the treaty not only removed what little basis of power the Carmadino families had left but also confirmed a communal system alien to the traditional imperialist structure that these families cherished. They had long been accustomed to dealing with the outlying feudality. Lanfranco Pevere, for example, served as the advocate for the marquis of Malaspina,[126] who was both the personification of the old ways and one of the great adversaries of the communal government. This nobleman, who still considered himself the feudal overlord of Genoa, emphatically resisted attempts to subjugate him to the authority of the Genoese *compagnia.* As late as 1174 the Genoese would be fighting him (interestingly, under the command of Ingo di Flessia, a son of Ingo della Volta), and it would be only in 1199 that Marquis Opizo's heirs would swear fealty to the commune.[127] Connections like this one, now lost to history and surely fortified by many family ties with the old-fashioned rural nobility, which also are unknown, surely made the Carmadino families fear the radical change that the policies of the della Volta faction were fast bringing to Genoa.

After 1162, then, the Carmadino families, alienated from the communal government that was destroying their feudal power and separating them from the comforting structure of the empire, and the della Corte family, angry over the della Volta faction's usurpation of the Byzantine connection that they themselves had begun, aligned themselves into a tightly knit opposition group devoted to the destruction of the ever-growing della Volta power. The incident which finally brought these families together must have been the election in 1163 of Ugo della Volta as the archbishop of Genoa by an electoral committee consisting of representatives of the clergy, members of the municipal *consiglio,* and the consuls, of whom four out of six—that is, Rogerono d'Ita, Guglielmo Cassicio, Guglielmo Vento, and Oberto Spinola—were staunch della Volta adherents.[128]

The Pisan sack of the Genoese compound in Constantinople not only played a large role in alienating the della Corte family from the della Volta and in consolidating the opposition, but also seriously weakened the della Volta position in the city. Many della Volta supporters lost money in the attack, and they must have begun to question the viability of the della Volta program. In fact, della Volta's strongest supporters, the Mallone family, were practically wiped out financially. Members of this family altogether lost the very large sum of 2,535 hyperpers, or £845. In Giovanni Scriba's documents after the summer of 1162 members of the Mallone family appear very rarely, and when they do, their purpose is usually only to witness contracts. In 1163 Ansaldo Mallone, the head of the family, was forced to return the dowry of Solomon of Salerno's daughter.[129] While this transaction might have been occasioned by Solomon's financial difficulties, it was more likely prompted by Solomon's realization that little could be gained by a marriage with the nearly bankrupt Mallone family.[130] In political matters, members of the family would not hold office again until 1183, twenty years later.

Other supporters, too, abandoned the della Volta group. The Doria family, who lost 1,802½ hyperpers in 1162, appeared in only one notarial contract after that fateful summer with members of the della Volta family until much later in the century.[131] Marchese della Volta tried to reconcile his family to the distinguished family of the annalist Caffaro, a staunch advocate of expansionism, by confirming the terms of a Constantinopolitan deal he had with the annalist's grandson, Ansaldo, and by agreeing to restore to Ansaldo one-half of whatever he might recover.[132] Finally, the Guercio bloc, which lost 2,535 hyperpers in the sack, must surely have become suspicious of the grandiose schemes of Ingo della Volta.

Death too was taking its toll on the expansionists. In early 1164 Ansaldo Spinola, the brother of Oberto Spinola, died. By mid-year Ogerio Vento and Enrico Guercio, the heads of their families, were dead. The old annalist, Caffaro, who had participated in the First Crusade, also must have died during this year because his portion of the annals ends in 1163.[133] Ingo della Volta increasingly found himself alone in executing his plans for Genoa and in facing the opposition to them from the della Corte and Carmadino families.

In an effort to restore political and economic strength to the expansionist cause, Ingo della Volta became involved in 1164 in a scheme to place a puppet king on the throne of Sardinia. Besides the enormous loans that the commune, led by the della Volta group, made to the royal candidate, Barisone, privately Ido Mallone gave the proposed king £600, which must have represented the residue of the Mallone fortune.[134] Although Emperor Frederick crowned Barisone, Pisan and Sardinian resistance to the Genoese puppet prevented his installation. Barisone lingered for many years in Genoa as a "hostage, a hopeless debtor, and embarrassing guest."[135] This last grand design of Ingo della Volta had also been a fiasco.

While Barisone was in Genoa on his way to receive his crown from Barbarossa, a skirmish broke out between Fulco di Castro and his followers and Rolando Avvocato and his men, giving expression to the tension in Genoa in the summer of 1164. This outbreak is the first violent clash between the della Volta and the new della Corte factions. Fulco di Castro was Ingo's son-in-law, and there is no doubt about the anti-della Volta feelings of Avvocato.

In the fray, Baldovino, the son of Enrico Guercio, and Gandulfo Usodimare, the son of Baldizone, were killed by arrows, and Sardo, Rolando Avvocato's son, was killed with a rock.[136] In August assassins, undoubtedly working for the della Corte people, stole into the house of Marchese della Volta, who was then serving as a consul of the commune, and killed him.[137] Genoa was now thrown into a factional war that would last for several years. The consuls for 1165 attempted to end the violence by tearing down the towers of the factions' leaders, Ingo della Volta and Amigo della Corte, but not even this drastic measure could quench the fire with which the factions' bitter hatred was burning their city.

Amid the development of factionalism in Genoa in the middle of the twelfth century, the city's connection with the Byzantine Empire played a considerable role. Not only did Byzantine considerations strongly affect the internal political maneuvering that took place during the decade from 1154 to 1164, but also Genoa's relations with Byzantium were heavily influenced by events in Genoa itself. Although the Genoese accepted the promise of privileged trade in Constantinople as part of a program of commercial expansion, Ingo della Volta and his associates, who were deeply involved in the Syrian and Sicilian trade, realized the potential harm that this new commercial link could bring to their business. Their eventual solution was to take over this trade too, so that they could maintain control over the closely connected economic and diplomatic picture. However, they could not control affairs in Byzantium, and the severe setback in Constantinople in the spring of 1162 started the process of political deterioration that the overtaxed della Volta organization could not stop. In the end, della Volta interests and the Byzantine connection had become so interdependent that the collapse of the one led to the fall of the other. Their handling of Byzantine matters alienated other groups in Genoa, who found ready allies in the old conservative Carmadino families who resented their exclusion from power and della Volta's active dismantling of the old system. In 1164 the della Volta machine was broken, ultimately as a result of the failure of its Byzantine policy, and with its fall, the first period of Genoese flirtation with the Eastern Roman Empire came to an end. When in 1164 the Genoese government sent an embassy to Manuel I, the careful emperor wisely refused to reopen his empire to the city until it could establish a stable government that could reasonably fulfill its treaty obligations to the Byzantine Empire.[138] Manuel saw that Ingo della Volta had gone far in separating his city from the German empire, but the politician's power was waning and the Germanophile opposition, if it succeeded in gaining control in Genoa, would surely be no more than fair weather friends to Manuel in any confrontations with the German emperor.

The potential clash of empires, German and Byzantine, would put Genoa in a very precarious diplomatic position for the rest of the century. The communal government existed at the pleasure of the German emperor, and the city needed German support in its confrontations with neighboring feudal magnates or with its arch-enemy, Pisa. Yet the agricultural lands of the German empire offered to the Genoese none of the potential profits that the economically sophisticated territories of the Byzantine Empire could give them. Now added to this monumental conflict of interest was the internal rift of the Genoese aristocracy itself, with one group, the della Volta faction, intent on pursuing an indepen-dent program of commercial expansion, and the other group, hoping perhaps nostalgically, to regain its lost political position in the community by restoring Genoa's close administrative associa-tion with the German empire. Thirty years later, in the 1190's, all these irreconcilable ambitions would destroy the consular form of government. These conflicting interests would also prevent Genoa from developing a stable relationship with the Byzantine Empire.

The eventual winners in the struggle of the early 1160's were undoubtedly the Guercio family and its associates. That family would support whatever political group that could advance its own interests, and it barely escaped the disaster that could have resulted from its close association with the della Volta machine. Members of the Guercio family would come into their own as masters of Genoa's relations with Byzantium. In Ingo della Volta's grand scheme of Mediterranean commercial dominance, the Guercii held unquestionably a secondary role, but the temporary removal of della Volta dominance gave the Guercii the opportunity to use their Byzantine influence for their own profit. The della Volta faction would soon regroup under new leadership, and the Guercii would use it to maintain Genoese involvement in the Byzantine east. The interaction of the Byzantine connection and of factional politics in Genoa would continue, but in the future, internal factionalism would affect relations with East Rome more than the other way around.

## Notes

1. On political factions in the medieval world in general and the Genoese experience in particular, see Heers, *Parties and Political Life.* I prefer the term, "faction," to "party," which gives the impression of a highly organized and self-regenerative association not found in medieval local alliances. Nevertheless, Heers's succinct statement of the aims of faction in the Italian communes can serve as the underlying assumption of this and subsequent chapters: "The party wanted to seize and keep all power and exclude other political forces completely. Rivalry was thus absolute and unforgiving" (ibid., 141). Heers devotes a whole chapter to the issue of the family and its friends as the foundations of medieval faction. He says: "The consular government's activity was limited to establishing a kind of division or alternation of power among the great families" (ibid., 18). Heers extends his investigation into the political role of the family in a separate study, *Le clan familial au moyen âge* (Paris, 1974). Many of the assumptions about the role of the extended family in Genoese life are taken not only from Heers, but also from Diane O. Hughes: "Urban Growth and Family Structure in Medieval Genoa," *Past and Present* 66 (1975): 3–28; and "Kinsmen and Neighbors in Medieval Genoa," in *The Medieval City,* edited by Miskimin et al. (New Haven, 1977), 96–111. Both articles contain extensive bibliography on the scholarship. David Herlihy has convincingly rebutted the earlier scholarly opinion of progressive nuclearization of the medieval family in his "Family Solidarity in Medieval Italian History," in *Economy, Society, and Government in Medieval Italy,* edited by Herlihy, Lopez, and Slessarev (Kent, Ohio, 1969), 174–79. In fact, the twelfth century was that period when families in Genoa were becoming what we can properly call lineages with a strong self-consciousness and a sense of continuation. Very recently David Herlihy and Christine Klapisch-Zuber have scrutinized quantitatively family institutions in fifteenth-century Tuscany in *Tuscans and their Families: A Study of the Florentine Catasto of 1427* (New Haven, 1985). Although the work deals with a later period and a different area of Italy, nevertheless, many of its general statements probably can be applied to twelfth-century Genoa. Some of the best work on the medieval family and a source for several general ideas that have been valuable in this work is the series of essays by European scholars published in Georges Duby and Jacques Le Goff, eds., *Famille*

*et parenté dans l'Occident médiéval: actes du colloque de Paris* (6–8 *juin,* 1974) (Paris, 1977).

2. A very good synopsis of scholarship relating to the origins of the *compagnia* can be found in De Negri, *Storia di Genova,* 232–37.

3. Ibid., 207.

4. Ibid., 195–208.

5. *Annali genovesi,* 1: 5.

6. This view is held by De Negri, *Storia di Genova,* 233–34, Hughes, "Family Structure," 5–6, and Vitale, *Breviario,* 1: 17.

7. This is the older interpretation presented by G. Doneaud, *Sull'origine del Comune e dei partiti di Genova e della Liguria* (Genoa, 1878). Perhaps it is simplistic, but it seems to me to fit the sense of historical development far better, especially the temporary nature of the early *compagnie* of Genoa, the very close connection made between the *compagnia* and the Genoese expedition on the First Crusade, and the dominance of one family group, the Maneciano, in the early affairs of the *compagnia.*

8. *Annali genovesi,* 1: 5.

9. Ibid., 13.

10. Ibid., 14

11. *Codice diplomatico,* 1: 77–80, doc. 65.

12. *Annali genovesi,* 1: 73–74.

13. Bertolotto, "Cintraco," 37.

14. Byrne, "Genoese Trade," 191–219; Krueger, "Post-War Collapse," passim. It is generally agreed among scholars that these two viscountal clans were rivals. See, for example, Hughes, "Family Structure," 7–8. Hughes does not mention, however, that the eponymous ancestors of the lineages were brothers, and that there was a third clan, the d'Isolis, whose role in Genoese factionalism seems, in the present state of research, to have been marginal.

15. These figures are taken from the lists of officials in Agostino Olivieri's work, "Serie dei consoli del comune di Genova," *Atti della Società Ligure di Storia Patria* 1 (1858): 155–479.

16. *Codice diplomatico,* 1:224–26, docs. 178–80.

17. *Ystoria captionis Almarie,* 80: "predicti vero consules post eorum electionem parliamentum statim fecerunt, in quo omnibus discordantibus pacem iurare preceperunt."

18. *Codice diplomatico,* 1: 355, doc. 285: "Si fuero consul de Communi ego mittam filium Philippi de Lamberto in consilium ut sit unus de consiliatoribus Ianue, si ipse fuerit in Ianua et consiliator esse voluerit."

19. *Ystoria captionis Almarie,* 80; *Codice diplomatico,* 1: 224, n. 1.

20. Codice diplomatico 1: 224, n. 1; and for the decision of 1141 on Vento's complaint, see 137, doc. 115.

21. Ibid., 226, doc. 180.

22. Ibid.

23. On this conservative interlude and the policies of the new consuls, see Krueger, "Post-War Collapse," passim. He calls the out-of-office group the della Volta faction (123). Similarly, Byrne, "Genoese Trade," 196 and 202–3.

24. *Codice diplomatico,* 2:, 129–31, doc. 108.

25. Krueger, "Post-War Collapse," 123–26.

26. Ibid., 123.

27. For their relationship, see below, chap. 5.

28. Olivieri, "Serie dei consoli," 463, 468, 471, 474, 475, and 477.

29. Krueger, "Post-War Collapse," 123.

30. Giovanni Scriba, *Il cartolare di Giovanni Scriba,* edited by Mario Chiaudano and Mattia Moresco, 2 vols. (Turin: 1935), no. 139, and Oberto Scriba de Mercato, *Notai* (1190), edited by Mario Chiaudano and Raimondo Morozzo della Rocca (Genoa, 1938), no. 140. Hughes considers the marriage of Pevere and Vento to be an unsuccessful attempt by the della Volta to come to terms with their political opponents ("Family Structure," 12). Hughes may be correct, but Pevere's business associations with della Volta people at this time and the fact that he married not one but two daughters to della Volta people make me doubt that he was an opponent in the 1150's and early 1160's.

31. See below, p. 93.

32. Richard D. Face has stated that Caffaro began writing his annals in the early years of the first decade of the twelfth century ("Secular History in Twelfth-Century Italy: Caffaro of Genoa," *Journal of Medieval History* 6 [1980]: 170). In 1152 the annalist presented his work to the consuls of the commune, who ordered that it be placed in the city's cartulary, thus giving it official status (*Annali genovesi,* 1: 3). Caffaro must have considered his work complete at that time, but his enthusiasm over his faction's restoration to power in 1154 motivated his resumption of the annals (ibid., 38).

33. "Isti namque consules, quando electi fuerunt, quoniam civitatem dormire et litargiam pati, et secuti navem sine gubernatore per mare pergentem cognoscebant, ad presens consulatum iurare noebant. at quia ab archiepiscopo moniti in remissione eorum peccatorum, et a populo coacti fuerunt, vix tandem consulatum pro honore civitatis iuraverunt. qui, postquam iuravere, statim multum cogitando quomodo civitatem a sompno eriperent, mox in initio eorum consulatus galeas pro munimine civitatis facere, quibus civitatis omnino carebat, et peccuniam feneratoribus civitatis ultra quindecim milia librarum numero solvere inceperunt. unde cives qui dormierant, a sompno aliquantulum surrexerunt, et in omnibus eorum preceptis obedire dixerunt" (*Annali genovesi,* 1: 37–38).

34. *Codice diplomatico,* 1: 326, doc. 270; Krueger, "Post-War Collapse," 127.

35. Krueger, "Post-War Collapse," 127–28.

36. Byrner, "Genoese Trade," pp. 198–99.

37. Ibid.

38. Giovanni Scriba, *Cartolare,* nos. 96, 97, 401, 696, 705, 798, 892, 900, and 901.

39. In Giovanni Scriba's cartulary members of the Mallone family appear in notarial contracts with the della Volte family 18 times and Vento family members 16 times with della Volta people.

40. Giovanni Scriba, *Cartolare,* nos. 450 and 1254.

41. Ibid., no. 375.

42. Hughes, "Family Structure," 8.

43. Giovanni Scriba, *Cartolare,* no. 864.

44. Byrne, "Genoese Colonies in Syria," 147–53.

45. Giovanni Scriba, *Cartolare,* nos. 124 and 125.

46. *Annali genovesi,* 2: 218; Guglielmo Cassinese, *Notai* (1190–1192), edited by Margaret W. Hall, Hilmar C. Krueger, and Robert L. Reynolds, 2 vols (Genoa, 1938), no. 58.

47. Hughes, "Kinsmen and Neighbors," 101.

48. Giovanni Scriba, *Cartolare,* no. 714.

49. For the list, see "Registrum Curiae," 2, 2: 24–26.

50. In one notarial entry, for example, Ingo della Volta is referred to as "dominus Ingo," a title rarely found in notarial materials. Giovanni Scriba, *Cartolare,* no. 1262. Interestingly, this contract was made in August, 1164, at the height of della Volta's power and immediately before his fall.

51. *Codice diplomatico,* 1: 291–93, doc. 243.

52. Krueger, "Post-War Collapse," 126–27.

53. The city's annals, far from being objective, were devoted under Caffaro's authorship to recording the actions and progress of the expansionist faction as articulated through the communal government, which was their creation. Only in Caffaro's continuators, who took up the task of compilation in 1164, do references to the della Corte faction appear in the text. The notarial cartulary of Giovanni Scriba, our one other extensive source for the period, like the annals, was concerned with della Volta people, and only eight entries have anything to do with the della Corte family (nos. 44, 81, 84, 577, 666, 871, 907, 2A II, 263). The later surviving register of Oberto Scriba is even more biased in catering to della Volta people and has no references at all to the della Corte. Nevertheless, the specific references to the faction in the annals and the few mentions of members of the family in Giovanni Scriba's cartulary and in the archbishop's

register (see nos. 70 and 71), do prove its existence. The problem is that the della Corte family was always on the outside trying to get into positions of power—and historical commemoration—in Genoa.

54. *Annali genovesi*, 2: 19.

55. Hughes, "Family Structure," 8 and n. 17.

56. Giovanni Scriba, *Cartolare*, no. 713.

57. Ibid., no. 871, for the "curia Amigonis"; Cassinese, *Notai*, nos. 89, 93, 279, and 285, for the "curia Gontardi"; and Archivio di Stato di Genova, "Cartolari notarili," 4.115r and 4.173r, for the "curia Embriachorum."

58. For example, Giovanni Scriba, *Cartolare*, nos. 122, 139, 158, 270, 296, 713, 940, and 1034. Note that the last entry dealing specifically with members of the della Volta family was no. 940, enacted in January 1162, several months before Ingo's treaty between Genoa and Frederick Barbarossa (June 1162).

59. See above, p. 78.

60. *Annali genovesi*, 2: 37.

61. Bach, *Gênes*, 161–63; Scarsella, *Il comune dei consoli*, 206.

62. De Negri, *Storia di Genova*, 231.

63. Scarsella, *Il comune dei consoli*, 138.

64. *Annali genovesi*, 1: 75.

65. Vito Vitale, "Guelfi e Ghibellini nel duecento," *Rivista storica italiana* 40 (1948): 526–31. He argued that a true Guelf-Ghibelline split in Genoese politics came only as a result of Frederick II's disruptive diet at Ravenna in 1232. Heers warns about oversimplifying the Guelf-Ghibelline issue: "It ties the political history of these towns directly to the great issues of Western history and reduces the internal rivalries to a relatively simple scheme which can be easily explained" (*Parties and Political Life*, 42).

66. Some scholars have recognized the "de Curia" as a family, most notably Chiaudano and Moresco in their edition of Giovanni Scriba's cartulary; but no one has really carried the matter further to investigate notarial references and to develop the family's role in factionalism (Scarsella, *Il comune dei consoli*, p. 217; Agostino Olivieri, "Serie dei consoli del comune di Genova," *Atti della Società Ligure di Storia Patria*, 1 [1858]: 412; and Bach, *Gênes*, 155–56). On the other hand, years ago Butler, in translating a passage from the Genoese Annals and unaware of the existence of the della Corte family, wrote "Dorias" for "isti de Curia," thus completely confusing the factional divisions (*Lombard Communes*, 191).

67. *Curtis* is a variant of *curia*, as the modern English "court" and the Italian "corte" testify. See Olivieri, "Serie dei consoli," 362. Also, the Genoese annalist, Caffaro, used the words *curia* and *curtis* interchangeably. While the usual word is *curia*, in one passage, for example, probably to

avoid repetition of the same word in one sentence, Caffaro wrote: "Verumtamen Ianuenses ad *curiam* vocati venire, de consulibus et melioribus civitatis Willelmum Ventum [other names follow] ubi tunc imperator *curtem* tenebat, sine more miserunt" (*Annali genovesi*, 1: 65).

68. "Registrum curiae," 2, 2: 24.

69. *Annali genovesi*, 1: 18.

70. "Registrum curiae," 2, 2: 89, 91, and 94, for example.

71. Ibid., 24.

72. Giovanni Scriba, *Cartolare*, nos. 44, 84, and 907; Olivieri, "Serie dei consoli," 464.

73. Giovanni Scriba, *Cartolare*, nos. 66, 70, 81, 218, 405, 406, 1233, 1234, and 2A; *Codice diplomatico*, 2: 327, doc. 172.

74. *Annali genovesi*, 1: 170.

75. In Giovanni Scriba's cartulary, members of the di Castro family appear 28 times with della Volta family members, more than any other family.

76. See above, p. 80.

77. *Annali genovesi*, 2: 45.

78. Giovanni Scriba, *Cartolare*, nos. 713 and 717.

79. Ibid., nos. 3, 4, 7, 587, and 602.

80. See chap. 5.

81. Olivieri, "Serie dei consoli," 464.

82. Ibid., 472.

83. Giovanni Scriba, *Cartolare*, no. 84.

84. Ibid., no. 666.

85. See chap. 5.

86. Giovanni Scriba, *Cartolare*, nos. 713 and 717.

87. Lusio, however, had been one of Ansaldo Mallone's partners in the *compera* of Spanish Tortosa in 1150 (*Codice diplomatico*, 1: 265, doc. 214, and 266, doc. 215). He is not, however, listed among the financial contributors of the combine (ibid., 267, doc. 216). This association is further indication that in the early 1150's della Volta's friends did not appear to the della Corte and Carmadino leaders as serious political threats.

88. *Annali genovesi*, 1: 38–39.

89. In fact, the consuls were preparing the city to fight Barbarossa if necessary (ibid., 41–43).

90. The document recording the loan for their journey east was dated June 8, 1156, and the imperial court was specified as the destination (Giovanni Scriba, *Cartolare*, no. 84).

91. Ibid., no. 97.

92. Ibid., no. 127. The city's inclusion in Byzantine territory is

deduced from references to Genoese problems there in the Genoese list of grievances to Manuel in 1174. In fact, one of the complaints speaks of four hundred hyperpers which the "duke" of Adalia confiscated from Ido Mallone, and another sum of £14 similarly taken from Nicola Berfolio by the Byzantine official. These items are indications of additional della Volta involvement in Byzantine commerce that have been lost from notarial sources (Sanguineti and Bertolotto, "Documenti," 386 and 401).

93. For the heavy involvement of della Volta adherents in the trade with Sicily, see Abulafia, *Two Italies,* 217–54.

94. Abulafia considers all the contracts of 1156 to have been made in conjunction with the departure of the Genoese embassy (ibid., 101–5). In Giovanni Scriba's cartulary, however, there is a hiatus in the Sicilian business from May 3 to August 9, with only one contract in the interim (June 30) (Giovanni Scriba, *Cartolare,* no. 89). It seems more likely that the documents of early 1156 covered a voyage of habitual Sicilian traders who left with the spring sailing. The later group of contracts was for a projected sailing in September, and when it was decided to send an embassy to the Sicilian king, more people took advantage of the diplomatic mission, thus explaining the large volume of activity in late August and early September that Abulafia himself notes (*Two Italies,* 103). The two ambassadors were still in Genoa on September 9, when the transaction concerning the dowry of Lanfranco Pevere's daughter (married to Guglielmo Vento's son) was made (Giovanni Scriba, *Cartolare,* no. 139). The voyage to Sicily in May was short enough to allow the traders to return to Genoa by July with their bad news, forcing the government to begin planning an embassy.

95. *Annali genovesi,* 1: 46.

96. *Codice diplomatico,* 1: 341–42, doc. 280, and 344–49, doc. 282 (the Genoese ratification, in which no member of the della Corte family appears as swearing to uphold the agreement, an indication that they, indeed, were at Manuel's court.)

97. The man's name, "de Ita," was a matronymic (Olivieri, "Serie dei consoli," 299).

98. *Annali genovesi,* 1: 48.

99. The Genoese swore in their ratification of the Sicilian treaty that no Genoese citizen would enter Byzantine service against the king of Sicily (*Codice diplomatico,* 1: 354, doc. 282).

100. Giovanni Scriba, *Cartolare,* no. 401.

101. Chalandon, *Les Comnène,* 2: 367–70.

102. Giovanni Scriba, *Cartolare,* no. 666.

103. Ibid., no. 615.

104. Ibid., no. 669.

105. Ibid., no. 673.

106. Ibid., no. 674. An undated contract in Giovanni Scriba's register calls Guglielmo Piperata a della Volta (ibid., 2: 311).

107. Ibid., no. 752.

108. Ibid., no. 840.

109. Ibid., nos. 223, 255, 864, 877, and 886.

110. Ibid., no. 899.

111. Ibid., nos. 705 and 901.

112. Ibid., no. 705.

113. Sanguineti and Bertolotto, "Documenti," 368-405.

114. Ibid., 395. Vsevolod Slessarev made the connection between the list of Genoese losses and Giovanni Scriba's cartulary ("The Pound Value of Genoa's Maritime Trade in 1161," in *Economy, Society and Government in Medieval Italy*, 97-99). He did not, however, notice Ingo della Volta's arrangements which follow.

115. Sanguineti and Bertolotto, "Documenti," 390.

116. Giovanni Scriba, *Cartolare*, nos. 899 and 900. Gioele di Bonico seems to have regularly acted as a factor for Ingo della Volta, for Giovanni Scriba has other contracts for partnerships between the two men (ibid., no. 379, and appendix 2, 309).

117. Sanguineti and Bertolotto, "Documenti," 390.

118. Giovanni Scriba, *Cartolare*, no. 799.

119. Sanguineti and Bertolotto, "Documenti," 395.

120. *Annali genovesi*, 1: 67.

121. Giovanni Scriba, *Cartolare*, nos. 741 and 746.

122. *Annali genovesi*, 1: 67.

123. *Codice diplomatico*, 1: 220, doc. 172; and 381, doc. 302.

124. De Negri, *Storia di Genova*, 289-92.

125. *Codice diplomatico*, 1:, 395-404, doc. 308.

126. Giovanni Scriba, *Cartolare*, no. 163. Yves Reynouard has linked the attitudes of the Avvocati, at least, with the rural nobility (*Les hommes d'affaires italiens du moyen âge* [Paris, 1949], 69).

127. *Annali genovesi*, 1: 258-60; and 2: 5-6; *Codice diplomatico*, 2: 184-91, docs. 89 and 90; and 3: 153-55, doc. 59.

128. *Annali genovesi*, 1: 74-75.

129. Giovanni Scriba, *Cartolare*, no. 1064.

130. Byrne, "Easterners in Genoa," *Journal of the American Oriental Society* 38 (1918): 176-87.

131. Giovanni Scriba, *Cartolare*, no. 1198.

132. Ibid., nos. 1014-16.

133. In May 1164, Oberto Spinola was settling the financial affairs of his deceased brother (ibid., nos. 1193-96). A document of July 11, 1164,

speaks of Rubaldo, "quondam Enrici Guercii" (ibid., no. 1235). Ogerio Vento had died in February (ibid., no. 1162). Epstein speaks of Vento's illness, but gives the impression that the man recovered. Epstein does not notice that this just-cited document involves Ogerio the Younger and Guglielmo acting as the guardians for their younger half-brother, Simon, in carrying out the instructions of their father's will (*Wills and Wealth*, 26-27).

134. *Annali genovesi,* 1: 158-67; *Codice diplomatico,* 2: 12, doc. 4.

135. Byrne, "Genoese Trade," 203-4.

136. *Annali genovesi,* 1: 160.

137. Ibid., 168.

138. See above, chap. 2., for this embassy.

## Chapter Five

~~~~

# The Byzantine Trade
# as a Family Business

IN THE FEW SURVIVING RECORDS of Genoese activity in the twelfth-century Byzantine world, the Guercio family figures as the one group that most successfully combined adventure, business acumen, family alliance, and political power to exploit the Byzantine connection for its own advancement and profit. Although the family did not try to exclude other businessmen from commerce with the Byzantines, their control became so complete that the Genoese twelfth-century trade with Byzantium might be considered to have been a family business. The story of the Guercio family clarifies the close relationship between the development of the Byzantine trade and internal politics at Genoa. The phenomenon of the Guercii was not atypical of the Genoese, for other great families acquired predominant influence in other markets, the most outstanding example being the Embriaco family in Syria.[1] The Genoese applied to commerce that same sense of individualism that was to emerge in the civil strife that ruined the twelfth-century commune, and the activities of the Guercio family provide one of our best examples of the Genoese view that the city's government had its significance only as an instrument by which politicians could most effectively advance their own private interests.

The family of Guercio was part of the viscountal house of Guercio, descended through a Filippo Guercio, who flourished in the late eleventh century, from a Viscount Waraco, the eponymous ancestor of the clan of the Guaracchi.[2] The history of the lineage is very obscure until the middle of the twelfth century when enough evidence becomes available to establish a tentative family tree. By then, the two branches of the Guaracco and Guercio families were still close enough to participate together in private family and business matters, and they must have felt a strong common lineage. As for the Guercio family itself, at least three branches are visible by the mid-twelfth century, even if their exact relationship to one another cannot be satisfactorily determined.

The central figures of our story are the three brothers, Enrico and Baldovino Guercio, and Rubaldo Bisaccia. Although the brothers' surnames are different, their fraternity is proved by two notarial entries. In 1158 Enrico and Rubaldo stood surety for a loan that Baldovino had taken out, and Baldovino is specifically mentioned as their brother.[3] Thirty-four years later, in Baldovino's donation of 1192 to the hospital of Santa Maria di Lanarolo, Baldovino mentioned Bisaccia as his brother.[4] Baldovino was an adventurer who commanded the confidence of the Byzantine emperors; Enrico used his diplomatic skill to win his city's entry into the market of Constantinople; and Rubaldo Bisaccia was a powerful politician who persuaded the municipal government to adopt the policies that affected Genoa's position with the Byzantines.

The primary representative of a second branch of the family was Lamberto Guercio, a very active merchant-financier in the middle of the twelfth century. In one document, a certain Aimelina is mentioned as are her brothers Lamberto Guercio and an otherwise unknown Oreglerio.[5] Several other documents mention another of Lamberto's brothers, Rubaldo Drogo, who was specifically designated as Lamberto's brother in the list of losses suffered by the Genoese in the destruction of their quarter in Constantinople in 1162.[6] Lamberto's exact relationship to the three brothers is unknown, but because he often appears in notarial documents with them or with their associates he must have been kin; perhaps he was an uncle, because he seems to have been older than the brothers.

A third branch of the extended family was that of Guglielmo Anfosso Guercio. This line included three sons of Guglielmo: Guglielmo the Younger, Ogerio Tanto, and Anfosso Simpato.[7] Tanto had at least one son, named Alinerio, and a daughter, Dandala, who had by her husband, Rubaldo di Gionata della Porta, a son named Pietro Dandala. The boy's name is a reminder of the tendency of some Genoese noble families to use matronymics.[8]

The Guercio family may have inherited its interest in Byzantium from Lamberto Ghetto, who was a Genoese spokesman at the Byzantine court sometime around 1104.[9] The man's name may be a corruption of "Guercio," especially in light of his first name, Lamberto, which was common to the family. In fact, he may be the same Lamberto Guercio or Getio who was a communal consul from 1114 to 1118.[10] This Lamberto may have been the father of the Lamberto Guercio who flourished in the mid-twelfth century, or perhaps he was the father of our brothers themselves. Nevertheless, too many uncertainties surround this Lamberto Ghetto and his relationship to later members of the Guercio family to do more than simply to offer him as the possible connecting link between the Guercio family and Byzantium in the absence of any other explanation.

Of the three brothers, Baldovino, probably the youngest, emerges with the clearest record. Like many other younger sons, he established himself apart from his family and native land by taking up service with the Byzantines. Baldovino was primarily a military man and only later in life did he settle down to a distinguished career in Genoa. Since he was old enough to enter military service under Emperor John II,[11] who died in 1143, Baldovino could not have been born later than 1120 or 1125, and he was still alive in 1206,[12] but he died by 1218.[13]

As a young Genoese of good family, Baldovino Guercio may have accompanied the embassy of Oberto della Torre and Guglielmo Barca to John II Comnenus in the principality of Antioch in 1142.[14] This possibility would best explain his introduction to the Byzantine world and his decision to remain in the East as a soldier in John's service. There is some evidence that the Byzantine military had a Lombard contingent similar to the more famous German, Scandinavian, Russian, and English troops, and it may have been this unit that Baldovino joined.[15] The young Baldovino soon proved himself to be a loyal servant of John's successor, Manuel I. Baldovino undoubtedly served in Manuel's campaigns against King Roger I of Sicily in Corfu and the Morea in 1147,[16] for he was imprisoned by the Sicilian monarch.[17] Probably, he served in Manuel's campaigns in southern Italy and perhaps partially influenced the Byzantines' decision to approach Genoa for aid in 1155 (such a plausible and convenient hypothesis, however, cannot be substantiated with hard evidence). At some other unknown time, the prince of Antioch also imprisoned Baldovino as a consequence of the Italian's duty to the emperor.[18] In spite of these temporary setbacks, Baldovino's career with Byzantium was successful enough for him to receive from Manuel a *pronoia* and to be honored as an imperial "lizios," which the feudally minded Genoese habitually translated as "vassal."[19]

Guercio enjoyed the confidence of Byzantine emperors for many years. In 1179 Agnes of France, betrothed to Manuel's heir, Alexius II, was entrusted to a Genoese fleet commanded by Baldovino for her passage east.[20] After the tumultuous years following Manuel's death had passed and Isaac II had given a pro-Latin flavor to Byzantine policy again, the emperor showed his trust in Baldovino by writing to him in 1188 when Guercio was a consul of the commune to request that he keep the Byzantine court informed about Western preparations for the Third Crusade.[21] In 1193, when the piracy of Guglielmo Grasso had angered Isaac to the point of withdrawing Genoese privileges, Genoa sent Guercio and Guido Spinola to placate the emperor.[22] Although Baldovino's nephew had been one of Grasso's henchmen,[23] so great was the Italian's prestige at the Byzantine court that he and his colleague were able to calm the piqued emperor and save their city's privileges.[24] Alexius III's wrath over Gafforio's piracy could not be so easily assuaged, and not only did the Genoese lose their quarter and privileges,[25] but also Baldovino had his *pronoia* taken from him, and it is unknown whether it was ever returned.[26]

Baldovino Guercio's influence in the Byzantine world was matched by his position of leadership back home in Genoa. The adventurer returned to his home city sometime before June 1158, when his brothers became guarantors for a sum of money he had borrowed.[27] The first reference to Baldovino in public office comes from 1161 when he, along with several other substantial Genoese, was elected to the office of public witness, whereby he was empowered to witness all public documents, charters, and contracts.[28] In 1164 Baldovino participated in one of the most important affairs of the commune by serving as the depository for a loan made by the envoy of the Genoese-backed Judge Barisone of Sardinia to Marquis Opizo Malaspina, one of the emperor's vassals assigned to escort the Sardinian to Frederick's court.[29] The transaction, interestingly, was

witnessed by both of Baldovino's brothers, with Bisaccia undoubtedly acting in his capacity as consul of the commune.[30]

Two years later Baldovino commanded a naval search and destroy
mission against the Pisans in waters off the Riviera. The operation
well illustrated the chronic political infighting at Genoa. One of
the six galleys under Guercio's command had been unwisely placed
in charge of Guglielmo Galleta, a political opponent of Baldovino's
then serving as a consul of the pleas for the city. After an unsuccessful search, Guercio anchored his ships at Corsica to rest the crews.
There a squabble broke out between the two factions, perhaps
occasioned by the consul's dissatisfaction with his subordination to
Guercio. After order had been restored, the force set sail and was
soon intercepted by a Pisan flotilla. In the ensuing battle, the
Genoese fought in their usual manly fashion, as the annalist assures
us, but neither Guercio not Galleta were willing to come to the aid
of the other, and the Pisans were able to capture both of them and
their ships.[31] Baldovino was released before 1170, for at the beginning of that year he was a member of a Genoese mission sent to
receive possession of the castle of Fraccario from the counts of
Lavagna, who had seized the fortress from the people of Passao
against the wishes of the Genoese commune.[32] Nearly a year later
Baldovino was part of an embassy sent to Lucca to arrange an
anti-Pisan alliance.[33]

Apart from Guercio's transportation of Agnes of France to
Constantinople in 1179, the existing record is silent about Baldovino
from 1171 until the 1180's. It is very likely that he spent much of
this period in the East, where, as a favorite of Manuel's, he may
have acted as a semi-official spokesman for Genoese interests at the
imperial court. Some years later he had the prestige under Isaac II
to be effective in such a role, for in Isaac's letter of 1192 to the
Genoese *podestà*, Manegoldo Tetoccio, the emperor refers to the
effectiveness of Baldovino's esteem in gaining for the Genoese a
renewal of their privileges.[34] At any rate, Guercio must have left
Romania in the aftermath of the Latin massacre of 1182 and
returned to Genoa, where he was to reach the culmination of his
political life by being elected consul of the commune for 1188.[35]
The major business of that year was to prepare the city's crusading
expedition for its passage to the Holy Land. Baldovino and his
fellow consuls arranged a peace treaty with Pisa in the summer to

expedite their preparations,[36] and it was in Baldovino's capacity as consul that Isaac wrote to him asking for information on the crusade's progress in Europe.[37] After the end of his consular year, Baldovino and three of his former colleagues, Nicola Embriaco, Simon Doria, and Spezapedra, joined the crusading host.[38] It is not known how long Baldovino stayed in the Holy Land, but he was back in Genoa in March 1191, when he witnessed a contract in his home.[39] Over a year later he naturally enough signed the Genoese officials' oath to abide by the terms of the new treaty with Isaac II.[40] His signature and those of his close relatives were undoubtedly required in this case on account of their active participation in Byzantino-Genoese affairs, since only Bisaccia held public office at the time.[41] Baldovino's mission to Isaac's court in 1193 over Genoese piracy appears to have been Baldovino's last public charge, and now a very old man, he settled down to semi-retirement, during which he occasionally hosted businessmen in his home or engaged in business or charitable transactions.[42]

While Baldovino is the best known of the Guercio brothers, Enrico, probably the eldest (based on his early consulships and death), is the least known. If he is distinguished from the homonymous marquis of Savona, as he should be, there are very few references to him at all. Enrico was consul of the commune for the first time in 1137, and he held the office three more times, in 1148, 1153, and 1160.[43] He therefore must have been a man of some political influence at home, although the annalist is suspiciously silent about events during Enrico's years of office.[44] Enrico's consulships of 1148 and 1153 came during the period of the commune's initial subjugation of the *contado,* but Enrico's role in the phenomenon is unknown. The repeated possession of the consulship by him and by his brother, Rubaldo Bisaccia, during these years, however, indicated that the family supported the commune's conservative group, which was in power during this period. As consul in 1153 Enrico traveled to the court of Count Raymond Berenger IV of Barcelona, where for a substantial sum he sold to the count all Genoese rights and possessions in Spanish Tortosa as part of the commune's efforts to dispose of its debt.[45] Enrico's greatest achievement for his city came in 1160 when he went to Constantinople to negotiate the specifics of the general agreement made between Genoa and Manuel Comnenus' deputies five years before.[46] Although Enrico Guercio's diplomatic victory was short lived, because the new compound was quickly destroyed by the Pisans in 1162,[47] Guercio had nevertheless broken ground for the continuing involvement of both his city and his family in Byzantium. His death sometime before the middle of 1164 ended a career that had contributed substantially to Genoa's political and economic advancement in the mid-twelfth century.[48]

The third brother, Rubaldo Bisaccia, was the driving force behind Genoa's intrusion into Byzantium. Probably the middle of the brothers, he was still active in 1201 in the private commercial enterprises of his fellow Genoese.[49] There is no question of Rubaldo's strong political influence at Genoa, for he held the consulship eleven times between 1149 and 1192, and often in years of considerable importance for Genoese affairs with the Byzantine Empire.[50] Throughout his career he served the commune in various other capacities as well. He assisted in the agreement made in 1150 with William of Montferrat.[51] In 1165, as a councillor of the commune, Bisaccia signed Genoa's anti-Pisan treaty with Raymond Berenger of Provence.[52] Although Rubaldo seems not to have been much of a warrior, he nevertheless served as a naval commander both in 1167 and in 1172 in expeditions against the Pisans.[53] Bisaccia continued to participate in communal affairs outside of the consulship, and he is included in a list of Genoese "senators" in 1173.[54]

The few surviving references to Rubaldo from the notarial registers demonstrate clearly that this illiterate Genoese nobleman also participated in the business life of his city.[55] In 1157, for example, he borrowed £200 from Vassallo di Gisulfo for a business enterprise,[56] and in the next year he and his brother Enrico borrowed another £100 from Marchese della Volta for a trading voyage to Alexandria.[57] In 1168 he had a small sum invested in Sardinia.[58] This kind of activity in Genoa's far-flung Mediterranean trade was a part of Bisaccia's personality that endured, at least to 1206 when he last appeared in extant notarial material. A combination of political power and commercial interest made Bisaccia more than anyone else the architect of Genoa's relations with the Byzantine Empire in the twelfth century.

From the first appearance of Bisaccia in a position of communal leadership in 1149, a clear testimony is left to the philosophy of the Guercio family of using public policy for the advancement of its own interests. Bisaccia and his consular colleagues of 1149 initiated the program of clearing the municipal debt by farming out the city's privileges and possessions both at home and abroad to private consortia.[59] Thus, Genoa's customs revenues at home were sold for a fifteen-year period to a group of businessmen of whom Guglielmo Anfosso Guercio, Bisaccia's own relative, was a member,[60] and later in the year other municipal revenues for twenty-nine years and the minting operation for ten years were sold to another consortium including Anfosso Guercio.[61] At the close of the consular year in January 1150, the city's banking rights were sold to the same businessmen for twenty-nine years.[62] The consuls of 1151 continued the government's policy of debt liquidation, as did those of 1152, when one of the consuls was again Bisaccia, to whose close relative, Lamberto Guercio, was given the castle and *pedagium* of Rivarolo.[63] During these years the Guercio family was by no means alone in turning the city's financial plight to its own profit, but it became accustomed to a method of operation by which official public policy was exploited, or even formulated, to serve its own private interests. When Genoa became directly involved with Byzantium in 1155, it was natural that the politically powerful members of the family of Guercio should use the means at their disposal to bring their commune closer to the Byzantines.

Enrico Guercio's successful embassy of 1160, five years after the Byzantines' initial approach to the Genoese, is the first time that the Guercio family can be clearly seen taking a leading part in Genoa's diplomacy with Constantinople. Not only may Enrico Guercio, as a consul, have had a part in making the decision to bargain with the Byzantines, but his brother, Rubaldo Bisaccia, consul for the third time the year before, very likely could have prepared the groundwork for the embassy. At any rate, Bisaccia was intimately connected with his brother's embassy, for he partially subsidized the diplomatic mission. In March 1160, Bisaccia made a sea loan with Marchese della Volta for his own voyage to Constantinople, surely to accompany his brother's mission.[64] In May he made another sea loan with Adalardo della Corte to insure the three galleys he was sending to the Byzantine capital,[65] and two weeks later Enrico Guercio accepted from a certain Gisla, the widow of Guiscardo di Guala, £23 to take to Byzantium.[66] A few days before that, Guidoto di Bonobello made an *accommendatio* contract with Guglielmo Burone, Simon Doria, and Guglielmo della Volta to raise capital for his trading voyage on "Bisaccia's galleys,"[67] and Guglielmo Pevere and his son borrowed £200 from the Guercio brothers for the same stated purpose.[68] Genoa, then, owed her entry into the Byzantine market to the diplomatic efforts of Enrico Guercio, paid for, in part at least, by his brother Bisaccia. All that is missing is some proof (although the speculation is highly likely) that the third brother, Baldovino, was at Manuel's court preparing the emperor for his brother's visit.

This episode only began Bisaccia's life-long connection with Genoa's Byzantine affairs. Bisaccia was again consul of the commune in 1162, the year that the Pisans destroyed the nascent Genoese quarter in Constantinople. The Genoese government's harsh reaction to the crisis in the form of an ultimatum to Pisa leading to renewed warfare was to be expected,[69] but Bisaccia contributed to the feeling of angry affront that must have pervaded the consular sessions in late June and early July. The unsuccessful embassy of Corso Sigismundi, Ansaldo Mallone, and Nicola di Rodolfo to Constantinople departed in 1164, when Bisaccia was consul for the next time.[70] Rubaldo may have spent some of his time during his consulship of 1167 preparing the way for the dispatch of Amico di Murta's more productive mission the next year.[71] Three years later, at any rate, Bisaccia, again a consul, led the escort flotilla sent to Terracina to transport to Genoa the Byzantine envoys who carried for ratification the tentative agreement reached between Manuel and di Murta at the end of 1169.[72] Another Genoese ambassador, Grimaldi, left Genoa in December 1174, to treat with the Byzantine government in the matter of Genoese grievances, and interestingly enough, one of the men already elected as the next year's consuls was Rubaldo Bisaccia,[73] who was consul again in 1181, the year that marked the high point of Latin infiltration of the Byzantine Empire under Alexius II's regency.[74] Between 1182 and 1191, when the Genoese officially had no facility at Constantinople, Bisaccia failed to hold public office. His last consulship in 1192, however, signaled the successful negotiations of Tornello and Spinola, which allowed the return of Genoese merchants to a privileged status in the Constantinopolitan market.[75] Of Bisaccia's nine consulships in the epoch of Genoa's twelfth-century connection with Byzantium, then, seven of them were held in years when significant events for Byzantino-Genoese affairs took place. The election of Bisaccia to consul for 1172, when the Genoese perhaps still hoped to improve their position in the Byzantine Empire in the wake of the Venetian expulsion can reasonably be attributed to the importance that his fellow citizens placed on the Byzantine situation.[76] Bisaccia's only other consulship in 1177 occurred during his city's uninterrupted prosperity in Constantinople's business. His control over Genoa's Byzantine policy is further demonstrated by the election of his son, Bisacino, to one of the consulships in 1189,[77] when Isaac II's agent, Constantine Mesopotamites, visited Genoa to bargain for the city's reentry into the Byzantine capital.[78] Indeed, extremely few events making up Genoa's twelfth-century diplomacy with the Byzantines did not involve either Bisaccia or one of his immediate relatives.

In order to accomplish such grandiose personal policies, the Guercio brothers had to be skilled manipulators of the political realities of twelfth-century Genoa, and they had to have supporters. By looking both at Genoa's consular lists and especially at notarial materials, it is possible to determine which individuals made the plans of the Guercio family achievable. First, the family had close relatives, such as Lamberto Guercio and Guglielmo Anfosso Guercio and his family, and it received the support of the Guaracci and other more distant relatives. Among other allies, as is to be expected, were members of the della Volta and della Corte families, but also the Guercio family had its own unique connections with people, both great and not so great, who can be said to have formed a third political bloc in Genoa. Although this Guercio group is much less well defined than the other two, it did have enough strength to be a definite factor in the squabbles of the other two factions. Under Bisaccia's leadership, the Guercio bloc always kept one program in the forefront of its policies: the establishment of closer relations with the Byzantine Empire. All other projects and loyalties were secondary to this one.

From the family relationships of the Guercii, Enrico apparently was married to a sister of Ido Porcello, or Porco,[79] who had been consul of the commune in 1136,[80] and was a member, if not the head, of another powerful Genoese clan. Perhaps the most distinguished member of the family was the archbishop of Genoa throughout the period of Genoa's first commercial entreaties with the Byzantine Empire. Moreover, a young relative of Ido Porcello's, Ogerio Porco, would be in 1191 one of the most active participants in the flurry of business deals made on the eve of the departure of Tanto's delegation to Isaac II's court.[81] He is probably the same Ogerio Porco who financed the voyage of another Porco to Thessalonica in 1206 to transport Agnes of Montferrat to her new husband, Emperor Henry of the Latin Empire of Constantinople.[82]

Ido's daughter, Enrico Guercio's niece, was married to Ido Gontardo, whose family had been one of the most active in city affairs.[83] His father had been consul of the commune three times, in 1148 (with Enrico Guercio), 1150, and 1154, while he himself had already been consul of the pleas in 1153 and would fill the commune's highest office in 1166 and 1168, the year that Amico di Murta went to Constantinople. Of considerable importance is that Gontardo, like Baldovino Guercio, was a "lizios" of the Byzantine emperor,[84] an honor he may have owed to Baldovino himself, although it is impossible to trace Ido's career with Byzantium any farther. The two men had mutual business interests, at least, for in June 1158, Gontardo lent money to Baldovino with Enrico and Bisaccia standing surety for their brother.[85] Among the witnesses, it may be noted, were Gontardo's in-laws, Ido Porcello, and Porcello's son, Corrado.

Perhaps some of the staunchest supporters of the Guercio program were members of the Malocello family. Oberto Malocello had been a consul in the years 1114 to 1117 on the same board as Lamberto "Getio," who may have been an ancestor of the Guercii in the mid-twelfth century.[86] Guglielmo Malocello had been a consul in 1140, and Giovanni Malocello in 1155 and 1158. Members of the family strongly supported the Byzantine program. Not only was Giovanni Malocello one of the consuls who accepted the initial Byzantine offer to the Genoese, but the family lost one of the larger sums, 1,070 hyperpers, in the Pisan sack of 1162.[87] Again in 1171, when the commune borrowed money to finance an expedition to assist Manuel I in his war with the Venetians, the most generous contributor was Enrico Malocello, and a few years later, when the Genoese tabulated all of their losses, the Malocelli had lost 5,390 hyperpers, second only to the Guercii themselves.[88] Although there is no proof of business partnerships between the

Guercio and Malocello families, nevertheless, members of the two families appear together as witnesses at least ten times in extant notarial entries, making the Malocelli one of the more frequent companions of the Guercii.[89] These few definite instances, along with the families' mutual interest in Byzantium, lead to the conclusion that at least a loose political alliance existed between the Guercii and the Malocelli.

The Guercii had dealings with some other very important people in Genoa. Bisaccia borrowed money twice from Marchese della Volta, once in 1158 and again in 1160, and both of these loans were guaranteed by Nicola Roza and Bonvassallo di Medolico.[90] The Roza family had been consular since 1114,[91] and Nicola himself had been consul of the pleas in 1155, 1160, and 1161, and would serve as consul of the commune in 1166, 1169, and 1171.[92] Bonvassallo di Medolico's ancestor, Bonmoto, had been one of the original consuls of the commune from 1099 to 1102,[93] although subsequent family members devoted their energies to business rather than to city politics.

There are traces of lesser men who seem to have attached themselves to the Guercio family. Perhaps the most notable person of this type was Guido da Lodi. He held political office only once in his life, when he served a term as consul of the pleas in 1161.[94] Guido was most closely associated with Merlo Guaracco, a distant cousin of the Guercio brothers, and with Lamberto Guercio.[95] Guido da Lodi lost 350 hyperpers when the Pisans destroyed the Genoese compound at Constantinople in 1162,[96] and in 1175 he went east with Grimaldi's delegation to accept compensation both for his own losses and for those of some other businessmen, most notably the sons of the annalist Caffaro, Oberto Guaracco, and his old friend, Lamberto Guercio.[97] Enrico Detesalve,[98] perhaps a native of the Genoese town of Portovenere,[99] also frequented the circle of Baldovino Guercio. He had been one of the two Genoese ambassadors to Kings Richard and Philip who were captured in 1189 by the marquis of Incisa.[100] Detesalve was interested not only in the Byzantine trade, but also in the Sicilian and North African markets. His connections served him in good stead, for he or his like-named son won a term as consul of the commune in 1210.[101] A third person who was associated with the Guercii was Ido di Pallo, one of five brothers engaged in various commercial enterprises.[102] He at least had one deal with Baldovino Guercio, for mention of a *societas* between the two was made in another contract of 1186.[103] These men are representative of many people just below the ranks of the great families who were using their connections with the noble houses of Genoa to improve their lot and even to rise to the lower fringes of the office-holding aristocracy.

From the very beginning the Guercii attached themselves to the powerful group of citizens headed by Ingo della Volta, who ruled twelfth-century Genoa like the Florentine de Medici of a later period. In fact, the Guercii appear in notarial documents with members of the della Volta family more often than with any other family, even more than with their own cousins, the Guaracci.[104] Ingo's brother, Guglielmo Burone, was one of Enrico Guercio's consular colleagues in 1137, 1148, and 1162, while his son and namesake shared the office with Bisaccia in 1192.[105] Ingo himself was also one of Bisaccia's colleagues in 1162,[106] and in 1164 his son, Marchese, served in the consulate with Bisaccia.[107] In that year Enrico Guercio's son, Baldovino, lost his life fighting for the della Volta group against the followers of Rolando Avvocato.[108] Marchese della Volta himself, who was assassinated in that same year as a consequence of the vendetta the disturbance generated,[109] was tied to the Guercii in business matters as well. In 1158 the young della Volta loaned Enrico and Rubaldo £100 for their business venture to Alexandria,[110] and in March 1160, he loaned Bisaccia £100 for his coming trip to Constantinople.[111] Marchese was also a witness three months later to the *accommendatio* contract mentioned above between his uncle, Guglielmo Burone, and Guidoto di Bonobello for the latter's trip east on Bisaccia's galleys.[112] Marchese also sometimes borrowed money from members of the Guercio family, as is evidenced by a contract of March 1, 1158, in which Lamberto Guercio loaned him £20.[113] In 1162 Bisaccia was a witness, along with Guglielmo Burone and Ingo della Volta, to Giordano di Gisulfo's loan to the master of the Hospitallers in Lombardy, and at the end of the same year, Bisaccia and Ingo witnessed Guglielmo Burone's sale of some real estate to Angelerio di Camilla.[114] Lamberto Guercio appeared twice in contracts with Guglielmo Burone, once in 1159 as a witness to a land purchase made by Burone and again in 1162 as a principal in a business arrangement witnessed by Burone.[115]

The Guercii are also known to have been in the company of people connected with the della Volta group. Both Bisaccia and Baldovino Guercio were witnesses to a private contract from 1159 involving Guglielmo Usodimare's marriage portion for the niece of a certain Guglielmo Filardo.[116] Among the other witnesses were Ansaldo Mallone, who had been a partner of Guglielmo Anfosso Guercio in the *compera* of 1150 for Spanish Tortosa,[117] and his son Ugo; Martino di Castro;[118] and Amico and Lamberto Grillo, whose family had a major interest in the commerce with Syria.[119] There surely were even more business and personal associations between the Guercio and della Volta families than these few examples that have survived.

Traces of Guercio family members associating with the della Corte family in the 1150's and very early 1160's have been found. In May 1160, Adalardo della Corte lent Bisaccia £200 for the latter's voyage to Constantinople with his brother's embassy.[120] Several months before, in September 1159, a cousin of the Guercii, Merlo Guaracco, lent Amigo della Corte £100, and Lamberto Guercio was a witness to the document.[121] Several years earlier, in June 1156, Lamberto Guercio also witnessed the contract in which the della Corte brothers, Amigo, Rubaldo, and Raimondo, borrowed £115 from Rubaldo Boleto to help finance their voyage to Manuel's court.[122] In another document, one from 1158, a possible member of the della Corte Family, Ogerio "Curtis," and his wife, Adalasia, sold two pieces of land with the counsel of Adalasia's "propinquus," Lamberto Guercio.[123] If "propinquus" means "relative," rather than simply "neighbor," this document provides evidence of a matrimonial tie between the della Corte and Guercio families, although the couple probably had sufficient regard for Lamberto to use him in place of the relative required in transactions involving a wife's dowry property even if no blood tie existed. In all, the notarial documents contain at least twelve associations of Guercio people with members of the della Corte family, a number higher than with any other family except the della Volta family and their Guaracco cousins.[124]

The larger Guercio family, as well as its cousins, the Guaracchi, enthusiastically engaged in trade with Byzantium. Unfortunately the notarial contracts for Genoese trade with Constantinople from 1170 to 1182 are all but lost; but even the scarce references that still survive testify to the large share that the clan had in Byzantine commerce, if a record of losses rather than of profits is accepted as a reliable and random indication of the true situation. The Guercii lost investments when the Pisans attacked the Genoese quarter in 1162. Bisaccia himself lost 500 hyperpers.[125] He had not been present in Constantinople, but the money had been entrusted to Rubaldo di Balneo, a young man who went on the trading venture with his kinsmen, Donadio and Pasquali di Balneo. Similarly, Baldovino Guercio had invested 170 hyperpers with Pietro di Pavarono, who lost the money in the raid.[126] Enrico Guercio's son and namesake was in the Byzantine capital at the time of the Pisan attack, in which he lost the large sum of 700 hyperpers, while a merchant named Girardo Scoto lost the small amount of 19 hyperpers which the young Enrico's wife had given him.[127] Lamberto Guercio lost 550 hyperpers through his brother Drogo.[128] Another probable relative, Guglielmo Guercio di Vulparia, lost 336 hyperpers,[129] and a probable cousin, Oberto Guaracco, lost 350 hyperpers in the attack.[130] The monetary losses of these seven members of the lineage was 2,625 hyperpers, or nearly 9 percent of the total 29,424 hyperpers claimed in 1175. Their individual investments were among the largest, and as a family, they lost more than any other.

If the investors outside the family with whom the Guercii had close connections are considered, an even more impressive picture of the pervasive influence of the bloc emerges.[131]

| | |
|---|---|
| Mallone family | 2,535 hyperpers |
| Doria family | 1,802 1/2 |
| Guglielmo Burone | 1,500 |
| Malocello family | 1,070 |
| Ingo della Volta | 997 |
| Guido da Lodi | 350 |
| Enrico Detesalve | 350 |
| Donadio di Balneo | 350 |
| Lamberto Grillo | 336 |
| Embriaco | 303 |
| Di Pallo family | 136 |
| Total | 9,729 1/2 hyperpers |

The amount over which it is certain that the Guercii had some influence, therefore, was 12,354 1/2 hyperpers, corresponding to

42 percent of the total investment lost. Other investors quite likely were involved with the Guercii, but no proof of any relationship can be found, so that the figures here presented indicate the minimum degree of Guercio involvement in the initial Genoese commercial enterprise in the Byzantine capital. There can be little question that they dominated the early business.

The immediate Guercio family escaped financial loss in the Venetian pillage of the new Genoese quarter in 1171, but the investment of a cousin, Oliverio Guaracco, amounting to 1,225 hyperpers, or 21.6 percent of the total, was wiped out, and an unidentifiable Pietro Guercio lost 16 hyperpers.[132] After the destruction of the Genoese compound in 1171, the commune floated a loan to subsidize its contribution to Manuel's subsequent war with the Venetians.[133] The contribution made by the Guercio family and its definite associates (using common agents as the connecting link) amounted to £2,415, or 26 percent of the total £9,419. If we add in the sums loaned by the Malocello, Doria, and della Volta groups, with whom we know that the Guercio family was close, the total investment under Guercio influence jumps to £5,715, or nearly 61% of the whole loan. Some of the other lenders not connected with these families may also have had links to the Guercii, especially Lanfranco di Pallo (£80 contribution), so that the Guercio influence in the loan may have been even larger than available evidence allows.

The evidence for later Genoese investment in Byzantium is much more sketchy than the detailed information available for the financial activity relating to the original quarter and to the loan of 1171, but it reveals continued and strong Guercio involvement. In the losses of Genoese ships that are cataloged in Grimaldi's instructions of 1174, various members of the Guercio family appear. One ship belonged to Lamberto Grancio and to Baldicio di Borgogno. Grancio himself may have been a member of the Guercio clan, since his name is sometimes written in the documents as "Guercio,"[134] and he appears in one private document with undisputed members of the Guercio family.[135] He lost 800 hyperpers when his ship was hijacked in Constantinople's harbor by the Pisans. But other Guercii and their definite associates lost money too. The mysteriously related Rufino Anne Guercie lost 640 hyperpers, Ido Gontardo lost 231 hyperpers, the unnamed son of Guglielmo Guercio lost

650 hyperpers, and Rubaldo Porco lost 660 hyperpers.[136] Bisaccia himself lost five hundred hyperpers on the ship of Villano Gauxono when it was shipwrecked and plundered by local inhabitants. An otherwise unidentified Guaracco lost 158 hyperpers on the same ship.[137] If we total up all of the known losses sustained by the Genoese in the Byzantine trade from 1155 to 1174, the Guercio bloc lost as much as 26,491½ hyperpers, or 33.5 percent of the total 79,112 hyperpers claimed, by far the largest amount of any of the political blocs, and the Guercio family by itself lost 11,434 hyperpers, again the largest amount for any single family.

While the three Guercio brothers played the leading political roles in Byzantino-Genoese relations, at least two other people who can be identified as members of the extended family also took significant parts in the diplomatic story, even if today the details of their contributions are impossible to work out. The more important of these two was a cousin of the Guercii named Ogerio Tanto,[138] who presumably followed Baldovino east and became known at Isaac's court, for in 1191 he was sufficiently important in Byzantine affairs to be entrusted with Genoa's negotiations with the Byzantines.[139] At the time he had already been involved with the Genoese quarter for twenty years because he and Otto d'Elia had loaned to the Genoese "viscount" (if, indeed, the Latin word in the document, *vicecomes,* is an official title and not simply a surname) 173 hyperpers to help repair the compound, perhaps after the Venetian attack of 1171.[140] He also made the substantial contribution of 2,900 hyperpers as a partner of Otto di Caffaro to the loan of 1171. He not only served as Genoa's ambassador to Isaac's court in 1191, but also was a signatory to the Genoese oath of 1192 to abide by the terms of the new treaty with the Byzantines.[141] Three months later, a second relative of the Guercio family, Pietro Dandala, brought to Genoa Isaac's complaint about Grasso's piracy.[142] Pietro was most probably the son of Tanto's daughter, Dandala, who was married to Rubaldo di Gionata della Porta.[143]

Although the administration of the Genoese quarter in Constantinople during the twelfth century is practically unknown today, nevertheless, members of the Guercio family seem to have had considerable influence over the compound. Baldovino carried much weight at the Byzantine court,[144] and perhaps his unofficial influence was translated into a more official position as a Genoese advocate or even as a governor of the colony. Grimaldi's instructions of 1174 make mention of a certain Viscount Guido, with whom the ambassador was to make contact on his arrival, and of a "Lombard viscount," undoubtedly the Greek title for the Genoese administrator.[145] The existence of a viscounty of Constantinople after the resumption of organized activity in the Byzantine capital in 1192 is certain, because a reference to the office was made in della Croce's instructions of 1201.[146] In fact, della Croce's instructions specifically ordered the ambassador to prevent the passing of the office into the hands of Alinerio, the son of Tanto.[147] Probably, from this specific instruction the Genoese government was attempting by this move to destroy a growing hereditary claim by the Guercii to the office.[148] This conjecture makes even more sense because of Guercio influence among the Byzantines, and because of an analogous situation in the crusading states after the Third Crusade, when fresh concessions of property and privileges allowed the commune to exert a new direct control through viscounts over the possessions that formerly had been enfeoffed to the Embriaco family.[149] Moreover, in 1200 Alinerio, whose father was now dead, was actively involved in business arrangements with the Guercio family, as was his probable kinsman, Guglielmo Dandala.[150] Any hereditary claim that Alinerio tried to put forth in 1201, then, the Genoese government was determined to block in order to break the family's long domination in the Byzantine business.

The Guercio family, to achieve its Byzantine goals throughout the second half of the century, had to be adept participants in the political maneuverings of their city's factions. As partisanship was developing in the 1150's and 1160's, the Guercii seem to have had no decided preference for one faction or another. Both Enrico and Rubaldo had served as consuls in the conservative governments from 1149 to 1153, and the willingness of the Guercii to continue cooperating with the old families and with the della Corte group in the early diplomacy with the Byzantines enabled these families to take an early lead in the diplomacy. In fact, the Guercio brothers probably approached the della Corte people for help in establishing the Byzantine link, because the della Volta combine, busy with the Syrian, Spanish, and Sicilian trade, may originally have had no desire to see the already complicated commercial network jeopardized by adding another element that conflicted with already existing interests. Toward the achievement of their Byzantine goal, however, the Guercii soon found that the orientation of their partners with a bygone past was of little use to them. Perhaps also, the Guercio leaders perceived in Amigo della Corte's visit to the Byzantine court in 1156 an unexpected and unwanted intrusion, or perhaps Amigo so botched his mission that the Guercii determined to find more competent partners. In any event, they soon realized that they needed to tap the economic and political resources of the other great Genoese families who were just as devoted to the expansion of Genoese trade. After the della Volta people decided to add the development of trade with Byzantium to their own larger expansionist program, it was only natural that the Guercii should become their allies. By 1160 the old Guercio–della Corte combination was still alive, since Adalardo della Corte contributed £200 to Bisaccia's Constantinople-bound fleet,[151] and the next year, a man connected with the Guercii, Elias, borrowed £100 from Amigo della Corte.[152] Nevertheless, at the same time Marchese della Volta had contributed £100 to Bisaccia's diplomatic project and the large della Volta investment on the whole in the mission of 1160 demonstrates their growing support.[153] Finally, the Guercii had found the right allies to advance their Byzantine aims.

As for della Volta ambitions, the move of the Guercii, with their strong political friends like the Malocelli and the Porcelli, over to the della Volta camp gave Ingo and his partners the leverage they needed to control the consequent Byzantine trade for themselves. The Guercii now became a necessary but subordinate part of the Mediterranean-wide della Volta commercial organization. The role of the Guercii was the same as that of the Embriaco family in the crusading states, where that family, with all Genoese property enfeoffed to them, controlled the trade at the eastern terminus and guarded over Genoese interests.[154] This system had been tried in Spain as well, where the Mallone family especially, had been given the Genoese possessions in Tortosa in 1150, but in 1153 the same bundle of property and privileges was sold by the nearly bankrupt commune to Raymond Berenger of Barcelona.[155] The political situation in the highly feudalized Kingdom of Jerusalem was not the same as the imperial framework of the Byzantine Empire, but the della Volta leaders, inexperienced in Byzantine matters, may not have been fully aware of the difference, and they made a parallel with regard to the operation of trade. While it was not possible for the Guercii to become great landed feudatories in the Byzantine Empire, as the Embriachi had become in Syria, because Manuel retained control over what he had granted, nevertheless Baldovino Guercio had his *pronoia* in the empire, and the della Volta traders saw in the strong position of the Guercii at the Byzantine court their usefulness in carrying out the same duties there as the Embriachi did in Syria.

This political and commercial alliance of the Guercio family with the della Volta faction would continue throughout the twelfth century, bringing power and profit to both parties. Only once was it temporarily broken in 1191, when a breakdown in the internal discipline of the della Volta system drove the Guercii into a temporary alliance with the della Corte people to advance their Byzantine interest, with the result of increased factional strife and constitutional turmoil in Genoa.[156] Soon, however, the Guercii would return to their traditional allies, even though by then the political and diplomatic situations were in such disarray that little durable headway could be made in the Byzantine connection until the Fourth Cusade ended it altogether.

The Guercii proved to be masters of political manipulation. The three brothers, Baldovino, Enrico, and Rubaldo, were responsible for turning the generous proposal made by Manuel's deputies in 1155 into a permanent association between Genoa and the Byzantine Empire. In the face of perilous challenges to the survival of Genoa's Byzantine trade, the brothers continually applied their skills and influence to the maintenance of their city's interest in the Greek-speaking world. The sagacious Rubaldo Bisaccia did not let the concerns of faction overwhelm his devotion to securing his city's presence in Byzantium and to advancing his family's interests there. Somehow, he guided his family through the vicissitudes of Genoese internal policies so that the Guercii always came out on top. That was no mean accomplishment in twelfth-century Genoa. Nearly every time he or a relative was in a position of authority in the commune, the city government took unmistakable steps to strengthen Genoa's involvement with the Byzantines. There can be little doubt that for him and for the members of his clan, the government served little other purpose than to execute the private policies of the family.

Perhaps the Guercii were not responsible statesmen, for they persistently led their city into Byzantine debacles, thus subordinating their city's welfare to their own family's objectives: Baldovino's glory and Rubaldo's profit. Although Genoa potentially could have derived much profit from the Byzantine connection, the actual benefit that the Guercio program brought to the city is questionable. The Byzantine interest cost Genoese merchants considerable financial losses in 1162, 1171, 1182, and 1198, and probably in 1204 as well. The number of Genoese lives lost in such attacks as the Latin massacre of 1182 will never be known, but the Genoese who died both in Constantinople and in the never-ending wars between Genoa and its commercial rivals that trace their origins in part to problems in Byzantium must have been many. In the eyes of the Guercio brothers, as for other great men of the twelfth-century commune of Genoa, the government, itself little more than a businessmen's consortium, promoted the common weal only when it promoted the private interests of the people making up the association. Perhaps the disastrous civil strife that overtook Genoa's political life in the late twelfth century and continued to plague it throughout the Middle Ages is best attributed to the eventual clash of irreconcilable private interests and the inability of the Genoese to refrain from their ingrained habit of manipulating public institutions for individual gain. The example offered by the Guercio family certainly leads to that conclusion.

## Notes

1. Byrne, "Genoese Colonies," 147–53. See also Franco Cardini, "Profilo di un crociato Guglielmo Embriaco," *Archivio storico italiano* 34 (1978): 405–36, and Richard D. Face, "The Embriachi: Feudal Imperialists in the Twelfth Century" (M. A. thesis, University of Cincinnati, 1952).

2. Belgrano, "Cartario genovese e illustrazione del registro archivescovile," *Atti della Società Ligure di Storia Patria,* 2, part 1 (1870), tables 40 and 41.

3. Giovanni Scriba, *Cartolare,* no. 398.

4. Cassinese, *Notai,* no. 1881. For brief biographies of Baldovino and Rubaldo, see Hilmar C. Krueger, *Navi e proprietà navale a Genova: seconda metà del sec. XII* (Genoa, 1985), 43–48 and 150–52. Krueger has also noticed the fraternity. Bisaccia is one of the few Genoese in this study who appears in the *Dizionario biografico degli Italiani* (Rome, 1960-), 10: 637–38. The other Genoese in the dictionary are the brothers Nuvelone

and Ottobono d'Albericis (cited as "Alberici" in the dictionary (ibid., 1: 636-37. Because the *Dizionario* is only up to "D" so far, perhaps other Genoese will appear in later volumes. The entry on Bisaccia, by the way, states that nothing is known of his family, and it confuses Bisaccia with his son, Bisacino.

5. Giovanni Scriba, *Cartolare,* no. 102.

6. Ibid., nos. 361, 744, 745, 1116, and 1199; Sanguineti and Bertolotto, "Documenti," 395.

7. Belgrano, "Cartario genovese," tables 40 and 41.

8. In a Genoese context matronymics raises the interesting problem of cognatic descent. For a brief, but very enlightening discussion of the phenomenon of descent through the female line in post-Carolingian Germanic society (which could very well have influenced the customs of the Genoese nobility), see Georges Duby, *The Chivalrous Society,* translated by Cynthia Postan (Cambridge, 1977), 100-3, where are cited pertinent German works on the topic by Gerd Tellenbach and Karl Schmidt. Paolo Cammarosano has stated that municipal legislation of the twelfth through fourteenth centuries reinforced and generalized the privileged custom of agnatic succession ("Les structures familiales dans les villes de l'Italie communale [XIIe-XIVe siècles]," in *Famille et parenté,* edited by Duby and Le Goff, 811-94). This legislation was necessary to enforce legally the imposition of a stricter male succession on a deeply entrenched habit of looking to the distaff side in tracing lineage, and such protective institutions for women as the *antefactum* were not new, but indeed, were vestiges of a once stronger position that women occupied in inheritance. On the other hand, it is possible that matronymic surnames in Genoa, as in ancient Rome, simply indicated illegitimacy.

9. See above, chap. 2, for Ghetto's visit to the Byzantine court.

10. See Olivieri, "Serie dei consoli," 254, for the man's office and a discussion of his possible family.

11. Sanguineti and Bertolotto, "Documenti," 471.

12. Giovanni di Guiberto, *Notai* (1200-1211), edited by Margaret W. Cole *et al.* 2 vols. (Genoa, 1939-42), nos. 1860 and 1870.

13. The Veneto-Genoese treaty of 1218 required the restoration of Baldovino's Byzantine *pronoia* to his heirs (*Liber iurium,* col. 613).

14. For this embassy, see above, chap. 2.

15. Girolamo Serra, *La storia della antica Liguria e di Genova,* 4 vols. (Turin, 1834), 1: 357.

16. On these campaigns, see Wieruszowski, "The Norman Kingdom," 13-14.

17. Sanguineti and Bertolotto, "Documenti," 471.

18. Ibid.

19. Ibid. Isaac called Guercio his "lizios," or "liegeman" (ibid., 406 and 456). See chap. 2, n. 49 for a cautionary statement regarding the use of the term "vassal" in a Byzantine context and for a discussion of the scholarship on the controversial term, "lizios."

20. *Annali genovesi,* 2: 13–14.

21. Sanguineti and Bertolotto, "Documenti," 406–7.

22. Ibid., 454–59. In the rubric accompanying the document, the editors mistakenly name as the ambassadors Guido Spinola and Guglielmo Tornello.

23. Ibid., 449 and 457.

24. See chap. 2.

25. Sanguineti and Bertolotto, "Documenti," 471.

26. Any chrysobull that may have been issued by Alexius III to confirm the Genoese in the restoration of their concession in Byzantium has been lost, and so has any proof that Baldovino's *pronoia* was returned. It is likely, however, that the honor was given back because the Veneto-Genoese treaty of 1218, which really was a return to the pre-1204 situation for Genoa, demanded the restoration of the property to Guercio's heirs.

27. Giovanni Scriba, *Cartolare,* no. 398.

28. *Liber iurium,* cols. 206–7.

29. Giovanni Scriba, *Cartolare,* no. 1254; *Annali genovesi,* 1: 158 and 160.

30. Olivieri, "Serie dei consoli," 314.

31. *Annali genovesi,* 1: 192–93.

32. Ibid., 232–34.

33. Ibid., 241.

34. Sanguineti and Bertolotto "Documenti," 409.

35. Olivieri, "Serie dei consoli," 367.

36. *Annali genovesi,* 2: 26; *Codice Diplomatico,* 2: 321–32, doc. 172; and 334–39, doc. 174.

37. "Documenti," 406–7.

38. *Annali genovesi,* 2: 32–33.

39. Cassinese, *Notai,* no. 386.

40. Sanguineti and Bertolotto, "Documenti," 447.

41. Olivieri, "Serie dei consoli," 392.

42. Cassinese, *Notai,* nos. 386, 818, 827, 1161, 1386, 1591, and 1629.

43. Olivieri, "Serie dei consoli," 469.

44. For Caffaro's displeasure with the consuls for the years 1149 to 1153, see Krueger, "Post-War Collapse," 123–24.

45. *Codice Diplomatico,* 1: 291–93, doc. 243.

46. *Annali genovesi,* 1: 60.

47. See chap. 2.

48. A document of July 11, 1164, speaks of Rubaldo "quondam Enrici Guercii." Giovanni Scriba, *Cartolare,* no. 1235.

49. Archivio di Stato di Genova, Oberto Scriba de Mercato "Cartolari notarili," 4.125v–126r.

50. Bisaccia held the consulship in 1149, 1152, 1159, 1162, 1164, 1167, 1172, 1175, 1177, 1181, and 1192. Olivieri, "Serie dei consoli," 463.

51. *Codice Diplomatico,* 1: 263, doc. 211.

52. Ibid., 2: 16–17, doc. 7.

53. *Annali genovesi,* 1: 202 and 255.

54. *Codice Diplomatico,* 2: 172, doc. 82.

55. "Ego Bisacia Consule Communis Litterarum ignaro Reverendo digno Crucis ab eo permisso ego W. Caligepolii" (Sanguineti and Bertolotto, "Documenti," 448). See also, Krueger, *Navi,* 43.

56. Giovanni Scriba, *Cartolare,* no. 304.

57. Ibid., no. 466.

58. *Codice Diplomatico,* 2: 12, doc. 4; and 88, doc. 37.

59. See chap. 4.

60. *Codice Diplomatico,* 1: 240–42, doc. 193.

61. Ibid., 254–55, doc. 202.

62. Ibid., 257–58, doc. 204.

63. Ibid., 284–85, doc. 234.

64. Giovanni Scriba, *Cartolare,* no. 615.

65. Ibid., no. 666.

66. Ibid., no. 676.

67. Ibid., no. 673.

68. Ibid., no. 674.

69. *Annali genovesi,* 1: 68–69.

70. Ibid., 1: 167–68.

71. On di Murta's extended embassy, see chap. 2.

72. *Annali genovesi,* 1: 234.

73. Olivieri, "Serie dei consoli," 469.

74. See chap. 3.

75. See chap. 2.

76. See chap. 2.

77. Olivieri, "Serie dei consoli," 387.

78. See chap. 2.

79. Giovanni Scriba, *Cartolare,* nos. 423–24. Porcello's daughter

calls Guercio her "patruus," a word that means a paternal uncle (as opposed to "avunculus," a maternal uncle). There is no record that the five Porcello brothers were brothers of the three Guercii, and the only other alternative is that Enrico became the girl's uncle by marriage to a sister of her father.

80. Olivieri, "Serie dei consoli," 256.

81. Cassinese, *Notai,* nos. 1088, 1101, 1102, 1129–31, and 1134.

82. Giovanni di Guiberto, *Notai,* no. 1997.

83. Olivieri, "Serie dei consoli," 466. On the family's commercial interests, see Hughes, "Family Structure," 16.

84. Sanguineti and Bertolotto, "Documenti," 378.

85. Giovanni Scriba, *Cartolare,* no. 398.

86. Olivieri, "Serie dei consoli," 234.

87. Sanguineti and Bertolotto, "Documenti," 390, 391, 396.

88. Sanguineti and Bertolotto, "Documenti," 368–405.

89. Giovanni Scriba, *Cartolare,* nos. 84, 398, 536, 666, 739, and 23A; Cassinese, *Notai,* no. 818.

90. Giovanni Scriba, *Cartolare,* nos. 466 and 615.

91. Lanfranco Roza was consul of the commune from 1114 to 1118. Olivieri, "Serie dei consoli," 233.

92. Ibid., 476.

93. Ibid., 226.

94. Ibid., 304.

95. Giovanni Scriba, *Cartolare,* nos. 19, 295, 398, 512, 558, 643, 644, 741, 962, and 1133.

96. Sanguineti and Bertolotto, "Documenti," 395.

97. Ibid., pp. 374, 387, 391, 393, and 395.

98. Cassinese, *Notai,* nos. 386, 1386, and 1591.

99. *Codice Diplomatico,* 2: 173, doc. 82.

100. *Annali genovesi,* 2: 30. On this incident, see chap. 3.

101. Olivieri, "Serie dei consoli," 424.

102. Hughes, "Family Structure," 16.

103. Oberto Scriba, *Notai* (1186), no. 28.

104. In Giovanni Scriba's cartulary Guercio appears with della Volta 18 times and with Guaracco 15 times.

105. Olivieri, "Serie dei consoli," 464.

106. Ibid., 305.

107. Ibid., 313.

108. *Annali genovesi,* 1: 160.

109. Ibid., 168.

110. Giovanni Scriba, *Cartolare,* no. 466.

111. Ibid., no. 615.

112. Ibid., no. 673.

113. Ibid., no. 361.

114. Ibid., nos. 964 and 1018.

115. Ibid., nos. 585 and 974.

116. Ibid., no. 806.

117. *Codice Diplomatico,* 1: 265–66, doc. 214.

118. In Giovanni Scriba's cartulary, Di Castro appears 32 times with della Volta, and later makes 59 appearances in various notarial entries done at the house of Bonifacio della Volta.

119. Della Croce's instructions of 1201, for example, speak of an Enrico Grillo, the son of the late Ansaldo Grillo "de Syria" (Sanguineti and Bertolotto, "Documenti," 473).

120. Giovanni Scriba, *Cartolare,* no. 666.

121. Ibid., no. 557.

122. Ibid., no. 44.

123. Ibid., no. 406.

124. Giovanni Scriba, *Cartolare,* nos. 84, 406, 557, 666, with each document containing several members of the families.

125. Sanguineti and Bertolotto, "Documenti," 392.

126. Ibid.

127. Ibid., 396.

128. Ibid., 395.

129. Ibid., 393.

130. Ibid., 392.

131. All of the following figures are derived from the list of Genoese claims contained in Grimaldi's instructions of 1174 (ibid., 389–97).

132. Sanguineti and Bertolotto, "Documenti," 383 and 384.

133. See chap. 2.

134. For example, Sanguineti and Bertolotto, "Documenti," 393 and 398.

135. Giovanni Scriba, *Cartolare,* no. 642.

136. Ibid., 378–80.

137. Ibid., 379.

138. He was the son of Guglielmo Anfosso Guercio. Belgrano, "Cartario genovese," table 41.

139. Sanguineti and Bertolotto, "Documenti," 408.

140. Ibid., 400.

141. Ibid., 448.

142. Ibid., 451.

143. Desimoni, "Memoria," 166, n. 1.

144. Sanguineti and Bertolotto, "Documenti," 409.

145. Ibid., 386–400. It was Schaube's conjecture that the first refer-

ence is to an official (*Handelsgeschichte,* 233, n. 2). In all fairness, however, the word, *vicecomes* may be no more than Guido's surname, for there was a noble family named Visconti at this time. Concerning the usual Greek usage of the general name, "Lombard," for the Genoese, see Fotheringham, "Genoa and the Fourth Crusade," 36 and n. 38.

146. Sanguineti and Bertolotto, "Documenti," 474.

147. Interestingly, one of the consuls issuing these instructions was a Guglielmo Guercio, perhaps Alinerio's own cousin (see Belgrano, "Cartario genovese," table 41). Either the younger Guercio did not have the clout of his predecessors or perhaps the prohibition against Alinerio was simply a personal matter in which Guglielmo concurred.

148. Byrne, "Genoese Colonies," 145–46 and 165–68.

149. See also Day, "Impact of the Third Crusade," 166–67.

150. Archivio di Stato di Genova, Oberto Scriba de Mercato, "Cartolari notarili," 3.131r and 3.134v.

151. Giovanni Scriba, *Cartolare,* no. 666.

152. Ibid., no. 871.

153. Ibid., no. 615.

154. Byrne, "Genoese Trade," 202–5.

155. See chap. 4.

156. See chap. 6.

## Chapter Six

⁓⁓⁓

# Factionalism and
# the Byzantine Connection,
# 1168–1204

THE DISASTER THAT BEFELL the della Volta faction in 1164 proved to be only an eclipse of the group's power rather than its demise. Immediately after the downfall of 1164, the della Volta forces began regrouping, and by 1170 they had renewed their struggle for dominance in Genoese politics. The return of strong della Volta influence in Genoese politics roughly corresponded to the second phase of Genoa's twelfth-century activity in the Byzantine Empire, beginning in 1168 with Amico di Murta's mission to the Byzantine court and continuing until the fall of Constantinople to the crusaders in 1203 and 1204. During this span of thirty-six years, Genoa's situation in the Byzantine Empire was stable and profitable only in the last ten years of Manuel's reign and in the two years of his minor heir's regency, that is, from 1170 to 1182. For the remainder of the twelfth century Genoa enjoyed only fitfully the commercial opportunities to which it had become so accustomed in the 1170's, from 1192 to 1198 and again at the very close of the Byzantine emperors' residence in Constantinople, beginning in late 1201. While Byzantine dynastic troubles contributed much to the Genoese failure to make a success of the Byzantine connection, the severe crisis of the Genoese government at home should receive most of the blame for the city's inability to overcome the dangers that threatened the maintenance of a solid commercial base in Constantinople. By the 1190's factional tension had erupted into open warfare in Genoa, and the consular form of government gradually gave way to the more impartial rule of a *podestà*. During these years of factional rivalry and constitutional transformation, Byzantine affairs continued to be intimately connected with the della Volta faction, and advances were made in Byzantino-Genoese affairs only when this faction was in power. In fact, if a profile of Genoa's relations with the Byzantines from 1168 to 1204 should be drawn, it would correspond quite closely to a similar outline of the vicissitudes of the reorganized della Volta faction.

While the factional warfare that broke out with the murder of Marchese della Volta in 1164 continued into 1167 and 1168, the consuls for those years still attempted to reacquire a privileged trading status in the Byzantine Empire. The board of Genoese consuls for 1167 was undoubtedly favorable to a renewal of their city's contacts with Constantinople. Not only was Rubaldo Biasaccia a consul, but also Corso Sigismundi, the ambassador to Constantinople in 1164, Ottobono d'Albericis, Enrico Mallone, and Oberto Spinola, all formerly associated with della Volta expansionism, and Lanfranco Pevere, who despite his Carmadino partisanship had a good record of supporting Genoese commercial expansion.[1] These consuls surely began making plans to send an ambassador to Constantinople, and they handed the project over to their successors, Nicola di Rodulfo, another envoy of 1164, Nuvelone d'Albericis (Ottobono's brother), Ido Gontardo, himself a liegeman of the Byzantine emperor,[2] and Lamberto Grillo, all of whom would continue the plan. The consuls of 1168 sent Amico di Murta east to reopen the negotiations.[3] The effectiveness of his embassy, however, was certainly impaired by the civil strife at home between the resurgent della Volta group and their old enemies. The feuding was escalated in late 1168 when another of Ingo's sons, Giacomo, was assassinated.[4]

Throughout the rest of 1168 and much of 1169 the city was in turmoil. Near the end of 1169 the consuls determined to take strong action to end the prolonged violence. Armed retainers hired by the commune were billeted in the houses of both Ingo della Volta and Amigo della Corte, much to the owners' displeasure, and additional retainers were posted along the street leading from the city's main gate to San Lorenzo. The consuls then unsuccessfully tried to persuade the chiefs of the warring factions to swear to obey their orders, but the temporary truce broke down when the government could not agree on a common plan for settling the complaints between the groups. Finally, toward the end of the year the consuls sought out the assistance of the archbishop, Ugo della Volta. The citizens were assembled in parliament in front of the cathedral, the city's entire clergy turned out in their festive vestments, the relics of John the Baptist were put on display, and the crosses from the city's churches were carried in solemn procession. Amid these trappings of civic and ecclesiastical awe, the archbishop implored the instigators of the factional war to make peace. The consuls called on Rolando Avvocato. The partisan leader, tearing his clothes and uttering a loud war cry, refused to come forward but sat down motionless on the ground. The man's relatives around him could not move him. Finally, the archbishop and some of his clergy carried a Gospel book over to Avvocato, and after some coaxing, they persuaded him to swear quietly to obey the consuls' orders. The assembled Genoese then called on Fulco di Castro to take a similar oath, but he refused unless his father-in-law, Ingo della Volta, gave him permission to do so. Thereupon the archbishop and his clergy went to his brother's house, where after some additional prodding, Fulco and Ingo begrudgingly swore their oath. The prelate's procession returned to the cathedral while church bells resounded throughout the city, and from his altar the prelate intoned the *Te Deum* with his clergy, filling the whole of San Lorenzo with the joyful chorus.[5] As the consuls left office, their successors took up the task of settling the many grievances between the two factions. The new consuls named Nicola Embriaco and Guglielmo Burone as representatives of the della Volta group and Baldizone Usodimare and Lanfranco Pevere for Rolando Avvocato and the della Corte faction. The arbitrators were charged to settle matters within twenty days of the next consulate, that is, within a year.[6]

The civil war in Genoa had made Emperor Manuel very cautious about extending his generosity to the Genoese. In 1169 Amico di Murta could persuade the emperor to give the Genoese no more than a quarter outside Constantinople's walls, and Manuel hoped to capitalize on Genoa's weak bargaining position by binding the Italian city to an offensive alliance. With the end of the civil war in Genoa, Manuel became more confident of Genoa's ability to observe the terms of an agreement, and he began negotiating much more generously with di Murta. In April 1170, the emperor reopened his capital to Genoese merchants, thus beginning the most prosperous period of Genoa's twelfth-century commerce with Byzantium.

The reconciliation of factions in 1170 had played a major role in opening Constantinople to Genoese merchants, and soon events in the Byzantine Empire would compel the city's government to honor its treaty commitment of helping to defend the Byzantines. In the wake of the Venetian expulsion in punishment for the attack on the newly reconstituted Genoese compound in early 1171, war broke out between the Venetians and the Byzantines. The Genoese hoped to profit from the turn of events, as evidenced by the instructions sent to di Murta, still at the Byzantine court, to wangle a new and more advantageous bargain from the emperor.[7] To finance the city's naval contribution to Manuel's war, the Genoese government collected the huge loan of £9,419.[8] In the details of this loan, which have been preserved in the list of Genoese losses presented to Manuel for compensation in 1175, the interests of various groups of Genoese at work can be seen. Most striking, but understandable, is the heavy contribution of the Guercio family and its associates, who, as we have seen, contributed as much as £4,240, nearly half of the total. People associated by kin, politics, or business with the della Corte faction lent £1,266. Della Volta people gave only £574 and, in fact, only £370 came from the della Volta family members alone, Fulco and Ogerio di Castro, Guido Spinola, Marchese Cassicio, and Bertolotto della Volta. Members of the very closely associated Mallone and Vento families are conspicuously absent from the list of creditors. Similarly, no contributions from the della Corte family itself are listed. Because so many people connected with the della Volta and della Corte families had contributed, the failure to do so resulted not so much from disinterest as from the devastating financial consequences of property destruction and confiscations that were inflicted as punishment upon these families for feuding in the 1160's. From the identities of the lenders, the Guercio and the still influential Doria and della Corte families seemed willing to embark on a venture with much potential benefit in spite of the temporary political enervation of the chief families. Power in the commune had for the moment passed to the Guercii, and the maintenance of Genoa's

Byzantine connection had become a prominent item on the commune's agenda.

The list of lenders shows that the della Volta family had much work to do to restore its leadership in the bloc of expansion-minded Genoese, but the political scene would be much different from what it had been during the decade of Ingo della Volta's control. The years from 1154 to 1164 had been a glorious period in Genoese history. The Genoese then had developed privileged trade with the Byzantine Empire, with Sicily, and with many coastal Tyrhennian ports while significant inroads, although still only at the level of unprivileged trade, had been made into the commerce of Moslem North Africa. Closer to home, Genoa had extended and solidified its power over the surrounding *contado*, so that in the Brief of 1157, an oath taken by the important members of the citizenry to abide by the city's laws, it was assumed that these laws and the authority of the Genoese government spread from Monaco in the west to Portovenere in the east, and from Vultabio, Savona, and Montalto to the sea.[9] In Genoa's treaty with Barbarossa in 1162, the city gained the independence within the framework of the Holy Roman Empire that other northern Italian cities would have to fight so hard to obtain in the 1170's. In the 1170's and the 1180's, however, the Genoese would be far more concerned with cultivating their newly developed commercial network and with keeping their city's position intact than in further expansion. Management of their commercial links was kept simple. The Embriaco family handled matters in Syria, and the Guercii managed affairs in Constantinople. Because of the long involvement of the della Volta family itself and of the Vento family in Sicily, they probably looked out for Genoese interests unofficially in the great island kingdom.[10]

The late twelfth century was far from peaceful for the Genoese. An earlier legacy of warfare with Pisa continued until 1188, and constant naval fighting with the Pisans exacted a heavy toll on the resources of Genoa. The Genoese government also was forced continuously to fight the arrogant feudal marquises whose fiefs surrounded the city, and the marquises of Malaspina and Gavi refused to submit to the almost inevitable control of the commune. Several revolts among the subject towns of the *contado* commanded much of the municipal government's attention.[11] On the other hand, though, the few extant notarial registers from the mid-1180's and the 1190's show greater numbers of people from the outlying areas coming into Genoa to do business, if not actually to take up their residences there.[12] In the same way, many of the feudal families of the *contado*, forced in the 1140's and 1150's to swear their allegiance to the communal government and to live in Genoa for part of the year, had found the conveniences and benefits of urban life so alluring that they had become permanent members of the commune and were fast becoming the great Genoese families of della Torre, Cavarunco, and Fieschi, to name just three.[13] Fortunately for Genoa, the city remained outside of the intense struggle of the 1160's and 1170's between Barbarossa and the Lombard League.[14] Not until the 1190's would Genoa become involved with the affairs of the Holy Roman Empire.

A new generation had come into its own. A few of the old guard, like Rubaldo Bisaccia and Guglielmo Burone, remained, but the sons and even the grandsons of the leaders of the 1150's and 1160's now controlled Genoa's destiny. The great Ingo della Volta was no longer active in city affairs. He was still alive in 1170, but his name does not appear in city documents and surviving contracts. His influence was still present, though, in his progeny. Similarly, Amigo della Corte and Rolando Avvocato would no longer be politically active, but their younger relatives, Rubaldo della Corte and Giovanni Avvocato, together with Lanfranco Pevere the Younger and the sons of other della Corte families, carried on their policies and animosities.

Indeed the della Volta family consolidated its position and became one of the great consorterial families of Genoa. In the notarial register of Giovanni Scriba, abundant evidence exists of family members already in the 1150's and 1160's buying property in the same blocks to become neighbors.[15] Very quickly the della Volta members, their adherents, clients, and relatives focused themselves on the church of San Torpeto, which became in essence a family church. The compound of the consorterial family was now a feature of Genoese life, decorated not only by palaces and churches, but also by plazas or courtyards and necessary towers, like the still present tower of the Embriachi, which dates from the twelfth century.[16] Ingo della Volta and his associates had thought about family considerations, but much of the confusion in the factional history of Genoa comes from the willingness of people in the middle of the twelfth century to collaborate in business and in politics with people from other families who by the 1180's would appear to be strange bedfellows. The association of Maneciano and della Volta families with Pevere and Usodimare are examples. Very little association with outsiders can be seen after the 1170's, however, especially by della Volta people. The various aristocratic families of Genoa had come together into intensely self-absorbed power blocs, the della Volta and the Guercio blocs being the most visible. The della Corte group, however, was also a powerful political force amid the many family groups of the late twelfth century.[17]

While Ingo della Volta's son, Marchese, had been the only one of his children to play a large role in public affairs in the 1150's and 1160's, now his other sons became not only the family's but also the city's leaders. Marchese and his brother, Giacomo, had already paid the highest price for family service. Three others would assume family leadership from their fallen brothers: Ingo di Flessia, Rubeo della Volta, and Guglielmo Cassicio. The last-named brother would not play a very active role in Genoese politics, although he served in 1161 as an ambassador to Ibn Mardanish, the ruler of Valencia, and as a consul of the commune in 1163.[18] Ingo di Flessia would be perhaps the most politically active of the brothers, serving as consul of the commune seven times and often commanding the city's military forces. He too would fall to an assassin's sword in 1193.[19] Rubeo, involved extensively in both business and politics, would be a consul in 1183 and 1187. All of these men had their own sons who enhanced family power by the end of the century. Except for Rubeo, they appeared in notarial contracts more as dabblers interested in expanding their fortunes than as serious businessmen. The political life of the city was their business, and they pursued it with an intensity that had little time for commerce. In fact, the family's business affairs were largely managed by another brother, Bonifacio della Volta. In the 1180's and 1190's Bonifacio would assemble in his house a coterie of businessmen over which he presided just as carefully as a baron would manage his feudal court.[20] From the nature of his recorded activities, Bonifacio must have been learned in the law, and he may even have served as the family's *consigliere*.

Ingo had taught his sons to form a united family bloc, and he used his two daughters as well to strengthen the family's position, by marrying them off to Oberto Spinola and Fulco di Castro. Both of these sons-in-law were influential statesmen and devoted champions of della Volta causes. Frederick Barbarossa once said of Oberto that whatever he said was right,[21] and Fulco in the late twelfth century would become the quintessential politician, capping his career in 1205 by being named as the only native *podestà* of his city.[22]

Surely the leading members of the della Volta family kept their financial objectives, but they were more intent on building a monopoly of political power. They nearly succeeded. In the early 1170's the della Volta family regained its political power in Genoa. In 1172, three people who can be connected with the della Volta family, that is, Simon Doria, Rubaldo Bisaccia, and Oberto Spinola, sat on the consular board. The next year Ingo di Flessia himself served as a consul. In 1174 only Guglielmo Doria can be clearly associated with the della Volta, although Ottobono d'Albericis and Otto di Caffaro were definitely expansionists. The consular board of 1175 reflected the recrudescence of della Volta strength, when four of the six consuls, Fulco di Castro, Rogerono di Castro, Ingo di Flessia again, and Rubaldo Bisaccia, were della Volta people. The consulships of Nicola Embriaco and Guglielmo Vento in 1176 marked the return of these old della Volta families to the political forefront. From then on, the della Volta group would supply several, if not the majority, of consuls every year. From 1172, when della Volta people reappeared in the consular lists, until 1216, when the consulship came to an end, one hundred and ninety-seven consuls of the commune were elected. Twenty members of the della Volta family itself filled this office—more than any other single family. If Fulco di Castro, his son, and members of the Spinola family are added, the number rises to twenty-eight. Adding the representatives of the old della Volta combine, that is Mallone (five), Vento (twelve), Embriaco (fifteen), and Doria (nineteen), the number of consulships held by the della Volta faction rises to seventy-nine or a little over 40 percent of the consulships.[23]

The della Corte families maintained some influence in city politics throughout these della Volta years. The most prominent member of this political faction was Lanfrano Pevere the Younger, who was a consul in 1183, 1185, and 1190, while his brother, Guglielmo, served in 1174 and 1186. Baldizone Usodimare was consul in 1176 and 1179, and his son, Oberto, held the office in 1192. Angelotto di Mari, consul in 1183 and 1187, and Ido di Carmadino, consul in 1180, 1187, 1190, and 1193, are others who probably represent the della Corte bloc. Ansaldo and Enrico Piccamiglio, who were consuls in 1175, 1182, 1189, and 1190,[24] may be tentatively added to the della Corte group. In all, perhaps twenty-three consulships between 1172 and 1216 can be assigned to della Corte people, a small number in comparison to the number of consulships held by the della Volta faction during the same period.

Although hardly any record of the trade between Genoa and the Byzantine Empire during the 1170's exists, still the della Volta people were participating in the eastern market. Two notarial entries from 1179 mention Constantinople, and in both of these chance survivals, della Volta people were involved. Vassallo and Guglielmo Balbo, sons of Fulco di Castro, accepted a small sum of money from Bernardo Clerico for a trading voyage to Constantinople. A few days later, Berbrammo the smith and his wife borrowed £16 from Rubeo della Volta for their trip to Constantinople, perhaps in the train of Agnes of France.[25] Probably a large part of the 228,000 hyperpers claimed by later Genoese ambassadors for damages suffered in the Latin massacre of 1182 was della Volta money.[26]

Not even the disaster of the Latin massacre was sufficient to dislodge the eastern combine from Genoa's government. Among the six consuls of 1183 were Ugolino Mallone, Guglielmo Doria, and Rubeo della Volta. The other two consuls, however, Angelotto di Mari and Lanfranco Pevere, represented the della Corte side. The year 1185 was nearly a complete victory for the della Volta group, when the communal consuls were Nicola Embriaco, Ingo di Flessia, Simon Doria, Guglielmo Vento, and Bisacino, the son of Rubaldo Bisaccia. Only Lanfranco Pevere was not in the inner group of della Volta politicians.

It is little wonder, then, that in the following year, with more della Volta consuls, the project was put under way to negotiate a return to Constantinople with the new Byzantine Emperor Isaac II Angelus.[27] Nicola Mallone, who had shared the consulship with Ingo di Flessia in 1182, was chosen as one ambassador, and Lanfranco Pevere, whose brother, Guglielmo, was one of the consuls for the year, was picked as the other, probably to accommodate the della Corte group, which was surely suspicious of the eastern combine's willingness to deal with the Byzantines. The della Volta clan seized on the trading opportunities provided by the new diplomatic mission. In the sixteen surviving Constantinopolitan contracts from Oberto Scriba's register for 1186, Fulco di Castro's son, also named Fulco, intended to accompany the embassy to trade the enormous sum of £675 entrusted to him by his mother and his uncle, Rubeo della Volta, and his cousins, Rufo and Bonifacio della Volta. Ugo Mallone was to trade £300 given him by his brother, the ambassador, Nicola Mallone. The wife of Guglielmo Ciriolo, who had invested with Guglielmo Burone and Ido Mallone in the Constantinopolitan trade of the early 1160's, now gave £50 to a certain Forzano for the Byzantine venture.[28] Unfortunately for the della Volta group, the delegation was unable to reach a settlement with Isaac II. The tensions that must have existed between the two ambassadors, with each one unwilling to agree to a deal particularly advantageous to his colleague's political friends, reasonably contributed to the ultimate failure of the mission. Perhaps Lanfranco Pevere, whose faction represented German interests in Genoa, could not conscientiously agree to whatever terms of future naval support that Isaac may have put in front of the ambassadors. In any event, the Genoese would have to wait several years before they could seriously reopen talks with the Byzantines.

Throughout the 1180's the animosity between the fast-rising della Volta faction and its della Corte enemies sometimes erupted into violence. The first flare-up occurred in 1179, when Amico Grillo the Younger and Pietro and Simon Vento fought.[29] Although the disturbance was settled by the consuls in 1180,[30] and it is not known whether the della Volta family was directly connected with the violence, at least, it is likely that the hard feelings engendered by this dispute meant that the Grillo family would not sympathize with della Volta interests. In 1183 Fulco di Castro and the Venti joined forces to fight one Bulbunoso and other expressly labeled della Corte adherents, perhaps over Bulbunoso's construction of a new tower in what the della Volta family considered to be its section of the city.[31] Open hostilities were renewed in 1187 when Lanfranco della Turca, the son of an incumbent consul, assassinated the della Corte consul, Angelotto di Mari. Although the young della Turca was a member of the Carmadino lineage, he must have been operating for the della Volta people in this crime since in the next year a papal legate, Cardinal Peter of St. Cecilia, restored peace between Lanfranco and Bulbunoso, who was clearly a della Corte partisan.[32] Soon after, Rubaldo Porcello and Opizo Lecavelo were murdered, perhaps by Doria adherents.[33] Both of these men were from families connected to the Guercio group, and Opizo's daughter was married to Giovanni Avvocato, the son and political heir of Rolando Avvocato. This particular incident illustrates that the connection between the Guercio and the della Volta blocs was not strong enough to prevent satellite families from becoming embroiled in discord and that a rift was developing in the expansionist families that would cause considerable damage in the 1190's.

Despite the continuing factional struggle, by 1188 the revivified della Volta machine nearly monopolized public office. All eight consuls of the commune for the year, led by Fulco di Castro, were intimate members of the della Volta circle. Moreover, Ingo Cassicio della Volta, a grandson of the famous Ingo, served as a consul of the foreigners that same year. Before the young della Volta's term of office had expired, however, he was assassinated by the sons of Filippo Malfanti.[34] While the assassination shows the continued animosity some Genoese held for della Volta power, the board of consuls for 1188 was still able to turn the energies of the commune toward preparing an expedition to support the upcoming Third Crusade. The next year, a new della Volta consul of the commune, Guido Spinola, led the city's forces to Acre, and in his company went the leaders of the della Volta group, Fulco di Castro, Rubeo della Volta, Nicola Embriaco, Simon Doria, and Baldovino Guercio.[35] These men surely did not foresee the devastating impact that their absence would have on the political and constitutional character of their city.

It has been said that the departure of the della Volta leaders on the Third Crusade left Genoa at the mercy of their political opponents,[36] but they did leave behind some people in the government to watch out for their interests. Ingo di Flessia apparently stayed home, and three consuls for 1189, Guglielmo Embriaco, Guglielmo Vento, and Bisacino, were in the della Volta camp. But in 1190, when Raimondo di Flessia, the son of Ingo, and Simon Vento represented the della Volta side, they were outnumbered by Lanfranco Pevere, Enrico Piccamiglio, and Ido di Carmadino. Di

Flessia was left to stand alone when his della Volta colleague sailed east to join the crusade.[37]

The mass exodus of della Volta leaders left their partisans who stayed behind to fight among themselves. Guglielmo Vento, married to a daughter of Lanfranco Pevere the Elder and, probably encouraged by his in-laws, made a bid for the leadership of the residual della Volta faction.[38] One skirmish was fought on May 2, 1189, and another a few weeks later on the feast of Pentecost.[39] The struggle must have continued throughout 1191, although the annalist is not specific about the matter, since the internal turmoil would not be settled until 1192 after the return of the crusaders.[40]

The absence of strong della Volta leaders and the internal dissension within the faction at home provided the della Corte people their long-awaited opportunity to seize control of the city government. To restore order to the commune, the Genoese *consiglio* decided to call in the first *podestà*, Manegoldo Tetoccio, from Brescia.[41] The move was undoubtedly a tactic of the della Corte faction, which was not strong enough to win a consular election, to take over the city and to remove the feuding della Volta people from power. Lanfranco Pevere himself must have been the sponsor of the constitutional change, for one evening, when he and other Genoese leaders met at the house of Ogerio Pane to discuss the organization of the new government, two of Fulco di Castro's sons and their cousin broke in and killed him. The *podestà* immediately took action: he razed the most expensive of Fulco's houses and outlawed the perpetrators of the crime, who fled to Piacenza.[42]

In spite of the attention Tetoccio had to pay to this factional warfare, the *podestà* also made an effort to reopen negotiations with the Byzantines. Tetoccio sent as his envoy a man named Tanto, himself a member of the Guercio family, but he was rejected by the Byzantine emperor on the grounds that he lacked sufficient authorization to negotiate.[43] In actual fact, the insufficiency was not so much in Tanto's authorization as in the insufficiency of the podestral government that sent him. Although Tanto had connections with the della Volta faction through his family, nevertheless, he was serving as an agent for a governor owing whatever legitimacy he may have had to a political strategem carried off by the opponents of that faction, whose power was now in eclipse. The notarial record demonstrates the apathy for the diplomatic project on behalf of the immediate members of the core della Volta families. Rubaldo della Volta was going on the trip with at least £407. 1s. contributed by friends and relatives, while Otto and Ottobono di Castro collected £134. 12s. to trade in Constantinople. Rogerio Nocenzio, probably a younger relative of Ingo della Volta's old confidant, Ingo Nocenzio, lent Enrico Tosano £188½.[44] These people, however, cannot be connected with the politically significant branches of their lineages.[45] On the other hand, the Guercio bloc participated actively in the mission, as evidenced by the heavy financial contributions of the Guaracco, Scoto, Porco, and Detesalve families.[46] The Guercio family, despairing of the problems facing the della Volta faction, gave its support to the della Corte, at least in the matter of installing a *podestà,* and was rewarded with the initiation of fresh Byzantine negotiations by the della Corte–backed *podestà.* Nevertheless, Tanto's mission lacked the endorsement of the della Volta leaders, who were still absent on crusade, and although some della Volta people invested in the embassy, it was still directed by the opponents of the della Volta group prompted by the self-serving Guercii. The emperor could not seriously negotiate with a revolutionary government whose survival in the face of della Volta opposition was so doubtful.

Isaac's caution rested not only on the questionable legitimacy of the podestral government but also on that government's reflection of renewed German influence in the affairs of the city. For nearly thirty years Genoa had governed itself with very little interference from Barbarossa except in matters pertaining to his feudal vassals in Liguria. But in 1191, with the della Corte faction in control, the group's nostalgia for the German imperial system led them into introducing the podestral form of government, the constitution which Barbarossa had tried to impose on the cities of northern Italy and which his grandson, Frederick II, would again in the 1230's try to use to administer his territory.[47] It is little wonder, then, that the della Corte–controlled municipal government began negotiating with the new German emperor, Henry VI, to aid him in his project to claim the crown of Sicily, which he had acquired through his marriage to Constance of Sicily. In early 1191 Henry was making preparations for an invasion of the island kingdom. To obtain the sea forces necessary to neutralize the formidable Sicilian navy, the German king concluded a treaty with Pisa in March,[48] and his ambassadors approached Genoa for similar assistance. Owing to Henry's diplomatic ineptitude in requiring unnecessary exchanges of embassies, an alliance was concluded with Genoa only in May, after Henry had begun the siege of Naples. By the time that the Genoese fleet arrived in southern Italy, the newly crowned emperor, whose Pisan force was insufficient to prevent the revictualling of Naples, had been forced to raise his siege and to discontinue the campaign.[49] In Constantinople, all that the emperor Isaac could do in this complex political situation, with Henry's demonstrated hostility to the Byzantines,[50] was to wait for the traditionally friendly della Volta faction to regain control before he could safely allow the Genoese back into his empire.

It must have been a shock to the della Volta leaders returning from crusade to see the state of affairs at home. Immediately they set about restoring their position in the city as well as in their own organization. By the end of 1191, they were sufficiently in control to dispense with the *podestà* and to renew the consulate. Elected as consuls for 1192 were Guglielmo Burone the Younger, Ogerio Vento, Rubaldo Bisaccia, Nuvelone d'Albericis, and Ido Picio, all della Volta adherents or nonpartisan. The inclusion of Bisaccia gives reason to believe that the Guercii, unhappy with Isaac's rejection of Tanto's embassy, had now returned to that traditional alliance that had proven so effective for them in the past. In August, one last fierce battle was fought in the della Volta section of the city between the della Volta stalwarts and "part of their adherents," probably led by Guglielmo Vento.[51] After that incident, the old della Volta alliances had been restored.

Toward the end of his term of office, the *podestà* dispatched a second delegation to the Byzantine court. It is very likely, in view of the late date of this embassy's departure, that Tetoccio acted on the advice of the della Volta group about who would rule the city in the upcoming year.[52] The two ambassadors, Guido Spinola and Guglielmo Tornello, were probably both della Volta supporters.[53] Unlike the embassies of 1186 and 1191, this one was totally controlled by the della Volta faction, and Spinola and Tornello were able to persuade Isaac to readmit the Genoese.[54] The conclusion of the new commercial agreement with the Byzantines thus coincided with the restoration of a della Volta consulate. The members of the expansionist group, eager to begin trading with the Byzantines once more, gladly swore to the oath demanded by Isaac to abide by the agreement's terms.

Throughout 1192 and 1193 the della Volta people went about consolidating their position, although their success was marred by the assassination of the head of the family, Ingo di Flessia, in August 1193. The murder set off a new round of intense factional strife that focused on the tower built by Bulbunoso, who had caused trouble ten years before. In late 1193 della Volta adherents captured the tower, but della Corte partisans soon reoccupied it. The fighting escalated in 1194. Both sides brought in siege machinery to destroy each other's houses and fortifications. Della volta people placed catapults on the towers of Oberto di Grimaldi and Oberto Spinola and bombarded Bulbunoso's tower until it was practically demolished. In retaliation, the della Corte partisans used a similar engine against the towers of Grimaldi and Spinola. The della Volta supporters, in their turn, bombarded the della Corte houses and fortifications. Finally, the della Corte group seceded from the commune and elected as their own consuls Rubaldo della Corte, Giovanni Avvocato, and Enrico di Embrone. Eventually the della Volta consuls in desperation acceded to the advice of Henry VI's seneschal, Markward of Anweiler, who was in Genoa to prepare for his master's second invasion of Sicily, and the Genoese again installed a *podestà*.[55] Although the consulate would be sporadically resurrected until 1216, for all practical purposes the institution now collapsed, and Genoa succumbed to government by imperially approved city managers.[56] The *podestà* prepared a fleet to help Henry VI in his new invasion of Sicily, a venture in which the Genoese governor would lose his life. This Genoese support at last gave the German emperor the resources he needed to make good his claim to the island kingdom.[57]

The young emperor demonstrated his unconscionable ingratitude to his Genoese allies by banning them from his new kingdom. When spokesmen for the Genoese approached the emperor in Palermo to ask him to make the promised concessions to their city, Henry tersely replied: "Your *podestà* is dead; I see no one who represents the commune of Genoa, and I know of no commune. But if I should ever see a man or men who represent the community, I shall well fulfill what I have promised."[58] The emperor subsequently revoked the privileges Genoa had won from previous Sicilian kings, he prohibited any Genoese from presuming to call himself a consul in his Sicilian domain, and he threatened to destroy Genoa if the Genoese dared to sail the seas.[59]

Henry's actions, and especially his words, showed his hostility to Genoa's twelfth-century consular form of government. Not only were communal consulates hard to control, but in the case of Genoa, they represented a tradition of independence from imperial authority. In Henry's words, the emperor refused to recognize the commune, and in his actions he attempted to prevent the resumption of the consular title. Thus, Genoa would not have another consular government until 1201, three years after Henry's early death in 1198. Again from 1202 to 1206 Genoa would have *podestà*, then consulates once more until 1216 with the exceptional *podestà* in 1211. Henry VI's hostility to communal consulates worked together with Genoa's internal strife to end the constitutional form that had effectively overseen the city's growth in the twelfth century.

Interestingly, the Genoese annals mention that Henry's action against Genoa was suggested in part by "some Genoese citizens,"[60] whose identity remains unknown. Probably, however, given the factional disputes that led to the appointment of a *podestà* in 1194, the della Corte partisans were involved, intent both on ingratiating themselves with their emperor and on destroying the profitable business on which at least some of their della Volta rivals' power rested. For the della Corte people, the imperially supported podestral form of government would restrict the communal control that the della Volta had enjoyed for so long.

If the della Corte leaders did hope to use the podestral constitution for their own political advancement, they were disappointed, because their influence cannot be seen in the wavering constitutional systems in Genoa from the 1190's to 1216. Any role played by della Corte people in the podestral regimes is hidden, and when the *podestà* was assisted by "rectors" (1196, 1199, 1202, 1203, 1205, and 1206), little factional information is to be gleaned from the names of these assistants.[61] Belmusto Lercario served four times (1196, 1199, 1202, and 1205), Nicola Mallone three times (1196, 1199, and 1205), Guglielmo di Nigrone twice (1196 and 1205), and a relative, Enrico di Nigrone once (1202). Four other families had two terms of service: Longo (1196 and 1199), Tornello (1202 and 1205), Carmadino (1203 and 1206), and Piccamiglio (1199 and 1206). It appears that an attempt was made to keep out of power representatives of the major political families of della Volta, Vento, di Castro (except in 1205 when Fulco di Castro was *podestà* himself), Embriaco (except for Ugo's term in 1196), Spinola (except for Guido in 1203), Guercio, Avvocato, della Corte, and Usodimare (except for Oberto Usodimare's term in 1206).

On the other hand, when the consular form of government prevailed, della Volta and Guercio people dominate (thirty-nine out of sixty consulships).[62] Thus, podestral government marked a restraint on della Volta power and consulates indicated their control of city policy.

During the first decade and a half of constitutional change from 1190 to 1204, there still is some evidence of activity by della Volta partisans in the Byzantine east. The two great pirates of the period, Guglielmo Grasso and Gafforio, were tied to the della Volta network. Grasso and his probable relatives frequented the circle of Bonifacio della Volta.[63] In one contract, Grasso even witnessed an arrangement made by Guglielmo Balbo, the son of Fulco di Castro, at Bonifacio's house, and another document places Grasso at the home of Raimondo di Balbo, perhaps a brother or other close relative of Guglielmo Balbo.[64] The esteem in which the della Volta people held Grasso was amply demonstrated several years after his piratical escapades when, in 1201, after a term as the Sicilian Grand Admiral and then a prisoner of Markward of Anweiler, the della Volta–backed government sent a fleet commanded by Guglielmo Embraico to Sicily to free the old corsair from his captor.[65]

Gafforio, the other notable Genoese pirate of the time, was also tied in with the della Volta. This pirate had been a naval commander in the della Volta-led Genoese contingent on the Third Crusade.[66] A certain Giacomo Gafforio, perhaps the corsair himself or a relative of his, was often linked with the della Volta group in notarial entries. In 1186, for example, he borrowed from Tommaso Vento £12½ in the house of Bonifacio della Volta.[67] Even earlier, in 1182, Giacomo had been a frequenter of Bonifacio's coterie, and in the same year he was associated in a notarial entry with Guglielmo Vento.[68] Two years later, this Gafforio was recorded in a business transaction with Guglielmo Burone, one of the most powerful members of the clan.[69] Surely then, Gafforio, like Grasso, had long been associated with the della Volta adherents, if not directly, at least through relatives.

Piracy threatened amicable relations with Byzantium because della Volta businessmen profited from it. When della Volta people served as consuls, the government displayed an understandable reluctance to restrain the actions of captains who were financially involved with its own interests. In this same context, Emperor Isaac's move to confiscate the goods of Enrico Nepitella, a Genoese merchant just arrived in Constantinople, in retaliation for Grasso's depredations, was intended to put pressure on the della Volta leaders of the city to restrain their henchman. Nepitella, the nephew of the eponymous ancestor of the later great Genoese house of the Streggiaporci,[70] had for years served as a traveling agent for della Volta investments.[71] Whether Nepitella was acting as a factor for della Volta investments in 1193 is not known, but the possibility is so likely that Isaac can be commended for his bold attempt to force compliance from the Genoese government, a della Volta consulate, by attacking the private pocketbooks of the people in charge. Because the Genoese quickly responded by sending Guido Spinola and Baldovino Guercio to Constantinople to assure the emperor of the city's good faith, Isaac's plan had the desired effect.[72]

Similar diplomatic maneuvers by Alexius III in 1198 were not to be so successful in maintaining harmony between the Genoese and the Byzantines. Gafforio's piracy so offended the Byzantine emperor that he jailed Genoese citizens in his capital and confiscated their property, and he went so far as to take back the Genoese facility and to close his capital to Genoese merchants.[73] The della Volta faction this time was out of power, and the city's *podestà,* either out of apathy or inability, failed to take the necessary measures to insure the safety of Genoa's presence in Byzantium. The della Volta camp, nevertheless, did make some private effort to ingratiate itself with the unfriendly emperor; at least, sometime in the late 1190's Oberto della Volta, a cousin of the powerful branch of the family, spent £500 of his own money on a galley to assist the Byzantine emperor in some fashion now unknown.[74] With a *podestà* in charge of the Genoese government from mid-1194 to 1200, however, the della Volta faction was powerless to demonstrate an official municipal policy of good faith to the Byzantines, and Genoese merchants remained excluded from Constantinople's business.

The momentary revival of a della Volta consulate in 1201 immediately occasioned the dispatch of Ottobono della Croce to Alexius. The emperor was looking desperately for allies to protect himself from the potential threat of the coalition that his nephew, Alexius, the son of Isaac II, was beginning to build against him among the potentates of the West.[75] Although Alexius III personally may not have liked the della Volta people, he must have realized that they at least could protect their Byzantine interests by honoring defensive treaty commitments. Perhaps the private support of the della Volta people had convinced Alexius of their friendliness, albeit the emperor now could not afford to be selective. At any rate, Alexius III returned to the Genoese their former properties and privileges, and even expanded on them in October 1201.[76] The frightened emperor's eleventh-hour effort, however, did not help.

The agreement of 1201 did not signal a new beginning for Genoa's relations with the Byzantines, but paradoxically, it was the harbinger of the end. The devastation of the Fourth Crusade virtually ended Byzantine power, and the permanent imposition of podestral government in Genoa broke the grip in which the della Volta and Guercio families had for so long held municipal politics. In the decade from 1192 to 1201, the della Volta faction had been heavily involved in Byzantine matters, while the day-to-day management of affairs in Constantinople had been delegated to their comrades, the Guercii. During this period of great political instability in Genoa, relations with the Byzantine emperors proceded favorably only when della Volta consulates were in power. Except for the administration of Manegoldo Tetoccio, who may have been influenced toward the end of his tenure of office by the della Volta group, government by *podestà,* supported by the sympathetic della Corte faction, meant inactivity in Genoa's precarious relations with the Byzantine Empire, either out of policy or out of disinterest. In 1203 and 1204 Genoa was again ruled by a *podestà,* and the city left the Byzantines to their fate at the hands of the Fourth Crusade. By naming Fulco di Castro as *podestà* for 1205 the Genoese may have hoped to reconcile podestral government and expansionist aims in an attempt to salvage something from the shambles into which their twelfth-century Byzantine policy had so unexpectedly fallen. The citizen *podestà* was not successful. Only some fifty years later, after the Genoese had helped Michael VIII Palaeologus recover his capital city, would the great Ligurian port begin to build the commercial empire in the East that internecine factional strife had prevented the Guercio and della Volta politicians of the twelfth century from obtaining.

## Notes

1. Olivieri, "Serie dei consoli," 330–31.
2. See chap. 5.
3. *Annali genovesi,* 1: 213.
4. Ibid., 213–14.
5. Ibid., 214–19.
6. Ibid., 230–31.
7. See above, chap. 2.
8. The Guercio contribution is the sum of Guercio and Malocello money.
9. *Codice diplomatico,* 1: 351, doc. 285.
10. For the involvement of the della Volta family and its associates in the Sicilian trade, see Abulafia, *Two Italies,* 217–37, passim. Abulafia gives little attention to the role of the Vento family in Sicilian affairs. Some notarial examples of the family's investments in the Sicilian trade, which Abulafia discusses, have survived. For the story of Pagano Vento's losses in his support of the rebel, Robert of Capua, against King Roger I, and his family's subsequent attempts to receive compensation from the Genoese government, see chap. 4. Of course, Guglielmo Vento was one of the ambassadors of 1156 who arranged Genoa's first commercial treaty with Sicily. Unfortunately, almost no business or notarial records have survived for the period from 1170 through 1185. The lack of such records makes it impossible to reconstruct in detail the commercial activity of twelfth-century Genoa.
11. For example, in 1170 Genoa had to step in when the count of Lavagna took the castle of Frascario from the people of Passano (*Annali genovesi,* 1: 231–32). In 1172 the marquis of Malaspina and the people of Lunisiana and Passano organized a conspiracy to seize several castles. The Genoese sent a force against the conspirators, and in the next year, Ingo di Flessia was able to recover at least the castle of Passano (ibid, 255–60). Although the marquises of Gavi appear to have been cooperative with Genoa throughout most of the second half of the twelfth century,

nevertheless, their peacefulness was only on the surface, for at the end of the century, in 1198, the marquis of Gavi and the people of Tortona conspired to take the castle of Gavi and others from their Genoese garrisons. The disturbance became much more serious for Genoa when the lords of Tassarolo and Malaspina's heirs joined him (*Annali genovesi,* 2: 72–76). Later in the same year the people of Tortona and the lords of Tassarolo submitted to Genoa (*Codice diplomatico,* 3: 131–33, doc. 50; and 124–25, doc. 47), and the marquis of Gavi gave in (ibid., 143–45, doc. 55). Malaspina held out until August, 1199, when he finally made his submission (ibid., 155–57, doc. 59). In 1199 the people of Ventimiglia revolted (*Annali genovesi,* 2: 77), and Genoa required new oaths of loyalty from several towns (*Codice diplomatico,* 3: 156–70, docs. 61–66). With regard to Genoa's relations with Liguria in general during the period, one should consult Calvini, *Genova e la Liguria Occidentale,* especially 34–65, dealing with the revolts of the 1170's and the 1190's.

12. A very good overview of Genoa's demographic relations with the outlying area, the *Genovesato,* and more distant lands is that of Robert L. Reynolds, "In Search of a Business Class in Thirteenth-Century Genoa," *Journal of Economic History,* suppl. 5 (1945): 1–10. For a recent and general description of Genoa in the Middle Ages, see Luciano Grossi-Bianchi, *Una città portuale del Medievo: Genova nei secoli X–XVI* (Genoa, 1979). Immigration from the countryside into the Italian cities in general is mentioned in Hyde, *Society and Politics in Medieval Italy,* 78–79.

13. Belgrano, "Cartario genovese," Tables 1–11.

14. Vitale, *Breviario,* 1: 42–43.

15. Giovanni Scriba, *Cartolare,* nos. 465, 505, and 864.

16. Hughes, "Kinsmen and Neighbors," 100. See Hughes' notes for additional bibliography, but especially important is the article by Enneo Poleggi, "Contrade delle consorterie nobiliari a Genova tra il XII e il XIII secolo," *Urbanistica* no. 42 (1965): 15–20, which includes a map (16) of the twelfth-century city indicating the enclaves of many of the most prominent families. Probably the best source for the topology and history of the physical medieval city, is Grossi Bianco, *Città portuale,* 51–163, and especially the maps on 68–69 (showing the parts of the city dominated by the various families); 86–90 (a general toponomastic map of the medieval city); and the diagrams on 97 (the area around S. Torpeto); 218–19 (showing the later *curiae* of the Pevere, Usodimari, Lercari, and Streggiaporco families); and 230 (the system of towers in the plaza of the della Volta family).

17. In the extant portions, both published and unpublished, of the notarial register of Oberto Scriba de Mercato (most entries coming from the 1180's), there are approximately 910 appearances of people in con-

tracts enacted at the house of Bonifacio della Volta. The five families whose members occur most frequently are: della Volta (131 times), di Castro (59 times), Vento (46 times), Pedicola (35 times), and di Pallo (27 times). These five families account, then, for 298 occurrences, or nearly one third of the total. The other two thirds are distributed among some 115 or more families. Clearly, the della Volta family associated with only a few other families regularly, although they marginally associated with a great many others. The registers for whatever notaries serviced the Guercio and della Corte families have not survived.

18. *Annali genovesi,* 1: 62.

19. Ibid., 2: 43.

20. See n. 17 above. Boniface himself hardly ever appears in the many contracts done at his house, meaning that he must have arranged or supervised these deals without participating in them as a businessman.

21. *Annali genovesi,* 1: 196.

22. Olivieri, "Serie dei consoli," 414.

23. These figures are taken from the lists of officials in Olivieri, "Serie dei consoli," *passim.*

24. With regard to the political alliance of the Piccamiglio family, see Hughes, "Family Structure," 12. Although a planned marriage between the Burone and Piccamiglio families was broken off by the death of Guglielmo Burone's daughter in 1160 (Giovanni Scriba, *Cartolare,* no. 790), three years later Guglielmo Cassicio, the son of Ingo della Volta, promised to marry the daughter of Ardizo Piccamiglio (ibid., no. 1144). Whether the marriage took place is not known, although Cassicio did eventually marry, as his sons prove. If the marriage did take place, perhaps the Piccamiglio family, at least in the generation after Ingo della Volta's, should be placed in the della Volta camp.

25. Archivio di Stato di Genova, "Manuscriptum 102 diversorum notariorum," 15v–16r and 18r.

26. Sanguineti and Bertolotto, "Documenti," 414.

27. On this mission, see chap. 2.

28. Oberto Scriba de Mercato, *Notai* (1186), nos. 15, 26, 27, 37, and 40. Bach first tabulated all the contracts from Oberto Scriba's register of 1186, *Gênes,* appendix.

29. *Annali genovesi,* 2: 12.

30. Ibid., 14.

31. Ibid., 19.

32. Ibid., 22 and 28.

33. Ibid., 23. Hughes mistakenly places this double assassination in 1179. "Family Structure," 8. The conjecture that the assailants were Doria people comes from the mention in the annals that in 1203 peace was

made between the Doria and the Porcelli and the son of the late Opizo Leccavelo (*Annali genovesi,* 2: 88).

34. Ibid., 26 and 28.

35. Ibid., 32–33.

36. For example, Bach, *Gênes,* 156.

37. *Annali genovesi,* 2: 30.

38. Ibid., 42; Hughes, "Family Structure," 12.

39. *Annali genovesi,* 2: 30.

40. Ibid., 42. By 1200 the Venti were once again solidly allied with their della Volta relatives, for they figure prominently in notarial entries with della Volta people (Archivio di Stato di Genova, Oberto Scriba de Mercato, "Cartolari notarili," 4.98v, 4.101v, 4.107v, 4.120r, 4.121r, 4.161r, 4.174v, 4.255r, 4.231r, 4.234r, and 4.237v). Even the della Volta and Vento marriage alliance was carried into the younger generation, since Tommaso Vento was the son-in-law of Rubeo della Volta (ibid., 247r). Rubeo was married to the sister of Guglielmo Vento's wife. A third sister was married to Bonvassallo di Antiocha, who had been a consul of the commune in 1174. Of course, these sisters were the daughters of Lanfranco Pevere the Elder (see chap. 4).

41. *Annali genovesi,* 2: 36.

42. Ibid., 2: 36–37.

43. Sanguineti and Bertolotto, "Documenti," 409.

44. Cassinese, *Notai,* nos. 1031, 1076, 1108, 1109, and 1116.

45. Louise Buenger (Robbert), "Genoese Enterprisers, 1186-1211," (Ph.D. diss., University of Wisconsin, 1955), 58–61 and 87–89.

46. Cassinese, *Notai,* nos. 1030, 1088, 1092, 1101, 1102, 1108, 1119, 1129-31, and 1134. The total of these investments comes to £1,243 ½. Guglielmo Guaracco entrusted £100¾ to Rubaldo della Volta, indicating at least some business ties between the della Volta and the Guercio blocs for this voyage (ibid., no. 1108).

47. See below, n. 56, and 149-50 for Henry's hostility to communes.

48. Weiland, *Constitutiones et acta publica imperatorum,* 472–77.

49. This opinion of Henry's handling of the negotiations is that of Dione R. Clementi, "Some Unnoticed Aspects of the Emperor Henry VI's Conquest," 339. The treaty between Henry and Genoa is in *Codice diplomatico,* 3: 4-12, doc. 2. The round of negotiations preceding the alliance is reported in *Annali genovesi,* 2: 37-41.

50. There is no consensus about Henry's ambitions. The best synthesis of scholarship on the German's relations with the Byzantine Empire is in Brand, *Byzantium,* 189-94. He emphasizes the necessity of imposing the *alleleggon,* a Byzantine tax raising tribute money to buy off Henry's threatened invasion of the empire.

51. *Annali genovesi,* 2: 36.

52. Isaac's letter to Tetoccio complaining of Tanto's diplomatic insufficiency was dated in October 1191, meaning that the unsuccessful ambassador could not have returned to Genoa before November. That Tetoccio, and not the new consuls, sent the second embassy is proved by Isaac's letter of April 1192, in which the emperor announced to the then out-of-office *podestà* the success of the new delegation (Sanguineti and Bertolotto, "Documenti," 409–10).

53. Members of the Tornello family were usually associated with della Volta adherents, although not too much with the della Volta family members themselves, in the 1150's and early 1160's (Giovanni Scriba, *Cartolare,* nos. 39, 88, 401, 669, 723, 882, 884, and 1056).

54. Sanguineti and Bertolotto, "Documenti," 445–48.

55. *Annali genovesi,* 2: 43–45.

56. On this phenomenon in Genoa itself, see Vito Vitale, *Il comune del podestà a Genova* (Milan, 1951). For Barbarossa's plan to use *podestà* to govern northern Italy, see Hyde, *Society and Politics in medieval Italy,* 101–2. For Frederick II's anger and retaliation against Genoa for appointing in 1231 a *podestà* who did not have the emperor's approval, see *Annali genovesi,* 2: 64–65.

57. *Annali genovesi,* 2: 45–53. Interestingly, of all the Genoese who participated in the adventure, besides the *podestà,* the only person mentioned by name in the account of the Sicilian expedition was Giovanni Avvocato, who was captured by the Pisans. This gives some indication of della Corte support for the expedition, or at least, of the faction's participation in it.

58. Ibid., 52: "potestas vestra mortua est; ego non video hic aliquem qui sit pro comuni (*sic*) Ianue, nec novi commune; set quandocumque videro per pertitudinem illum vel illos qui pro communitate sit, ego bene complebo quicquid promisi."

59. Ibid., 52–53. For a discussion of the whole matter, see Vitale, *Breviario,* 1: 44–49.

60. *Annali genovesi,* 2: 52: "unde contigit quod ipse (Henry) tanquam pernitiosus parvipendens promissiones quas fecerat, diabolica suggestione quorundam civium Ianue et aliorum provorum et malignorum, non solum promissa non observavit, verum etiam in cuncta asperrime erga civitatem Ianue . . . nerozavit . . ."

61. Olivieri, "Serie dei consoli," 398, 404, 409, 411, 414, and 415–16.

62. Ibid., 407–8, 417, 418, 421, 424, 428, 429, 430, 432, and 435.

63. There are at least eight instances scattered in the published and unpublished notarial entries.

64. Oberto Scriba de Mercato, *Notai* (1190), nos. 74, 80, 83, 84, and

184. The relationship between di Castro and Balbo is documented in Archivio di Stato di Genova, Oberto Scriba, "Cartolari notarili," 2.188r.

65. *Annali genovesi,* 2: 81.

66. See chap. 2.

67. Archivio di stato di Genova, Oberto Scriba de Mercato, "Cartolari notarili," 2.1r, 2.1v, 2.7r, 2.30v, and 2.33v.

68. Ibid., 2.139r.

69. Ibid., 2.5v.

70. Streggiaporco, who died in 1170, was the son of Giovanni Nepitella. This information comes from the epitaph on his tomb, published by Olivieri in "Serie dei consoli," 361.

71. He and his brothers, Bonvassallo and Oliverio, appear nearly a hundred times in both published and unpublished notarial records stretching back to Giovanni Scriba's cartulary of the 1150's, and they are nearly always associated with della Volta people. The connection was carried over into the second generation by Enrico's son, Oglerio (Archivio di stato di Genova, Guglielmo de Sauro, "Cartolari notarili," 3.124v).

72. Sanguineti and Bertolotto, "Documenti," 471.

73. See chap. 2 for Alexius' retaliation for Gafforio's piracy.

74. Sanguineti and Bertolotto, "Documenti," 471.

75. Brand has said of the Byzantine prince, "The young Alexius' presence may not have suggested to them (the crusade's leaders), the idea of attacking Constantinople, but it at least reinforced any plan they had had" (*Byzantium,* 155–56). Brand's statement summarizes scholarly opinion about the subordinate role that Alexius played in the diversion. However, the adolescent prince represented a serious challenge to the throne. Prince Alexius had fled to the West in late 1201, at the very same time that Emperor Alexius reached his trade agreement with the Genoese. Since the prince escaped Byzantium on a Pisan ship, perhaps Alexius III's willingness to come to terms with the Genoese was a punishment meted out to Genoa's Pisan rivals for their fellow citizens' complicity in the prince's escape. Such a move would surely have been in keeping with Alexius III's methods of handling the Italians. Prince Alexius, before he eventually enlisted the support of the Fourth Crusade, had visited the court of his brother-in-law, Philip of Swabia, and had seen the pope to find support for his plot to depose his uncle. Queller reports that even while in captivity, Prince Alexius had schemed with Latins in Constantinople and had written to his sister, the wife of Philip of Swabia, to plot the overthrow of the emperor (*Fourth Crusade,* 31). Emperor Alexius wrote to Pope Innocent III sometime before December 1202, when the pope's letter of response is dated, expressing his fears about his errant nephew's actions. Innocent's letter appears in his correspondence (Innocent III,

*Epistolae,* in *Patrologiae cursus completus, series Latina,* edited by Jean P. Migne, Vols. 214–217 [Paris, 1855], no. 122). Although Prince Alexius' conspiratorial activities in the West came after the emperor concluded a treaty with the Genoese, the emperor must have realized that his fleeing young nephew presented a danger to his throne and began building an alliance to forestall expected threats.

76. Sanguineti and Bertolotto, "Documenti," 475–99.

## Chapter Seven

*Chapter Seven*

✧✦✧

# Genoa's Byzantine Connection

WHEN THE GENOESE MADE their first formal agreement with the Byzantines in 1155, they had only a few places in the Mediterranean where they enjoyed a privileged commercial position, but by 1204, when Constantinople fell to the forces of the Fourth Crusade, Genoa had built up a considerable network of privileged trade, improving its situation in the crusading states and adding ports of call from Alexandria in Egypt to Ceuta in Morocco as well as in Sicily.[1] During this period of commercial expansion, the Genoese slowly learned better methods of administering their far-flung trading outposts, while at home the strains of commercial expansion disrupted politics to the point where a more efficient, even if more controlled, method of internal government became necessary with the imposition of the *podestà*. Not only on the diplomatic scene, but also on the local level the twelfth-century Genoese felt the attraction of Byzantium, and through the records they left, it is possible to trace the outlines of the role that the Byzantine Empire played in the political and economic lives of the Genoese.

This great eastern empire, still an important power in most of the twelfth century under the Comneni emperors, attracted an understandably large share of Genoa's attention. The Eastern Roman Empire, the Holy Roman Empire, and the Kingdom of Sicily were the three most powerful political systems in the world of the twelfth-century Genoese. Byzantium's position forced the Genoese to give careful consideration to the interests of the eastern empire in the many dealings they had with the other two powers, and often the Genoese must have thought that the tightrope they walked was very thin indeed. In Genoa's internal political life, the Byzantine Empire, like the Holy Roman Empire and the Kingdom of Sicily, had a group of sympathetic Genoese who were devoted to the promotion of their city's attachment to its interests, and the conflicts and tensions of the eastern empire with its counterparts figured in the conflicts and tensions among the political factions within Genoa. In terms of business, Byzantium's impact on Genoa was less significant because of the checkered history of Genoa's commercial intercourse with the Byzantines; but in the few years when the Genoese did enjoy unimpeded trade with Constantinople (1160–62, 1171–82, 1192–98, and 1201–3), the few shreds of evidence point to the importance of this commerce for Genoese business.

The year 1154 was crucial in Genoese commercial history, for then the municipal government decided to launch an ambitious program to develop privileged trade throughout the Mediterranean. From that time until new opportunities opened with the Third Crusade, the Byzantine Empire was a vital market for the Genoese to tap. In Syria, Genoa could do little to break the stranglehold that the Embriaco family had on affairs. In Moslem North Africa, western European sentiments and various papal prohibitions against trading with the infidel discouraged the development of privileged trade.[2] Although treaties were struck with the Almohads in Spain and Morocco, the Genoese participated only in regular, unprivileged trade elsewhere in the Moslem world until late in the twelfth century or early in the thirteenth. As for commerce with northern Europe, the rudimentary technology of navigation and the dangers of overland travel encouraged the Genoese to wait in their city for bolder northern merchants to come to them. The Byzantine Empire and the Kingdom of Sicily were the two most accessible markets for Genoese merchants.

The Sicilian trade prospered in the twelfth century,[3] but there is little evidence regarding Byzantine trade. Most of the information from notarial sources concerns special trading voyages in the retinue of diplomatic missions. The removal of surviving contracts connected with Genoese embassies to the Byzantine court in 1156 (perhaps) and 1157, 1160, 1164, 1186, and 1191 leaves only a minuscule number of business records that specifically deal with the normal functioning of Genoese trade in the Byzantine world. Moreover, some of these contracts involved with diplomacy may not even have been intended for trade so much as for offering naval services as mercenaries.[4] Unfortunately, too few examples of this exist to confirm this suspicion. The testimony of notarial evidence for Genoese trade with the Byzantine Empire in the twelfth century is then virtually silent.

Only the diplomatic record of Genoese efforts to develop this important commercial link with Constantinople remains. The list of losses contained in the Genoese government's instructions to Grimaldi, its ambassador to the imperial court in 1175, provides an unusually full picture of Genoese trade with the Byzantine Empire in the early years of its existence. The absence, however, of practically all information concerning Genoa's Byzantine commerce during the important years from 1175 to the middle of 1182 is a major lacuna. In the summary of negotiations contained in Isaac II's chrysobull of 1192 in favor of the Genoese, mention is made of the Genoese claim for 228,000 hyperpers lost in the Latin massacre of 1182.[5] Considering that the Genoese in 1175 claimed only 29,443 hyperpers for their losses in the Pisan sack of their quarter in 1162 and only 5,674½ hyperpers as compensation for their losses in the Venetian pillage of the Coparion in 1171, it is likely that between 1171 and 1182 the Genoese substantially expanded their commercial interest in Constantinople. This increase in investment, coupled with Genoese requests in diplomatic negotiations for a larger compound and for additional docking space, along with their rental of more space in Constantinople leads clearly to the conclusion that the Genoese were concentrating much effort on the Byzantine trade and realizing large profits from it.[6] In general, however, the Genoese, who enjoyed privileged trade in the empire for less than half of the forty-nine years from 1155 to 1204, did not realize the kind of success they must have anticipated from the considerable efforts they expended on the Byzantine connection.

Genoa's prolonged attempt to achieve its expansionist goals in the Byzantine empire had more important ramifications on Genoese diplomacy than on the moderate trade that actually existed. Genoa became a part of the intricate diplomacy that maintained a Europe-Mediterranean balance of power in the twelfth century. The Byzantine and German emperors and the Sicilian king viewed Genoa, like the other Italian maritime cities, simply as a pawn in their diplomatic games, but the Genoese utilized that lowly position to gain much. Genoa with the treaty of 1162 with Frederick Barbarossa obtained virtual independence from the German system, and for nearly thirty years thereafter, the Genoese carried on their business with very little interference from the western emperor. The breakdown of internal order in Genoa on account of intense factional strife forced Genoa to succumb to German influence once more in the 1190's, but the interval of separation had allowed Genoa to grow. Genoa's treaty of 1156 with King William of Sicily was the beginning of a very profitable privileged trading position for the city in that island kingdom, and throughout the second half of the twelfth century, the Genoese carefully piloted their city between the Sicilian Normans and the Byzantines. It is a tribute to Genoa's diplomatic skill that it could continue commerce with both sides. The reason for this success lies at least partially in Genoa's constant refusal to be brought into offensive alliances with either power and by the tense peace maintained between the two powers themselves in what may almost be called a twelfth-century cold war. When hostilities did break out in the 1180's, Genoa was already excluded from the Byzantine trade for a far different reason: the anti-Latinism of Andronicus I. Only when the German emperor acquired Sicily in 1194 was a severe strain placed on Genoa's Byzantine connection. Henry VI's dishonorable refusal to meet his promises to his Genoese assistants prevented a break in Genoa's relations with the Byzantine Empire, especially because the weakened empire, in the inept hands of the Angeli, sought help wherever it could. As the Fourth Crusade so dramatically proved, the Byzantines were not successful in their search for protectors.

Genoa had its own impact on Byzantine politics. Genoese naval strength gave Manuel I a valuable weapon against the Sicilian fleet. The Byzantines had relied on the Venetians for naval help for generations, but Manuel thought the Venetians were too unmanageable, and their attack on the Genoese quarter in 1171 convinced Manuel to expel them from the empire. The Pisans too were a source of naval support, but their attack on the Genoese quarter in 1162 had made the emperor suspicious of them as well. In 1170 both the Pisans and the Genoese were given convenient compounds in Constantinople as a manifestation of Manuel's anti-Venetian sentiments, and after 1171 they were a mainstay in the Byzantine commercial and naval nexus. Both the Pisans and the

Genoese resided in Constantinople peacefully for the remainder of Manuel's reign, surely disliking each other's presence but afraid to take action that would anger the disciplinary emperor. Manuel must have favored the Genoese over the other Italians because the Genoese alone had given him no trouble and had faithfully honored their treaty commitments in 1171 when Manuel needed help to thwart the invasion of the Venetians. After Manuel died, both the Genoese and the Pisans backed particular court cliques to improve their positions in Constantinople. The Genoese, however, made the mistake of comparing their situation in Byzantium with the one they had in the crusading states, where Genoese sea power had been of great assistance in conquering much of the Palestinian coast and in maintaining the precarious Latin kingdom's links with the West. In 1182 the Latin massacre in Constantinople showed the Genoese that their long-time partners, the Montferrats, could not protect them as the Embriachi did in Syria and that the Byzantines thought that the benefits of Genoese trade were expendable. The ineffective Angelan dynasty allowed Italian influence to return to Constantinople and to grow stronger than it had been during Manuel's reign. Isaac II constantly relied on the Italians to quell revolts, to protect him from the Sicilians, the Germans, and the crusaders, and finally to police his own waters. Once again, the Genoese failed to understand the Byzantine view of their involvement in the eastern empire, and when the Genoese balked in their responsibility of helping to keep Byzantine waters safe for shipping, the frustrated Alexius III excluded them from Constantinople. Alexius III, however, found the Italians to be his only source of economic and naval strength, and his dependence on them prevented him from disciplining them effectively. His failure threw the situation out of control and eventually cost him his throne. Italian meddling in Byzantine affairs was a very dangerous sport that cost the Genoese dearly both in money and in lives and virtually cost the Byzantines their empire.

Some of Genoa's troubles in the Byzantine Empire after Manuel's reign can be attributed to the Byzantines themselves. The antiwestern bias of the Byzantines explains only the Latin massacre of 1182; the Angeli proved themselves to be more favorable to western merchants than Manuel himself had been. This family of emperors, however, could not cope with the problems of rule. The resulting instability of the Byzantine government in the last years of the twelfth century prevented the existence of predictable, long-term conditions with regard to such matters as market availability, taxing policy, and administrative procedures, which were prerequisites for substantial Genoese investment. In view of the sporadic nature of Genoa's endeavors to penetrate the Constantinopolitan market in the last fifteen years of the twelfth century, it appears that a large segment of the Genoese business community had considerable reservations about the value of developing Byzantine commerce. The Guercio family and its comrades alone stood to gain particularly from the Byzantine trade, and Genoa's diplomatic movements closer to Constantinople were often prompted by that group's manipulation of the political scene in Genoa. The commercial milieu offered by Constantinople in the closing years of the twelfth century was simply too risky, given the profit margin and the convenience of other fast-developing markets, for most Genoese. It must not be forgotten that the Genoese, unlike the Venetians, who remained deeply involved with the Byzantines, had already developed very profitable markets in the crusading states, North Africa, and the western Mediterranean. The failure of the Genoese to build a strong trade with the Byzantines in the late twelfth century, then, is in large part not an indication of Genoa's diplomatic or commercial inadequacy so much as it is an example of that city's preoccupation with other more profitable areas; the politically troubled market of Constantinople was too much of a risk.

The Genoese, nevertheless, did not fare well in Constantinople largely because they did not understand the unique Byzantine view of loyalty. Although the dynasty of the Comneni had added many western trappings to the empire, there still existed a mystique of the empire as an entity in itself that transcended the purely personal relationships and loyalties on which feudal European society was based. In Byzantium, real power did not reside in the participants in court intrigues so much as in well-established field armies and bureaucracies whose loyalty was to the abstractions of office rather than to the persons who happened to fill them. For hundreds of years, emperors had come and gone, and revolution was seen by the Byzantines as a legitimate method of changing governments, as the many revolts and usurpations in Byzantine history attest. Throughout these personnel changes, the constitutional form of the emperor continued unassailed, and the bureaucracy and the army for the most part followed the commands of the emperor in performing their functions regardless of the person who sat on the throne. When some group found the rule of a particular emperor intolerable, it simply replaced that person with one whose will was more compatible with its goals. For the Byzantines it was far better to remove an incompetent emperor than to risk the possibility of one man's mistakes destroying the office of emperor altogether.

Indeed, the westerners who participated in the Fourth Crusade did not understand this profoundly different conception of government and social cohesion, in which loyalty was directed to the office and not to the person. The crusaders' surprise that the Byzantines rejected their "true" emperor and his son was soon replaced by discouragement and frustration caused by the ineffectiveness of personal loyalty in the Byzantine system. What the westerners perceived as treachery the Byzantines considered to be stratagems that did no harm to the bonds that held their society together. In the end, the crusaders despaired to trying to work with the unfamiliar Byzantine conception of loyalty and replaced that political structure with the more amenable feudal system based on personal loyalty.

As for the Genoese, in feudal Spain, Sicily, and the crusading states, they had been able to use the influence of powerful people like the Embriachi and the Montferrats to maneuver informal personal association to their advantage. In Byzantium, this Genoese practice worked under the Latinophile Manuel, to whom the Genoese were unswervingly loyal, but it quickly broke down when people of a more traditional Byzantine character ascended the throne, and the past loyalties of the Genoese prevented them from building a new impersonal loyalty to the emperor's office. Because the Genoese were not sufficiently powerful in Byzantium to maintain a particular person on the throne, whenever other forces beyond the control of the Genoese toppled their "patron" from power, their whole protective system vanished, and they were left to look to the Byzantines like disloyal intriguers and to the new powers in Constantinople like political enemies.

The Genoese compounded their mistaken response to the Byzantine system by habitually relying on westerners to champion their interests in Byzantium. The Byzantines were openly contemptuous of the less sophisticated Latins, resulting in a national consciousness that the Genoese could not manage. The Genoese overgeneralized Manuel I's friendliness to Latin culture and that of the court aristocrats in his favor to assume that other Byzantines shared the same sentiments.[7] The Genoese used the Montferrats and the Embriachi in the crusading states, where a western mentality prevailed, but the western origins of the Montferrats and the Guercio family greatly diminished the influence that they could exert over the ethnocentric Byzantines. If the Genoese insisted on using their personal attachment to powerful people as the means of advancing their interests, they should at least have found Byzantines to act as their patrons, but they did not. In spite of occasionally honoring treaty obligations, the Genoese could never prove to the Byzantines that they could be directly loyal to Byzantine institutions and would refrain from cooperating with various western intriguers to whom they were personally tied in order to insure the abstractions of "Romania" and the forms that constituted it.

The overwhelming importance of personal relationships shows through the tangled account of Genoese internal politics in the late twelfth century. The Genoese political organization of the twelfth century, although expressed through such institutions as the consulate, the *consiglio,* parliament, and the courts, nevertheless had much of the character of the short-term, limited contracts with which the citizens carried on their business. Throughout the twelfth century the constitution was changed as it pleased the people who controlled the city. Indeed, every year it was voted on anew whether or not to continue the *compagnia* by which the city was governed. There never was a fixed number of communal consuls, and every year the Genoese decided how many municipal officers they would have for the following year. Strangely, not until 1164 did the Genoese *consiglio* actually decree that the consulate was annual and that ex-consuls returned to private status.[8] New offices were created from time to time, while others fell into desuetude within a few years. The most telling proof of the transitoriness of offices and of particular constitutional forms in twelfth-century Genoa was the relative ease with which the communal consulate, in use for nearly a hundred years, was replaced by the institution of the *podestà* at the end of the century. The civil strife that accompanied the change in the constitution, it must be remembered, was the cause and not the result of the alteration, and it reflected a breakdown of the system of personal alliances that had ruled the city for so long. The Genoese saw their government only as a means to achieve private goals, and whatever respect the Genoese had for political institutions developed only from the effectiveness of those institutions in serving individual interests. Unlike the Byzantines, the twelfth-century Genoese could not apply the attribute of permanence to political institutions, at least not to their own.

Only intensely personal associations based largely on family or business had the continuity to command the loyalty of Genoese citizens. That was why there grew up alongside the official political system unofficial paragovernmental organizations that effectively established communal policy and struggled with one another to control the city. The phenomenon stems from the feudal background of the politically significant people in Genoa. This urban patriciate, descended from the viscountal families who had ruled the city for the bishop in the eleventh century, had not severed their ties to the feudal world. Many of these men were vassals of the archbishop in the middle of the twelfth century, they still possessed fiefs in the Genoese countryside, and they were still jealous of their rights to feudal exactions, as the story of Rolando Avvocato and the men of Recco demonstrates. The urban towers of the Genoese nobility and the skirmishes that made those fortifications necessary were continuations in a new setting of a lifestyle that had been practiced by their forebears for years in the countryside. Genoese families maintained their ties to the feudal world through marriages with the outlying aristocracy, a practice that for years pumped additional feudal blood and views into the patriciate of the city. The adage, "civis Ianuensis, ergo mercator," simply did not apply to the people who ruled the twelfth-century city.

The Genoese responded to the expectation of commercial connections with Byzantium by using personal bonds to create political blocs that would either encourage or discourage the further development of those links. In the first years of the Byzantine connection, the new trade played perhaps the deciding role in splitting the city's patriciate into hostile factions. There is no evidence that some factional rivalry existed in Genoa before the

1150's with the divisions into the Carmadino and Maneciano clans. Even the first instance of discord, the conspiracy against Filippo di Lamberto in 1147, cannot be placed into this lineage confrontation. The frustration of trying to line up people into factions at so early a date as 1160, leaves one with the strong impression that even if ill feelings existed in the early twelfth century, factionalism had not yet taken on the rigid delineation that would mark it in the later years of the century.

Genoa's expansionist policy after 1154 created the situation in which maneuvering over control of the Byzantine trade and over safeguarding other interests threatened by the Byzantine connection forced the people of the Genoese patriciate to choose sides and to hold firm their ground. The resultant factions are most clearly represented by the della Volta, the della Corte, and the Guercio blocs, all tied together by family, business, and historical viewpoint. More groups may have existed, but these three were the most prominent and powerful. The Guercio group was decidedly pro-Byzantine; the della Corte group, after its exclusion from the Byzantine connection and its consequent alliance with the backward-looking Carmadino families, would be pro-German; and the della Volta group, connected with the Maneciano families who had begun the commune and the most powerful of the three factions, would encourage trade wherever it was, even though it concentrated on Syria and Sicily. Perhaps the power of the della Volta organization can be best ascribed to its wider view of Genoese interests and its ability to accommodate more specialized interests, like those of the Guercio family, within its broad policy or commercial expansion. Guercio and della Volta people, with their common interest in expansion, could easily work together, while the della Corte people, favoring the old German imperial system and resenting the growing monopolization of power by those leaders who were drawing Genoa farther away from that comfortable situation, could only wait for an opportunity to regain a dominant place in city government. They attempted to remove their opponents in 1164 soon after the factional lines had taken shape, when problems in Byzantium had contributed to a weakening of the Guercio-della Volta alliance, but they were not strong enough to repress the forces of growth in their city. Until the last decade of the century, the greatest effect that the Byzantine interest had on

Genoese politics was its advancement of the della Volta faction by insuring Guercio support for that faction's political power. If the Byzantine trade of the 1170's was as profitable as the sources hint, then money made in Byzantium must have gone to strengthen the della Volta bloc to the point where by the 1180's it almost completely monopolized the political and business life of the commune.

In the 1190's, a breakdown within the della Volta organization encouraged the Guercio bloc, now despairing of the ability of their long-time allies to assist effectively in promoting the family's Byzantine ambitions, to realign itself temporarily with the della Corte group, thus allowing the reintroduction of German influence into Genoa. Although Guercio and della Volta would return to their traditional comradeship, the power of Henry VI had strengthened the della Corte faction, and his acquisition of Sicily in 1194 had perhaps strangely connected him with della Volta interests. Della Volta and della Corte people now found themselves temporarily to be strange bedfellows, tied to the German emperor for different reasons but still alienated from each other by over thirty years of violent animosity. Henry's unexpected prohibition of Genoese commerce with Sicily not only threw into chaos the strong della Volta business with the island, but also was the death blow to della Volta's stranglehold on the commune. The Genoese factions were at war, and violent solutions to the tangled skein of interests and personalities became chronic in the city. Order could be restored only by the imposition of a *podestà,* which embodied the constitutional form favored by the German emperor. The cross-purposed Genoese could no longer honor their city's responsibilities to Byzantium. The Guercio bloc continued to promote its Byzantine interests, but only with extreme difficulty. Even more devastatingly, by supporting piracy, some Genoese in the della Volta group had found, in almost Veblenian fashion, a way of profiting from a disregard for their Byzantine obligations. By 1203 and 1204, many Genoese whose fathers and grandfathers had loyally served the Byzantine Empire had little concern for the fate of East Rome.

The twelfth-century Genoese responded to Byzantium by slowly learning from their mistakes and by developing a more sophisticated approach to government and administration. Twelfth-century

Genoa was a paradise for rugged individualism and free-wheeling economics, and it offers perhaps the best historical example of business running government. This system brought about Genoa's rise to economic and political prominence, but it was insufficient to maintain Genoa's new position. At the end of the twelfth century, the Genoese began to realize that drastic revision of their system was required. Political organization was directed to the institution of the *podestà*, which superseded the power of the violence-ridden personal alliances that had been so strong in municipal affairs. At the same time, the Genoese used the rebuilding program of the Third Crusade to install municipally supervised administrators in the city's Syrian colonies,[9] replacing the quasi-feudal system used by the della Volta faction and controlled by the Embriaco family. In Constantinople as well, Genoa appears to have broken the hold that the Guercio family enjoyed over Genoese interests when a new arrangement with Alexius III in 1201 excluded a member of that family from the viscounty of the Genoese quarter. Although the Fourth Crusade prevented the new organization from proving its effectiveness in Byzantium, the later Genoese commercial network in the Levant certainly indicates a marked improvement over the twelfth-century practice of tying the city's commercial fortunes to particular individuals. The Genoese were fast being taught a new attitude, one much closer to the Byzantine view, that constitutional forms and offices had an importance and a permanence that overshadowed the individuals who happened to hold them. The Genoese were learning that the authority of political and administrative positions arose from the offices themselves and not from the personal power of the people who held them. By the end of the twelfth century, the Genoese had abandoned the feudal attitude that office was secondary to personality built around inheritance, lordship, and private immunities. The repeated Genoese failures in the Byzantine world and the more advanced Byzantine example must certainly have contributed a large share to this course of instruction.

Perhaps the old Genoese aristocracy did not learn as fast as the new people prominent by the end of the twelfth century, people who could not base their positions in Genoese society on the traditional institutions. New people became much more numerous in notarial entries at the end of the century and were more active in serving as investors rather than simply as traveling partners, and at the same time, members of the great families receded more into the background.[10] In addition an influx of outsiders into Genoa in the late twelfth century occurred.[11] These new people, either rising from the nonaristocratic elements of the city or coming from other places, took over the business of the city as the old feudal families became paralyzed in factional warfare. Even in these old families, the younger generation had grown up in a world dominated by business considerations and not solely by feudal issues. Therefore, a two-pronged attack on the old feudally oriented ways was launched. This blend of commoners and younger aristocrats, both placing the businessman's premium on coordination and efficiency, restructured Genoa's government and its commercial network by replacing basically feudal lords and advocates with municipal bureaucrats. The last years of the twelfth and the first half of the thirteenth centuries mark an intellectual transition in the Genoese to a "bourgeoise" and bureaucratic orientation that would build and supervise Genoa's later commercial empire in the region of the Black Sea. One can very accurately say of the Genoese during that later time, "civis Ianuensis, ergo mercator."

By the end of the twelfth century, the Genoese were coming of age, and the Byzantines had been one of their principal tutors. The Genoese saw that their method of building a commercial network on the old-fashioned personal bonds of feudalism was unworkable. It depended far too much on the fortunes and fickleness of individuals. The Genoese also saw that the unrestrained rivalry of personally based political power blocs weakened the free-wheeling consulate to the point where the government could no longer subordinate individual interests to the public good. These early city-dwellers eventually came to terms with the unfamiliar world outside the feudal Ligurian mountains, and by experiencing the far more sophisticated system of the Byzantine Empire, they learned that bureaucratic organization in which individual identity was subordinated to the abstraction of the group provided an impartiality and continuity that alone could insure administrative efficiency and commercial success. The development of an impersonal colonial administrative system and government by *podestà* signified the triumph of the Byzantine conception of loyalty to office over loyalty to individuals. The powerful aristocratic families of twelfth-century Genoa would continue to exist, and they would even consolidate their positions and place even more emphasis on family solidarity in the formation of the *alberghi* of late medieval Genoa.[12] Unlike the political factions of the twelfth century, these later family associations were largely defensive measures taken in a futile attempt to ward off the threats presented by the slowly growing power of the bureaucratic institutions of a state inspired by a hostility to all associations and organizations, public or private, that could motivate political action without its own approval. This change in political philosophy was necessary not only in Genoa but also in the West as a whole before strong governments, based on impersonality, continuity, and corporateness, could develop. One of the earliest places for this crucial change in outlook was in twelfth-century Genoa.

## Notes

1. Although references have been made in the text to most of the Genoese treaties, in 1177 the Genoese government sent Rubeo della Volta to Saladin, the sultan of Egypt, "cum quo pacem firmavit" (*Annali genovesi*, 2: 10). No other information about this diplomacy exists, but at least Saladin and the Genoese were willing to cooperate for their mutual benefit. For more information about Saladin's negotiations not only with the Genoese, but also with other Italian cities, see Day, "Impact of the Third Crusade," 161–62.

2. In 1198, for example, Innocent III gave the Venetians license from the ban imposed by the Third Lateran Council (Tafel, *Urkunden*, 1: 234–35).

3. Abulafia, *Two Italies,* passim.

4. Lilie, *Handel und Politik,* 635.

5. "Documenti," 414.

6. Evidence of rented property can be found in the "verbal processes." or descriptions of Genoese concessions in Constantinople issued in April 1192 by Isaac II and in October 1201 by Alexius III (ibid., 434–45 and 475–99).

7. Brand, *Byzantium,* p. 35, for the pro-Latin sentiments of the Byzantine military aristocracy during Manuel's reign.

8. *Annali genovesi,* 1: 169–70: "Fuerat quondam tempus, quod consulatus aliquando biennio, triennio, aliquando quadriennio durabit. demum senatui nostro placuit, qui semper rem publicam augere studuit, ne consulatus officium longius quam annum haberent, ne per diuturnitatem

potestatis insolentiores redderentur, sed civiles semper essent qui post annum scirent esse privatos."

9. Byrne, "Genoese Colonies," 160–82.

10. Byrne, "Genoese Trade," 210–11.

11. Vitale, *Il comune del podestà,* 120–60.

12. Although much has been written about these extended and sometimes artificial families grouped together in their own neighborhood compounds in late medieval Genoa, perhaps the most accessible and latest descriptions are those of Heers, *Gênes au XVe siècle,* and Eduardo Grendi, "Profilo storico degli alberghi genovesi," *Mélanges de l'École Française de Rome; Moyen Âge-temps modernes,* 87 (1975): 241–302.

# Bibliography

## Unpublished Sources

Genoa. Archivio di Stato. "Cartolari notarili" (also called "Notai Ignoti").
———. Cartulary 2, folia 1r–59v, 137r–154v, and 183r–193v (Oberto Scriba de Mercato, September 1182–September 1184).
———. Cartulary 3, folia 121r–134v (Guglielmo de Sauro, June–August 1200).
———. Cartulary 4, folia 68r–135v, 157r–174v, and 331r–258v (Oberto Scriba de Mercato, April 1200–April 1201).
———. Cartulary 6, folia 79v–80r (Guglielmo Cassinese, September 1188).
———. "Manuscriptum 102 notariorum diversorum" (August 1179–September 1202).

## Published Sources

Airaldi, Gabriella, ed. *Le carte di Santa Maria della Vigne di Genova (1103–1392)*. Genoa, 1969.
Basili, A., and Pozza, L., eds. *Le carte del monastero di San Siro di Genova dal 952 al 1224*. Genoa, 1974.
Belgrano, Luigi, T., ed. "Registrum curiae archiepiscopalis Ianue." *Atti della Società Ligure di Storia Patria*, Part 2, Vol. 2 (1862) and Vol. 18 (1887).
———, ed. *Regni Iherosolymitani brevis historia*. Vol. 1 of *Annali genovesi*. 125–50.
Benjamin of Tudela. *The Itinerary*. Edited and translated by Adolf Asher. 2 vols. London, 1840.
Boldorini, Anna M., ed. *Il cartario del monastero di S. Stefano di Genova dal 965 al 1300*. Genoa, 1980.
Bonvillano. *Notai (1198)*. Edited by Joyce E. Eierman, Hilmar C. Krueger, and Robert L. Reynolds. Genoa, 1939.

Caffaro et al. *Annali genovesi di Caffaro e de'suoi continuatori dal MXCIX al MCCXCIII.* Edited by Luigi T. Belgrano and Cesare Imperiale di Sant'Angelo. 5 vols. Rome, 1890-1929.

———. *Cafari de libertatione civitatum Oriente liber.* Edited by Luigi T. Belgrano. Vol. 1 of *Annali genovesi.* Pp. 95-124.

———. *Cafari ystoria captionis Almarie et Turtuose ann. MCXXXXVII et MCXXXXVIII.* Edited by Luigi T. Belgrano. Vol. 1 of *Annali genovesi.* 77-89.

Cassinese, Guglielmo. *Notai* (1190-1192). Edited by Margaret W. Hall, Hilmar C. Krueger, and Robert L. Reynolds. 2 vols. Genoa, 1938.

Cinnamus, John. *Ioannis Cinnami epitome rerum ab Ioanne et Alexio Comnenis gestarum.* Edited by August Meineke. Vol. 26 of *Corpus scriptorum historiae Byzantinae.* Bonn, 1836.

Comnena, Anna. *Alexiade.* Edited and translated by Bernard Leib. 3 vols. Paris, 1937-45.

Da Varagine, Giacomo. *Iacopo de Varagine e la sua cronica di Genova dalle origini al MCCXCVII.* Edited by Giovanni Monleone. 3 vols. Rome, 1941.

*L'estoire de Eracles Empereur et la conquête de la terre d'Outremer.* Edited by Louis de Mas Latrie Vol. 2 of *Recueil des historiens des croisades, historiens occidentaux.* Paris, 1859. 1-481.

Eustathius of Thessalonica. *De capta Thessalonica narratio.* Edited by Immanuel Bekker. Vol. 47 of *Corpus scriptorum historiae Byzantinae.* Bonn, 1842. 365-512.

Geoffrey of Villehardouin. *La conquête de Constantinople.* Edited and translated by Edmond Faral. 2 vols. Paris, 1938-39.

Giovanni di Guiberto. *Notai* (1200-1211). Edited by Mario Chiaudano and Mattia Moresco. 2 vols. Turin, 1935.

Hugh of St. Pol. *Epistula.* In *Annales Colonienses maximi.* Edited by Karl Pertz. Vol. 17 of *Monumenta Germaniae historica, scriptores.* Hanover, 1861. 812-14.

Imperiale di Sant'Angelo, Cesare, ed. *Codice diplomatico della repubblica di Genova dal MCLXIIII [sic] al MCLXXXX [sic].* 3 vols. Rome, 1936-42.

Innocent III. *Epistolae.* Vols. 214-17 of *Patrologiae cursus completus, series Latina.* Edited by Jean P. Migne. Paris, 1855.

Lanfranco. *Notai.* Edited by Hilmar C. Krueger. 2 vols. Genoa, 1951-52.

Maragone, Bernardo. *Gli annales pisani di Bernardo Maragone.* Edited by Michele Lupo Gentile. Vol. 6, Part 2, of *Rerum Italicarum scriptores, editio altera.* Rome, 1936.

Miklosich, Franz, and Müller, Giuseppe, eds. *Acta et diplomata Graeca res Graecas Italasque illustrantia.* Vol. 3 of *Acta et diplomata Graeca medii aevi sacra et profana.* Vienna, 1865.

# Bibliography

Müller, Giuseppe, ed. *Documenti sulle relazioni delle città toscane coll'Oriente e coi Turchi.* Florence, 1879.

Nicetas Choniates. *Historia.* Edited by Jan-Louis Van Dieten. 2 vols. Berlin, 1975.

Oberto Scriba de Mercato. *Notai* (1186). Edited by Mario Chiaudano. 2 vols. Genoa, 1940.

———. *Notai* (1190). Edited by Mario Chiaudano and Raimondo Morozzo della Rocca. Genoa, 1938.

Otto of Freising. *Gesta Friderici I imperatoris.* Edited by Roger Wilmans. Vol. 20 of *Monumenta Germaniae historica, scriptores.* Hanover, 1868. 338-493.

Richard of Devizes. *Itinerarium peregrinorum et gesta regis Richardi.* Edited by William Stubbs. Vol. 38, Part 1 of *Rerum Britannicarum medii aevi scriptores.* London, 1864.

Ricotti, Ercole, ed. *Liber iurium rei publicae Genuensis, Tomus I.* Vol. 7 of *Historiae patriae monumenta.* Turin, 1854.

Roger of Howdon. *Gesta Henrici secundi Benedicti Abbatis: The Chronicle of the Reigns of Henry II and Richard I, AD 1169-1192, known Commonly under the Name of Benedict of Peterborough.* Edited by William Stubbs. Vol. 69, Parts 1 and 2, of *Rerum Britannicarum medii aevi scriptores.* London, 1867.

Sanguineti, Angelo, and Bertolotto, Gerolamo, eds. "Nuova serie di documenti sulle relazioni di Genova coll'Impero bizantino." *Atti della Società Ligure di Storia Patria* 28 (1896-98): 337-573.

Simonsfeld, Henry, ed. *Historia ducum Veneticorum.* Vol. 14 of *Monumenta Germaniae historica, scriptores.* Hanover, 1883. 72-97.

Tafel, Gottlieb L. Fr., and Thomas, Georg M., eds. *Urkunden zur älteren Handels- und Staatsgeschichte der Republik Venedig.* 3 vols. Vienna, 1856-57.

Weiland, Ludwig, ed. *Constitutiones et acta publica imperatorum et regum, Tomus I. Monumenta Germanicae historica, leges. sectio IV.* Hanover, 1893.

William of Tyre. *Historia rerum in partibus transmarinis gestarum.* Edited by Louis de Mas Latrie. Vol. 1, Parts 1 and 2, of *Recueil des historiens des croisades, historiens occidentaux.* Paris, 1844.

## Literature

Abulafia, David. "Ancona, Byzantium, and the Adriatic 1155-1173." *Papers of the British School at Rome* 52 (1984): 195-216.

———. "Henry Count of Malta and his Mediterranean Activities, 1202-

1230." In *Medieval Malta: Studies on Malta before the Knights.* Edited by Anthony T. Luttrell. London, 1975. 104–25.

———. *The Two Italies: Economic Relations between the Norman Kingdom of Sicily and the Northern Communes.* Cambridge, 1977.

Ahrweiler, Hélène. *Byzance et la mer: la marine di guerre, la politique et les institutions maritimes de Byzance aux VIIe–XVe siècles.* Paris, 1966.

Ascheri, Giovanni Andrea. *Notizie storiche intorno alla riunione delle famiglie in alberghi in Genova coll'aggiunta dei nomi de'casati nobili e popolari che seguirono le fazioni guelfa e ghibellina . . .* Genoa, 1846.

Bach, Erik. *La cité de Gênes au XIIe siècle.* Copenhagen, 1955.

Balard, Michel. "Amalfi et Byzance (Xe–XIIe siècles)." *Travaux et memoires du Centre de Recherches d'Histoire et de Civilization de Byzance* 6 (1976): 85–96.

———. "Les génois en Romanie entre 1204 et 1261: recherches dans les minutiers notariaux génois." *Mélanges d'archeologie et d'histoire* 78 (1966): 467–502.

———. *La Romanie génoise.* 2 vols. Genoa, 1978.

Baldwin, Marshall W. "The Decline and Fall of Jerusalem, 1174–1189." In Vol. 1 of *A History of the Crusades,* edited by Setton, 590–621.

Battilana, Natale. *Genealogia delle famiglie nobili di Genova.* 3 vols. Genoa, 1825–33.

Bautier, Robert Henri. *The Economic Development of Medieval Europe.* Translated by Heather Karolyi. London, 1971.

Belgrano, Luigi T. "Cartario genovese et illustrazione del registro archivescovile." *Atti della Società Ligure di Storia Patria,* Vol. 2, Part 1 (1870).

Bertolotto, Gerolamo. "Cintraco." *Giornale ligustico di archeologia, storia e belle arti* 21 (1896): 36–40.

Brand, Charles M. "The Byzantines and Saladin, 1185–92: Opponents of the Third Crusade." *Speculum* 37 (1962): 167–81.

———. *Byzantium Confronts the West,* 1180–1204. Cambridge, Mass., 1968.

Bratianu, George I. *Recherches sur le commerce génois dans la Mer Noire au XIIIe siècle.* Paris, 1929.

Brown, Horatio F. "The Venetians and the Venetian Quarter in Constantinople to the Close of the Twelfth Century." *Journal of Hellenic Studies* 40 (1920): 68–88.

Buenger, Louise (Robbert). "Genoese Enterprisers, 1186–1211." Ph.D. diss., University of Wisconsin, 1955.

Bury, John B., *et al.,* eds. *The Cambridge Medieval History.* 8 vols. Cambridge, 1936–49. New Vol. 4 of *The Byzantine Empire.* Edited by Joan M. Hussey, 1966–67.

Butler, William F. *The Lombard Communes.* London, 1906; reprint, 1969.

Bibliography

Byrne, Eugene H. "Commercial Contracts of the Genoese in the Syrian Trade of the Twelfth Century." *Quarterly Journal of Economics* 31 (1916–17): 128–70.

———. "Easterners in Genoa." *Journal of the American Oriental Society* 38 (1918): 176–87.

———. "Genoese Colonies in Syria." In *The Crusades and Other Historical Essays Presented to Dana C. Munro.* Edited by Louis Paetow. New York, 1928. 139–82.

———. *Genoese Shipping in the Twelfth and Thirteenth Centuries.* Cambridge, Mass., 1930.

———. "Genoese Trade with Syria in the Twelfth Century." *American Historical Review* 25 (1919–20): 191–219.

Calvini, Nilo. *Relazioni medioevali tra Genova e la Liguria occidentale (secoli X–XIII).* Bordighera, 1950.

Cammarosano, Paolo "Les structures familiales dans les villes d'Italie communale (XIIe–XIVe siècles)." In *Famille et parenté dans l'Occident médiéval,* edited by Duby and Le Goff.

Cappellini, Antonio. *Dizionario biografico di Genovesi illustri e notabili.* Genoa, 1932.

Cardini, Franco. "Profilo di un crociato Guglielmo Embriaco." *Archivio storico italiano* 2–4 (1978): 405–36.

Caro, Georg. *Genua und die Macht am Mittelmeer,* 1257–1311. 2 vols. Halle, 1895–99.

Castagna, Domenico. *Genova nella storia.* Genoa, 196?.

Chalandon, Ferdinand. *Les Comnène.* 2 vols. Paris, 1900–12.

Classen, Peter. "La politica di Manuele Comneno tro Federico Barbarossa e le città italiane." In *Popolo e stato in Italia nell'eta di Federico Barbarossa: Alessandria e la lega lombarda. Relazioni e comunicazioni al XXXIII congresso storico subalpino.* Turin, 1970. 263–80.

Clementi, Dione R. "Some Unnoticed Aspects of the Emperor Henry VI's Conquest of the Norman Kingdom of Sicily." *Bulletin of the John Rylands Library,* 26 (1953–54), 328–59.

Cognasso, Francesco. "Un imperatore della decadenza: Isaaco II Angelo." *Bessarione* 31 (1915): 29–60.

———. "Parti politici e lotte dinastiche in Bizancio alla morte di Manuele Comneno." *Memorie della Reale Accademia delle Scienze di Torino,* 2d ser., 52 (1912): 213–17.

Costamagna, Giorgio. *La triplice redazione dell'instrumentum genovese: con Appendice di documenti.* Genoa, 1961.

Danstrup, John. "Manuel's Coup against Genoa and Venice in the Light of Byzantine Commercial Policy." *Classica et Mediaevalia* 10 (1949): 195–219.

Day, Gerald W. "Byzantino-Genoese Diplomacy and the Collapse of Emperor Manuel's Western Policy, 1168–1171." *Byzantion* 48 (1978): 393–405.

———. "Genoese Prosopography (12th–13th Centuries): The State of the Question and Suggestions for Research." *Medieval Prosopography* 4 (1983): 31–44.

———. "The Impact of the Third Crusade on Trade with the Levant." *International History Review* 3 (1981): 159–68.

———. "Italian Churches in the Byzantine Empire to 1204." *Catholic Historical Review* 70 (1984): 379–88.

———. "Manuel and the Genoese: A Reappraisal of Byzantine Commercial Policy in the Late Twelfth Century." *Journal of Economic History* 37 (1977): 289–301.

De Negri, Teofilo Ossian. *Storia di Genova.* Milan, 1974.

De Roover, Raymond. "The *Cambium Maritimum* Contract according to the Genoese Notarial Records of the Twelfth and Thirteenth Centuries." In *Economy, Society, and Government in Medieval Italy,* edited by Herlihy, Lopez, and Slessarev. 15–34.

Desimoni, Cornelio, ed. "Alberi genealogici compilati dall'annalista Iacopo D'Oria." *Atti della Società Ligure di Storia Patria* 28 (1896–1898): 299–310.

———. "Due documenti di un marchese Arduino crociato nel 1184–85." *Giornale ligustico di archeopogia, storia e belle arti* 5 (1878): 335–44.

———. "I Genovesi ed i loro quartieri in Constantinopoli in XIII secolo." *Giornale ligustico di archeologia, storia e belle arti* 3 (1876): 217–74.

———. "Il marchese Bonifacio di Monferrato e i trovatori provenzali alla corte di lui." *Giornale ligustico di archeologia, historia e belle arti* 5 (1878): 241–71.

———. "Il marchese di Monferrato Guglielmo II vecchio e la sua famiglia." *Giornale ligustico di archeologia, historia e belle arti* 13 (1886): 321–56.

———. "Memoria sui quartieri dei Genovesi a Constantinopoli nel secolo XII." *Giornale ligustico di archeologia, historia e belle arti* 1 (1874): 137–77.

———. "Sulle marche d'Italia e sulle loro diramazioni in marchesati." *Atti della Società Ligure di Storia Patria* 28 (1896–98): 1–338.

Di San Quintino, Giulio de'Conti. "Osservazioni critiche sopra alcuni particolari della storia del Piemonte e della Liguria nei secoli XI e XII." *Memorie dell'Accademia Scienze in Torino,* 2d ser., 13 (1853): 1–340.

*Dizionario biografico degli Italiani.* Rome, 1960–.

Douglas, David C. *The Norman Fate.* Berkeley, 1976.

Bibliography

Duby, Georges. *The Chivalrous Society*. Translated by Cynthia Postan. Cambridge, 1977.

————, and Le Goff, Jacques, eds. *Famille et parenté dans l'Occident médiéval. Actes du colloque de Paris (6–8 juin, 1974)*. Paris, 1977.

Epstein, Steven. *Wills and Wealth in Medieval Genoa 1150–1250*. Cambridge, Mass., 1984.

Face, Richard D. "The Embriachi: Feudal Imperialists of the Twelfth Century." M. A. thesis, University of Cincinnati, 1952.

————. "Secular History in Twelfth-Century Italy: Caffaro of Genoa." *Journal of Medieval History* 6 (1980): 169–84.

Ferluga, Jadran. "La ligesse dans l'empire byzantin: contribution à l'étude de la féodalité a Byzance." *Zbornik radova Vizantoloskog Instituta* 7 (1961): 97–123.

Fotheringham, John K. "Genoa and the Fourth Crusade." *English Historical Review* 25 (1910): 26–57.

Geanakoplos, Deno J. *Emperor Michael Palaeologus and the West, 1258–1282: A Study in Byzantine-Latin Relations*. Cambridge, Mass., 1959.

Gomes Perez, Jose. *Guia de los archivos de estados italicanos.*

Grendi, Eduardo. "Profilo storico degli alberghi genovesi." *Mélanges de l'École Française de Rome. Moyen âge—temps modernes* 87 (1975): 241–302.

Grillo, Francesco. *Origini storichi delle localita e antichi cognomini della repubblica di Genova*. Genoa, 1960.

Grossi Bianchi, Luciano. *Una città portuale del Medioevo: Genova nei secoli X–XVI*. Genoa, 1979.

Haberstumpf, Walter. "Ranieri di Monferrato: richerche sui rapporti fra Bisanzio e gli Aleramici nella seconda metà del XII secolo." *Bolletino storico-bibligrafico subalpino* 81 (1983): 603–39.

Halphen, Louis. "Le role des 'Latins' dans l'histoire interieure de Constantinople à la fin du XIIe siècle." *Études sur l'histoire et sur l'art de Byzance: mélanges Charles Diehl*. 2 vols. Paris, 1930. Vol. 1. 141–45.

Heers, Jacques. *Le clan familial au moyen âge*. Paris, 1974.

————. *Parties and Political Life in the Medieval West*. Translated by David Nicholas. Amsterdam, 1977.

————. *Gênes au XVe siècle: activité économique et problèmes sociaux*. Paris, 1961.

Hendy, Michael F. "Byzantium 1081–1204: An Economic Reappraisal." *Transactions of the Royal Historical Society*, 5th ser., 20 (1970): 31–52.

Herlihy, David J. "Family Solidarity in Medieval Italian History." In *Economy, Society, and Government in Medieval Italy*, edited by Herlihy, Lopez, and Slessarev. 173–84.

————, and Klapisch-Zuber, Christiane. *Tuscans and Their Families: A Study of the Florentine Catasto of 1427*. New Haven, 1985.

————, Lopez, Robert, and Slessarev, Vsevolod, eds. *Economy, Society and Government in Medieval Italy.* Kent, Ohio, 1969.

Herrin, Judith. "The Collapse of the Byzantine Empire in the Twelfth Century: A Study of a Medieval Economy." *University of Birmingham Historical Journal* 12 (1970): 188–203.

Heyd, Wilhelm. *Le colonie commerciali degli italiani in Oriente nel medio evo.* Translated and edited by Giuseppe Müller. 2 vols. Venice, 1866–68.

————. *Histoire du commerce du Levant au moyen âge.* Translated and revised by Furcy Reynaud. 2 vols. Leipzig, 1885–86.

Heywood, William. *A History of Pisa.* Cambridge, 1921.

Hughes, Diane O. "Kinsmen and Neighbors in Medieval Genoa." In *The Medieval City,* edited by Harry Miskimin *et al.* New Haven, 1977. 95–111.

————. "Urban Growth and Family Structure in Medieval Genoa." *Past and Present* 66 (1975): 3–28.

Hyde, John K. *Society and Politics in Medieval Italy: The Evolution of the Civil Life,* 1000–1350. London, 1973.

Italy. Ministero dell'Interno. *Archivio di Stato di Genova: cartolari notarili genovesi, 1–149, inventario.* 2 vols. Rome, 1956–62.

Janin, Raymond. *Constantinople byzantine.* Paris, 1950.

————. "Les sanctuaires des colonies latines à Constantinople." *Revue des études byzantines* 4 (1946): 163–78.

Jehel, Georges. "*Januensis ergo mercator* ou le petit monde d'un homme d'affaires génois, le juge Guarnerius (1210–21)." *Journal of Medieval History* 4 (1978): 243–66.

Johnson, Edgar N. "The Crusades of Frederick I and Henry VI." In Vol. 2 of *A History of the Crusades,* edited by Setton. 87–122.

Kazhdan, Alexander, and Constable, Giles. *People and Power in Byzantium: An Introduction to Modern Byzantine Studies.* Washington, D. C., 1982.

Krueger, Hilmar C. "The Commercial Relations between Genoa and Northwest Africa in the Twelfth Century." Ph.D. diss., University of Wisconsin, 1932.

————. "Genoese Merchants, Their Associations and Investments, 1155 to 1230." In *Studi in onore di Amintore Fanfani.* 2 vols. Milan, 1962. Vol. 1. 415–26.

————. "Genoese Merchants, Their Partnerships and Investments, 1155 to 1164." In *Studi in onore di Armando Sapori.* 2 vols. Milan, 1962. Vol. 1. 257–71.

————. "Genoese Trade with Northwest Africa in the Twelfth Century." *Speculum* 8 (1933): 377–95.

———. *Navi e proprietà navale a Genova: seconda metà del sec. XII.* Genoa, 1985.

———. "Post-War Collapse and Rehabilitation in Genoa (1149–1162)." In *Studi in onore di Gino Luzzatto.* 2 vols. Milan, 1949. Vol. 1. 117–28.

Laiou, Angeliki E. "Observations on the results of the Fourth Crusade: Greeks and Latins in Ports and Market." *Mediaevalia et Humanistica,* new ser., 12 (1984): 47–60.

Lamma, Paolo. *Comneni e Staufer: richerche sui rapporti tra Bizancio e l'Occidente nel secolo XII.* 2 vols. Rome, 1955–57.

Lane, Frederic C. *Venice: A Maritime Republic.* Baltimore, 1974.

Langer, Otto. *Die politische Geschichte Genuas und Pisas im 12. Jahrhundert.* Leipzig, 1882.

Lilie, Ralf-Johannes. *Handel und Politik zwischen dem byzantinischen Reich und den italienischen Kommunen Venedig, Pisa, und Genua in der Epoche der Komnenen und Angeloi (1081–1204).* Amsterdam, 1984.

Lopez, Robert S. "Aux origines du capitalisme génois." *Annales d'histoire économique et sociale* 9 (1937): 429–54.

———. *The Commercial Revolution of the Middle Ages.* Englewood Cliffs, New Jersey, 1971.

———. "Foreigners in Byzantium." *Bulletin de l'Institut historique belge de Rome.* Fascicule 44 (1974): 341–52.

———. "Market Expansion: The Case of Genoa." *Journal of Economic History* 25 (1964): 445–64.

———. "Medieval Trade: The South." In Vol. 2 of *The Cambridge Economic History of Europe,* edited by Postan. 257–354.

———. *Storia delle colonie genovesi nel Mediterraneo.* Bologna, 1938.

———, and Raymond, Irving W., eds. *Medieval Trade in the Mediterranean World: Illustrative Documents Translated with Introduction and Notes.* New York, 1955.

Luzzatto, Gino. *An Economic History of Italy from the Fall of the Roman Empire to the Beginning of the Sixteenth Century.* Translated by Philip Jones. London, 1961.

McNeal, Edgar H., and Wolff, Robert Lee. "The Fourth Crusade." In Vol. 2 of *A History of the Crusades,* edited by Setton, 153–85.

Maire-Vigueur, J. C. "Les institutions communales de Pisa au XIIe et XIIIe siècles." *Le Moyen Âge* 79 (1973): 519–27.

Manfroni, Camillo. "Le relazioni fra Genova, l'Impero bizantino e i Turchi." *Atti della Società Ligure di Storia Patria* 28 (1896–98): 575–858.

———. *Storia della marina italiana dalle invasioni barbariche al trattato di Ninfeo.* 3 vols. Leghorne, 1897–1902.

Martinez, Lauro. *Power and Imagination: City-States in Renaissance Italy.* New York, 1979.

Moresco, Mattia. "Parentele e guerre civili in Genova nel secolo XII." In *Scritti giuridici in onore di Sancti Romano.* Padua, 1940. 431–40.

―――, and Bognetti, Gian Piero. *Per l'edizione dei notai liguri del secolo XII.* Genoa, 1938.

Musso, Gian Giacomo. *Navigazione e commercio genovese con il Levante nei documenti dell'Archivio di Stato di Genova.* Rome, 1975.

Olivieri, Agostino. "Serie dei consoli del comune di Genova." *Atti della Società Ligure di Storia Patria* 1 (1858): 155–479. Published separately, Genoa, 1860.

Ostrogorsky, Georg. "Der Aufstieg des Geschlechts der Angeloi." In *Zur byzantinischen Geschichte.* Darmstadt, 1973.

―――. "Observations on the Aristocracy in Byzantium." *Dumbarton Oaks Papers* 25 (1971): 1–32.

Parker, John S. F. "The Attempted Byzantine Alliance with the Norman Kingdom (1166–7)." *Papers of the British School at Rome* 24 (1956): 86–93.

Paspati, Alexander. "To emporion ton Genouension en Konstantinoupolei kai Euxeino ponto." *Byzantinai meletai topographikai kai historikai.* 4 vols. Constantinople, 1877. Vol. 2. 127–276.

Pistarino, Geo. "Genova e l'Islam nel Mediterraneo occidentale (secoli XII–XIII). *Annuario de Estudios medievales* 10 (1980, issued in 1982): 189–205.

―――. "Genova medievale tra Oriente e Occidente." *Rivista storica italiana* 81 (1969): 44–73.

Pontieri, Ernesto "La madra di re Ruggero." *Atti del convegno internazionale di studi ruggeriani.* Palermo, 1955. 327–435.

Poleggi, Ennio. "Contrade delle consorterie nobiliari a Genova tra il XII e il XIII secolo." *Urbanistica,* no. 42 (1965): 15–20.

Poole, Austin Lane. "The Emperor Henry VI." In Vol. 5 of *The Cambridge Mediaeval History,* edited by Bury, 454–80.

―――. *From Domesday Book to Magna Carta,* 1087–1216. 2d ed. Oxford, 1955.

Postan, Michael M., *et al. The Cambridge Economic History of Europe.* Vol. 2, *Trade and Industry in the Middle Ages.* Cambridge, 1952.

Prawer, Joshua. *The Crusaders' Kingdom: European Colonialism in the Middle Ages.* New York, 1972.

Previte-Orton, Charles. "The Italian Cities till c. 1200." In Vol. 5 of *The Cambridge Mediaeval History,* edited by Bury, 208–41.

Pryor, John H. "The Origins of the *Commenda* Contract." *Speculum* 52 (1977): 5–37.

Queller, Donald E. *The Fourth Crusade: The Conquest of Constantinople,* 1201–1204. Philadelphia, 1977.

———, and Day, Gerald W. "Some Arguments in Defense of the Venetians on the Fourth Crusade." *American Historical Review* 81 (1976): 717–37.

Renouard, Yves. *Les hommes d'affaires italiens du moyen âge.* Paris, 1949.

———. *Les villes d'Italie de la fin du Xe siècle au debut du XIVe siècle.* 2 vols. Paris, 1969.

Reynolds, Robert L. "Genoese Trade in the Late Twelfth Century: Particularly in Cloth from the Fairs of Champagne." *Journal of Economic and Business History* 3 (1931): 362–81.

———. "In Search of a Business Class in Thirteenth-Century Genoa." *Journal of Economic History,* Supplement 5 (December 1945): 1–19.

———. "Position Report as of June, 1951, on Reproduction of Notarial Archives, 'Archivio di Stato,' Genoa, Italy." *Proceedings of the American Historical Association* (1951): 49–54.

Rossetti, Gabriela, ed. *Forme di potere e struttura sociale in Italia nel medioevo.* Bologna, 1977.

Runciman, Steven. "Byzantine Trade and Industry." In Vol. 2 of *The Cambridge Economic History of Europe,* 86–118.

———. *A History of the Crusades.* 3 vols. Cambridge, 1951–55.

Sauli, Ludovico. *Della colonia di Genovesi in Galata.* 2 vols. Turin, 1831.

Sayous, Andre-E. "Aristocratie et noblesse à Gênes." *Annales d'histoire économique et sociale* 9 (1937): 366–81.

Scarsella, Attilo R. *Il comune dei consoli.* Vol. 3 of *Storia di Genova delle origini al tempo nostro.* 4 vols. Milan, 1942.

Schaube, Adolf. *Handelsgeschichte der römanischen Volker des Mittelmeergebiets bis zum Ende der Kreuzzüge.* Munich, 1906.

Scorza, Angelo M. G. *Le famiglie nobili genovesi.* Genoa, 1924.

Serra, Girolamo. *La storia della antica Liguria e di Genova.* 4 vols. Turin, 1834.

Setton, Kenneth M., ed. *A History of the Crusades.* 5 vols. Madison, Wisc., 1969–77.

Slessarev, Vsevolod. "*Ecclesiae mercatorum* and the Rise of Merchant Colonies." *Business History Review* 41 (1967): 177–97.

———. "The Pound Value of Genoa's Maritime Trade in 1161." In *Economy, Society and Government in Medieval Italy,* edited by Herlihy, Lopez, and Slessarev, 95–112.

———. "Die sogenannten Orientalen im mittelalterlichen Genua: Einwanderer aus Subfrankreich in der ligurischen Metropolis." *Vierteljahrschrift fur Sozial- und Wirtschaftsgeschichte* 51 (1964): 22–65.

Tobacco, G. "Le rapport de parenté comme instrument de domination consorteriale: quelques examples piémontais." In *Famille et parenté*, edited by Duby and Le Goff, 153–85.

Usseglio, Leopoldo. *I marchesi di Monferrato in Italia ed in Oriente durante i secoli XII e XIII.* 2 vols. Turin, 1926.

Vasiliev, Alexander A. *A History of the Byzantine Empire, 324–1453.* Madison, Wisc., 1952.

Violante, Cinzio. "Quelques characteristiques des structure familiales en Lombardie, Emilie et Toscanie aux XIe et XIIe siècles." In *Famille et parenté*, edited by Duby and Le Goff, 85–148.

Vitale, Vito. *Breviario della storia di Genova: lineamenti storici et orientamenti bibliografici.* 2 vols. Genoa, 1955.

———. *Il comune del podestà a Genova.* Milan, 1951.

———. "Economia e commercio a Genova nei secoli XII e XIII." *Rivista storica italiana* 54 (1937): 61–88.

———. "Guelfi e ghibellini nel duecento." *Rivista storica italiana* 60 (1948): 525–41.

———. "Vita e commercio nei notai genovesi dei secoli XII e XIII; parte prima: la vita civile." *Atti della Società Ligure di Storia Patria* 72, Part 1 (1949).

Wieruszowski, Hélène. "The Norman Kingdom of Sicily and the Crusades." In Vol. 2 of *A History of the Crusades*, edited by Setton, 3–42.

Wolff, Robert Lee. "The Latin Empire of Constantinople, 1204–1261." In Vol. 2 of *A History of the Crusades*, edited by Setton, 187–234.

# Index

# Index